SOME TRACES OF THE PRE-OLYMPIAN WORLD
IN GREEK LITERATURE AND MYTH

SOME TRACES OF THE PRE-OLYMPIAN WORLD
IN GREEK LITERATURE AND MYTH

BY

E. A. S. BUTTERWORTH

WITH SEVENTEEN PLATES

1966

WALTER DE GRUYTER & CO · BERLIN
VORMALS G. J. GÖSCHEN'SCHE VERLAGSHANDLUNG · GUTTENTAG, VERLAGS-
BUCHHANDLUNG · GEORG REIMER · KARL J. TRÜBNER · VEIT & COMP.

PREFACE

It is a pleasure to have this opportunity of acknowledging publicly the obligation under which I stand to those who have helped me in my work on this book. To Professor Dr. Roland Hampe, now of the University of Heidelberg, I am grateful for encouragement given me years ago, and to Fräulein Dozentin Dr. Erika Simon, of the same university, for numerous kindnesses which have saved me much labour. Dr. E. J. Lindgren, of Harston, Cambridgeshire, has, out of her close acquaintanceship with Siberia and Siberian shamanism, been generous of counsel and practical help far beyond the deserts of my importunity. To Dr. K. Birket-Smith of the Ethnographical Department of the National Museum, Copenhagen, and Dr. Ulla Johansen, of the Museum für Völkerkunde und Vorgeschichte, Hamburg, I owe an especial debt of gratitude both for the information and for the admirable illustrations with which they have taken so much trouble to supply me. Professor T. B. L. Webster, of University College, London, courteously gave of his time to read and comment on a draft of what are now the first and last chapters of the book. Professor Dr. Hans Schwabl of the Free University of Berlin, who very kindly read the last three chapters, has not only rescued me from error but has prompted the inclusion of some valuable material.

All these whom I have named, as well as all those critics and correspondents whom I have not named but whose assistance I have not forgotten, are, of course, to be acquitted of any responsibility for the views expressed or for any defects in the following pages.

My chief debt, however, is to my wife, who, over the course of years, has, with unfailing patience, typed and retyped, and typed again, the pages of this book.

CONTENTS

ILLUSTRATIONS

Plate I   One of the side panels of the Hagia Triada sarcophagus. (From the repro-
           duction in the Ashmolean Museum, Oxford).

Plate II   Clay plaque of the seventh century B. C. from Gortyn, Crete, showing Aga-
           memnon, Clytaemnestra and Aegisthus. (By kind permission of Professor Doro
           Levi) (Heraklion Museum).

Plate III Attic black-figured vase (from Vulci) showing Hermes carrying the "three-
           leafed" caduceus. (Brit. Mus. Vase Cat. B. 248).

Plate IV   Black-figured vase, possibly Chalcidean, showing Hermes' caduceus with
           cross-bar. (Brit. Mus. Vase Cat. B 16).

Plate V   Poseidon and trident with cross-bar on Attic black-figured vase. (The shape
           to the left of the trident is the back of Herakles' lion-skin head-dress. Herakles
           has his head turned away from Poseidon). (Brit. Mus. Vase Cat. B 166).

Plate VI   Poseidon and trident with cross-bars on Attic black-figured vase. (Brit. Mus.
           Vase Cat. B 212).

Plate VII (a) and (b) Shaman staves of the Yenisei Ostyaks or Kets with trident heads.
           (c) Shaman staff of the Yenisei Ostyaks with bident head. (V. J. Anučin,
           Očerk šamanstva u jeniseiskich ostjakov in Sbornik Muzeja Antropologii i
           Etnografii pri Imp. Akademii Nauk, II, 2. St. Petersburg, 1914).

Plate VIII Shaman staff of the Yenisei Ostyaks adapted to carry pennant at the mast-
           head of a boat. (Anučin, *op. cit.*).

Plate IX   Mongolian Cham dancer holding trident-headed sceptre. (National Museet,
           Copenhagen).

Plate X   Tibetan medium, robed, with trident, entering into a trance (at Kalimpong).
           (*Oracles and Demons of Tibet* by R. de Nebesky-Wojkowitz. O. U. P./Mouton
           & Co., The Hague).

Plate XI   (a) Trident from a pariah altar at Vellore, S. India. (National Museet,
           Copenhagen).
           (b) Shaman's staff from Korea. (National Museet, Copenhagen).

Plate XII Siva holding the trident with his consort Parvati. From Hullabid, Mysore,
           India. (National Museet, Copenhagen).

Plate XIII Siva as Bhairava, holding the trident. From Siddapur, Mysore, India. (Natio-
           nal Museet, Copenhagen).

INTRODUCTION

The difficulty of interpreting myth has been recognised for so long, and the unreliability of legend as a basis for reconstructing the past so emphatically asserted, that a general reluctance to attempt interpretation at all is now perceptible. This is not the place, nor am I indeed at all inclined, to try to set forth the general principles, if any such there be, on which myth may be understood; nonetheless, there are a few observations which should be made by way of preface to the sequence of four essays that make up this book. The student of myth need not despair altogether of finding, here and there, some meaning and sense in the ancient stories.

One must first keep in mind a simple fact: the Olympian movement was a revolution, and like all important revolutions was accompanied by great zeal *de fide propaganda*. An aspect of this zeal was obscuration or denigration of the past. That this was so will, I think, appear from the following chapters. Secondly, the past which the Olympian revolution sought to efface was itself no uniform world: although it had very marked general characteristics, cults, clans and peoples were at strife with each other about more matters than territory and wealth. A consequence of this is that we often only learn about some figures or events or movements of the remote past through hostile mouths, for the victorious cause naturally influenced poets and reciters. Moreover, every myth, of whatever type, even the simplest statement, implies certain beliefs and an outlook (of which the narrator of the myth may himself be unconscious); because this is so, the myth excludes various other conceptions or possible accounts. For this reason, it is often as important to ask oneself what a story denies as what it means: against whom or what is it directed?

There is therefore a purposive element in myth, and the more times a myth has been re-told, the more varied the purposes to which it has been subjected. Some of these purposes may be, as has just been said, quite frankly propagandist. More myth, perhaps, is of a propagandist kind, or has been adapted and used for very widely different propagandist purposes, than is generally known. This has added very greatly to the difficulty of interpretation. Yet interpretation is needed, for there are few myths which do not contain contradictions or puzzle us by the narration of things the very nature of which we do not really understand. The strangenesses of myth

have been rendered acceptable to the modern world in two main ways: they
have either been dismissed as the arabesques of fancy, perhaps under the
scientific severity of some such term as 'folk-tale', or they have been explained by means of some concept comprehensible to people to day. A word
of comment is needed on both these ways of dealing with the inexplicabili-
ties of myth.

As to the former, if we allow for both adventitious error and deliberate
distortion, and exclude the aetiological myth, we may be categorical: no
myth, in its essentials, is the work of fancy, and, further, all myths, with
their differing elements of constructive thought, are expressions of experience. That experience, of course, may be very different from any that
is familiar to us to-day. In this context we must remember that, though it
can be abused, the imagination is a faculty. There are vain imaginings, and
there are imaginings which are not vain. If by 'folk-tale' is meant a kind
of story which appears in the mythology of many peoples, then this simply
means that, if the myth was not carried from one to another, these peoples
each had behind them a similar experience. This is true of Hydra, Chimaera,
and the faery hosts of King Gwynn. The difficulty is to discover the nature
of the experience.

As to explaining the incomprehensibilities of myth in terms familiar to
our day, it is obviously a dangerous proceeding. Rationalising mythographers
were at work in antiquity, and we ourselves in trying to interpret myth are
in danger of committing faults which are not very different from those
which they were guilty of. Against our own preconceptions it is difficult to
guard, and, since we can recover the outlook of earlier ages to only a limited
extent, it is inevitable that to some degree we should impose an explanation,
rather then enable the myth to speak for itself (so far as an original myth
is left to speak).

Among the distortions and falsehoods that arise from the interference of
others, however, there is one kind of evidence which yields us reasonable
certitude. This is the evidence of involuntarily-disclosed pattern, that is, of
pattern which has survived the refashionings of new *Weltanschauungen*, of
the rationalising mythographer, of sheer misunderstanding. It is the mark
of ancient tradition in late authors. To take a simple example from our field
of Greek myth: it seems fairly clear that certain names are characteristic of
one clan, while they are not found in another. For instance, names ending
in -*m(n)estra* seem to be distinctive of the Danaidae and of the sacred Tyndarid dynasty associated with them. Again, one may be reasonably sure that

persons to whom myth gives the names Tantalus, Sipylus and Pelopia belong to the people or clan or dynasty commonly called Tantalid or Pelopid. If, in an ostensibly patrilineal context, it prove impossible to trace in either case a consistent lineal descent of those who bear such names, while a matrilineally-traced genealogy reveals just such a connection, it is a reasonable conclusion that the patrilineal descent given in the myths is not the true one and that in fact these two dynasties, clans or peoples were matrilineal.

The principle of the involuntarily-disclosed pattern must of course be used very carefully, especially when comparisons are being made. The death of Pelias, his dismemberment and boiling in a cauldron, as we shall see, have a genuine identity of kind with some other events recorded in myth, but they are not identical in kind with the dismemberment of Pelops and his boiling in a cauldron by Tantalus, for Pelops did not die but lived on. This care is of course equally necessary when comparisons are made between apparently identical patterns in an ancient and in a modern context. From the examination of such patterns one may make out features which are characteristic of certain kinds of mythical figure or of certain clans, or of a certain type of myth, and such conclusions if reached with enough care, may be regarded as reasonably firm.

But at this point we encounter a difficulty which is scarcely touched on in this book (except to some extent in connection with the Danaidae), namely, the question of the historicity of the persons (I will not speak of the events) of myth. We live in an age of materialist thought, and behind the major names and events of legend usually seek to find some allusion to persons who, if we could but disentangle them from the accretions and conflations of time and the tendency to build up the memory of a great man into an ideal and superhuman figure, would appear as individual human beings. Pelops, we read, having slain Oinomaos, the son of Ares, whose wife was, in most traditions, Sterope, married their daughter Hippodameia. No doubt a 'Pelops' did slay an 'Oinomaos'. But Sterope, Lightening-flash? There is some reason to think that the cult of Ares may have involved an ascetic psychosomatic practice which culminates in momentary flashes of mystical vision that have been compared to flashes of lightening. In this moment the ascetic is united with a mystical bride. If Sterope should be after all a mystical bride, is not the daughter, Hippodameia (who bears a name significant, as we shall see, of shamanism), a figure from the same world? She may be, but on the other hand, in the pre-Olympian religious world it seems that living men and women, members of a sacred dynasty, on occasion embodied, represented, and took the name of the divinity or power they cultivated.

Helen was, besides being a tree-goddess, a visionary power, but she was said to be the sister of Clytaemnestra. If Clytaemnestra was a real person, Helen, in her essence, certainly was not[1]. In what sense, then, was she Clytaemnestra's sister? Agamemnon married Clytaemnestra, and Menelaos married Helen. Menelaos had a spring and a plane-tree, Pausanias tells us (8.23.3), near Kaphyai in Arcadia. The name of Menelaos surely implies the presence of Helen, and the plane-tree reinforces the inference. Menelaos, indeed, had a temple at Therapne (Paus. 3.19.9), where he and Helen were said to be buried, and their joint cult was popular in Egypt[2], at any rate in later times. Helen as a tree-goddess has become a sufficiently familiar concept: what then of Menelaos? Menelaos belongs to Helen rather than to Agamemnon, and would seem possibly to be, not a hero, but her equally divine consort, and originally perhaps her brother[3]. Are Helen and Clytaemnestra the goddess and her living embodiment (if we take Clytaemnestra to have been a historical figure)? If they are, then, had Agamemnon been of the same clan and cult as Helen, Menelaos might well have been his brother in a similar sense. But Agamemnon was a Pelopid and so of another cult; he and Menelaos cannot have been brothers. The marriage of Agamemnon and Clytaemnestra was traditionally a forced one, and the Danaid Artemis pursued the Pelopidae with unassuaged hatred. In other words, the Homeric tradition does not make sense. It is hard indeed to know in what world one is moving.

What does emerge from a study of the involuntarily-disclosed patterns of myth, even if there can be so far little certainty about some of its most celebrated figures, is a good deal of general information about the remote past, its beliefs and its customs. We can learn something of its religion and its society. This is not superficial information, for myth does not deal with superficial things; we need to look at Greek literature with other eyes than those with which we regard the modern world. When we have caught a glimpse of the Olympian revolution engaged in presenting the world that preceded it, and have peered beyond the revolution into that earlier world,

---

[1] This does not mean that no individual human beings were involved in the events from which the story of the abduction of Helen by Paris arose.

[2] Plutarch, *De Malign. Herodoti*, 12. See also, for the tree-cult in ancient Egypt, Appendix I.

[3] See Chapter I, § iv, on the Danaidae.

we cannot but see some of the Greek classics in a deeper perspective. Until we learn to recognise in particular the untruths that Homer told, and why he told them, this insight into pre-Olympian Greece will be denied us. Dio Chrysostom said that Homer was a great liar, but fortunately Homer nods, and when he does we sometimes learn some remarkable things.

One word more: it has seemed to me that the study of the early world of Greece has so far lacked a sufficiently detailed treatment of matrilineality. This foundation I have tried to give in Chapter I. It may, I fear, be hard work for the reader, but it is a necessary preparation for the arguments and unorthodox conclusions of Chapters II and III. Without some knowledge of the matrilineal dynasties and of the nature of their system and its practices, more of Greek literature will (as the author at any rate believes) remain obscure to us than need otherwise be. Moreover, only with this knowledge does a neglected aspect of the world destroyed by the Olympian revolution begin to move into the field of view.

A second aspect, of even greater importance, and one which has implications beyond the field of Greek studies, is the shamanism of that earlier world. About this we may, I hope, leave the final chapter to speak for itself.

CHAPTER I

The Matrilineal World

τοὺς ὁμογάλακτας οὓς γεννήτας καλοῦμεν. —Philochoros, fr. 94.

Athena.—ἐμὸν τόδ᾽ ἔργον, λοισθίαν κρῖναι δίκην·
ψῆφον δ᾽ Ὀρέστῃ τήνδ᾽ ἐγὼ προσθήσομαι.
μήτηρ γὰρ οὔτις ἐστὶν ἥ μ᾽ ἐγείνατο,
τὸ δ᾽ ἄρσεν αἰνῶ πάντα, πλὴν γάμου τυχεῖν,
ἅπαντι θυμῷ, κάρτα δ᾽ εἰμὶ τοῦ πατρός.—Aeschylus,
Eumenides, 734 ff.

I. The Loyalty to the Clan

The earlier world reflected in much Greek myth seems, as far as its society was concerned, to have been based on the clan. It is a world in which a man's or woman's loyalties are, first and foremost, either to the father's or to the mother's relations. Individual family affections mean little or nothing in the scheme of social loyalties, and the household family, at any rate among the ruling class, did not exist as a unit of society. This we can see from a function of the Erinyes in Homer. Just as Phoenix' father was ready to call down dreadful punishment on his son for supporting his mother against him, and all the father's kinsmen stood by him, while the mother's relations stayed away[1], so Althaea prayed for her son Meleager's death because he had killed one of her brothers[2].

---

[1] *Iliad* 9.444 ff. The suggestion of M. Miller in 'Greek Kinship Terminology', *Journal of Hellenic Studies,* LXXIII (1953), that ἔται means paternal kinsmen appears to be justified. See also *Il.* 9.529 ff.

[2] *Il.* 9.529 ff. I think that here at any rate Miller's suggestion (*loc. cit.*) that ἑταῖροι likewise means 'paternal kinsmen' is right. The context precludes their being maternal kinsmen. Nor can they be companions chosen at random (i.e. unrelated), for the phrase ἔθνος ἑταίρων (*Iliad* 13.648; 17.581,680) seems to imply at least supposed common blood. Of course the relationship may be very remote indeed, and I take the word to amount to something like 'fellow-clansmen of fighting age'. Miller points out that Patroclus was Achilles' second cousin once removed. κασίγνηται means 'maternal kinswomen', as Miller rightly holds.

So too in the *Odyssey*[3] Telemachus says, in reply to the suitors who had urged him to send his mother away from his home, that if he were to do so, not only would he have to pay compensation to her father, Ikarios, but she herself would call down the hateful Erinyes on him as she left. That is to say, the father of Penelope would be regarded as having a right to compensation if she were no longer maintained in her husband's house and this implies that the head of the family from which a woman came had rights in connection with her which were not extinguished by her marriage. This right would be supported by the Erinyes. Indeed, the very fact that the suitors made the suggestion at all to Telemachus shows that the ties that in later Greece united the individual family were in earlier times relatively weak. It was clan loyalty, and the rights of the clan, that were then in the ascendant, and it is these relationships, not those of the individual family, that the Erinyes uphold and of which they are summoned to punish a breach.

Even in classical times it was known that this was the outlook of early Greece, as we can see from the famous reply of the Chorus of Erinyes-Eumenides in Aeschylus' play to the question put by Orestes:

Ορ. τί δ' οὐκ ἐκείνην (sc. Clytaemnestra) ζῶσαν ἤλαυνες φυγῇ ;

Χο. οὐκ ἦν ὅμαιμος φωτὸς ὃν κατέκτανεν. (605).

Likewise a polluted fugitive does not seem to turn to any king indifferently for refuge and purification. Usually, it is true, our information is too exiguous for us to judge of the reasons why a particular king (or, sometimes, god) is asked by the polluted one to cleanse him. In two cases, however, we see what is apparently a significant connection. The Pelopid Kopreus was purified by Eurystheus at Mycenae. Eurystheus was the son of the Perseid Sthenelos and Nikippe, daughter of 'Pelops' and Hippodameia. Among the children of 'Pelops' and Hippodameia, as we shall see, the matrilineal rule was observed. In turning to Eurystheus for purification, therefore, Kopreus was turning to a fellow clansman[4]. The second case is that of Amphitryon, who fled with Alkmena and Likymnios to Kreion of Thebes for purification. According to one tradition, Amphitryon's mother was Hipponome, daughter of Menoikeus[5], ruler of Thebes. 'Kreion' would appear to have been her

---

[3] 2.135.

[4] Apollod. 2.5.1. makes it clear that Kopreus was not at Mycenae when he killed Iphitos. He made his way there to be cleansed.

[5] Apollod. 2.4.5. Euripides, *Hercules F.*, 5–8, makes Menoikeus one of the old 'earthborn' stock of Thebes.

brother[6]. The ruling house of Thebes at this time was apparently matrilineal. The name 'Kreion' seems to have signified 'regent' and to have been used of the brother or maternal uncle of the queen. Amphitryon therefore sought purification at the hands of his mother's brother, if we may rely on this tradition of his parentage[7].

The effect of the system of succession to the kingship and of the inheritance of property on the life of the times was immense. The majority of the clans were matrilineal by custom, and the greatest revolution in the history of early Greece was that by which the custom was changed from matrilineal to patrilineal succession and the loyalty to the clan destroyed. This revolution was still a theme for tragedy in the middle of the fifth century.

An examination of the myths enables us to see something of the detail of this world of matrilineal and semi-patrilineal dynasties. The first task is to reconstruct the custom of descent in three great clans, the Pelopidae or Tantalidae, the Perseidae and the Danaidae.

II. The Pelopidae or Tantalidae

The name of the clan to which Agamemnon and Menelaos are supposed to have belonged, if indeed it had one, is not apparent. Agamemnon and Menelaos are commonly known as the Atreidae, the sons or descendants of Atreus. But they and Atreus and other relations are known also as the Pelopidae, Tantalidae or Pleisthenidae. The Pleisthenidae, it will appear later, are unlikely to have been a clan at all, and may be struck out. There is also reason to doubt whether there was any family called the Pelopidae, for the Pelopes seem likely to have been a distinct racial type, of which an immigrant clan became famous.

That the Pelopidae or Tantalidae were a matrilineal clan would seem at first sight to be clear from the following table[8]:

---

[6] Apollod. 3.5.8.

[7] It is certainly more probable than the tradition that he was a Pelopid, for he seems to have been connected with the cult of Zeus (Apollod. 2.4.8), which no true Pelopid ever was. About the Guneus whom a third tradition gives as Amphitryon's father I can discover nothing.

[8] Drawn from Apollod. 1.9.8.–13 and 3.5.6.

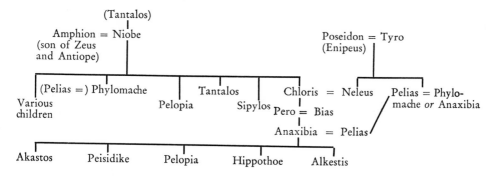

In its essential relationships the table is doubtless correct. It seems likely, however, as we shall see[9], that 'Niobe' was not originally a Tantalid, and her marriage to Amphion the son of Zeus probably belongs to her pre-Tantalid past. ('Niobe' here doubtless represents more than one generation of a dynastic line.)

There is also an element of uncertainty about the fifth generation after Tantalos, for the two traditions recorded by Apollodorus of Pelias' marriage place the alternative brides in different generations. This, however, makes no difference to the matrilineal pattern of descent, which is already clear in the names of the children of Niobe: the names Pelopia, Sipylos[10], and Tantalos reveal that they were thought of in the first place as the children of the mother. In the line of descent through Chloris the principle is again apparent, for the name Pelopia recurs among the children of Anaxibia and Pelias. This can hardly be due to anything other than matrilineal descent: Pelias was not the son of Bias, nor was Bias the son of Neleus. One might, it is true, urge that Pelias may have been a Pelopid. This is certainly possible, but the legends about Pelias in Iolkos plainly point to a matrilineal system there too. Pelias is embedded in matrilineal tradition. Furthermore, Anaxibia seems to be a Pelopid name: Agamemnon had a sister Anaxibia. Nevertheless, the table of descent is somewhat unsatisfactory because of the qualification of which it stands in need, and we must look more closely into the clan and its relationships.

It appears, in spite of the doubts expressed by some, to be certain that 'Pelops' was an immigrant into Greece from Asia Minor[11]. He is plainly a

[9] See Appendix I.
[10] See Paus. 5.13.4.
[11] See, for example, Herodotus, 7.8; Paus. 5.13.4; Pindar, *Ol.* 1.24 (36), 9.9 (15); Thuc. 1.9.

composite figure. A scholiast on Pindar[12] gives, in the last of three lists of
Pelops' children, a 'Pelops the Younger'. Another scholion[13] says that among
the suitors slain by Oinomaos was a Pelops Ὀπούντιος. As we shall later
have occasion to notice, Oinomaos' 'charioteer' Myrtilos was at least a rival
for Hippodameia and almost certainly the successor of Oinomaos and predecessor of 'Pelops'[14]. Pelops was said to have been a son of Tantalos and
Euryanassa[15].

Pelops married Hippodameia, the daughter of Oinomaos and his wife
Sterope or Asterope[16]. He is supposed to have lived at Pisa, near the river
Alpheios and the border of Elis and Triphylia, though some of the evidence
associates him with the region south and west of Corinth (especially with
Sicyon) and with Boeotia[17]. According to one tradition[18], Oinomaos had
been warned by an oracle that he would die if Hippodameia married. He
consequently subjected her many suitors to a severe test of eligibility: each
was challenged to a chariot race, and when the suitor lost, as, until the arrival
of Pelops, all of them did, Oinomaos killed him. To this subject, and the
first of the curses on the dynasty of the 'Pelopidae', we shall return later.
For the moment, we are concerned with the marriages made by the descendants of Pelops.

Pelops and Hippodameia had many children, about whose names and
number the traditions do not wholly agree. About two of them, however,
there is agreement, namely, Atreus and Thyestes. Some traditions mention
a daughter Nikippe[19] and a son Pleisthenes. Thucydides[20] apparently accepts
Nikippe as a daughter, for he says that Eurystheus, who was the son of
Nikippe[21], committed the government of Mycenae into the hands of Atreus,

---

[12] *Ol.* 1.89 (144).

[13] *Ol.* 1.70 (114).

[14] See also below on the Perseids.

[15] Schol. Eurip. *Orest.* 4. The name Tantalos recurs in the generation of his great-grand-
son, and may represent the family name of a Pelopian dynasty (unless it simply means
'seer' or 'shaman'). In Seneca's *Thyestes* Tantalos is one of Thyestes' sons.

[16] Hyginus, *Fab.* 84, makes O. the son of Ares and Asterope, his wife Euarete, daughter
of Akrisios. Hippodameia remains his daughter.

[17] See Paus. 2.14.3; 6.19.3; 9.40.6.

[18] Apollodorus, *Epitome* 2.2.4., where the other tradition, of O.'s incestuous passion, is
also mentioned.

[19] Schol. Eurip. *Orest.* 4. For Pleisthenes see below.

[20] 1.9.

[21] Apollod. 2.4.5.

his mother's brother, when he went off to fight the Heraclidae. As Eurystheus did not return from the campaign, Atreus, with the agreement of the people, took up the kingship of Mycenae and the rest of the dominions of Eurystheus.

There are two traditions about the marriage of Atreus. One asserts that he married Aërope, a Cretan, daughter of Katreus[22] and granddaughter of Minos. The other story makes Atreus marry Kleola, a daughter of Dias, by whom he has a son, Pleisthenes[23]. According to some lists of Pelops' children[24], Dias was a son of Pelops. A struggle arose between Atreus and his brother Thyestes for the kingship[25]. There are several accounts of the course of events, but in their essentials they agree[26]. Hermes, embittered by the death of his son Pelops, sends by a herdsman a golden lamb to Atreus, which Atreus takes as a sign that the kingdom belongs to him[27]. Thyestes, however, secretly seduces Aërope, Atreus' wife, and with her help steals the golden lamb. Zeus then shows by heavenly portents that the kingship belongs to Atreus, the people recognise this, and Thyestes has to flee. According to another version, Thyestes returns, and, in virtue of signs from heaven, is restored[28]. A third version says that Atreus had vowed the finest lamb in his flocks to Artemis, but that when the lamb was born he did not fulfil his promise, but strangled it and put it into a chest. Thyestes, however, seduced Aërope, and stole the lamb. Zeus intervened with celestial portents, and the

---

[22] Apollod. *Epit.* 2.10.

[23] Schol. Eurip. *Orest.* 4.

[24] Schol. Eurip. *Orest.* 4. Dias is also mentioned in the second of three versions of Pelops' children in Schol. Pindar, *Ol.* 1.89 (144).

[25] Aeschylus, *Agam.* 1585; Apollod. *Epit.* 2.11–13.

[26] Apollod. *Epit.* 2.10–13 gives the clearest account. See also Seneca, *Thyestes*, 220 ff.; 641–783; 784–8 and the following chorus. For other sources see Frazer's Apollodorus (Loeb Classical Library), vol. 2, pp. 164 ff., footnote 1.

[27] The implication of Hermes' 'embitterment' is apparently that Thyestes caused Pelops' death.

[28] The heavenly signs took the form of the reversal of the sun's course from east to west, both in the case of the portent that favoured Atreus and in the case that favoured Thyestes. Why should the sun in particular have manifested his displeasure at the way things were going? If Aërope observed the cult of Helen, this would be easy to understand (see Appendix I). It is a possible pointer to the dynasty and cult of Aërope (see next footnote). If a man did not marry his sister's daughter, as sometimes happened, an exogamic rule seems to have been at least commonly observed, and it would have been perfectly possible for Atreus, a 'Pelopid', to have married a Cretan princess of another clan and another cult.

lamb was restored to Atreus. From this arose Artemis' anger, which prevented the fleet from sailing to Troy[29].

One fact stands out plainly from these stories: union with Aërope, and her consent, were necessary to the conferring of sovereignty, represented by the golden lamb, upon the man who aspired to it. The will of Zeus was also involved in the choice of sovereign. We cannot fail to be reminded of Menelaos, to whom it was promised that he should not die, because he had Helen, and by her was the son-in-law of Zeus[30]. Through marriage with the princess one became related to the supreme deity. The right to the throne apparently descended through the female line, to the husband of the heiress, or in certain circumstances to her nearest male relation on her mother's side, as we see in Thucydides' account of Atreus' accession[31]. Access to the divine was through the queen.

This inference is remarkably confirmed in a work called the *Ephemeris Belli Trojani*, by a writer who goes under the fictitious name of Dictys, and pretended to be a companion of the Cretan Idomeneus at Troy[32]. Dictys[33] says that after the death of Atreus all those great-grandchildren of Minos who ruled in Greece came together to Crete, to take their share in the distribution of Atreus' possessions. Atreus had left gold, silver and herds to the grandchildren whom his daughters had borne. By Atreus' order, Idomeneus and Meriones, son of Molos, held the sovereignty of the land, that is, of Crete. Those who came together were Palamedes and Oiax, the sons

---

[29] Apollod. *Epit.* 3.21–22. The story tends to support the suggestion in the preceding footnote that Aërope represented Helen-Artemis in cult (for Helen-Artemis see Appendix I).

[30] *Odyssey* 4.569.

[31] The brother or uncle of the queen seems, however, to have been regent rather than king. See p. 16, with footnote 45.

[32] As this work may not be familiar to every reader, a few words about it should not be out of place. It was translated into Latin by one L. Septimius in the fourth century A. D., and has two prefaces. The first preface asserts that the Greek original, inscribed in Phoenician lettering, was found in Nero's time in the grave of Dictys at Knossos, and that it had been abbreviated in translation into Latin. The second preface, however, says that the original was written in Phoenician characters and language, and that Nero had it translated into Greek. In the *Ephemeris* Crete comes more strongly into the foreground than it does in the *Iliad*. Female characters, such as Hecuba, Cassandra and Polyxena, play an outstanding part in the narrative. Few scholars, perhaps, will share T. W. Allen's view of Dictys as an authority, but it seems improbable that the matrilineal pattern referred to immediately below can have any other origin than ancient tradition.

[33] I.1.

of Klymene (who is also known as Aërope) and Nauplios, and Menelaus, Anaxibia and Agamemnon, the children of Aërope and Pleisthenes[34].

If we can admit, as it would seem that we quite fairly may[35], that Idomeneus and Meriones really succeeded to the rule of Crete through the female line (Idomeneus through his wife Meda; the name of Meriones' wife we do not know), the whole passage is in agreement on the principle of matrilineal succession. For Atreus is said to have left his wealth to the children whom his daughters had borne, and this is certainly only a way of saying that his wealth was left to the children of the daughters of his wife,

[34] In this story, one detail strikes us as strange, namely, that Idomeneus and Meriones should succeed to the rule of Crete by order of Atreus. Idomeneus is said to be a son of Deucalion, and Meriones the son of Molos, who was a bastard son of Deucalion (Apollod. 3.3.1). They thus belonged to the ruling house of Crete. (In the Iliad, Idomeneus is the leader of the Cretan contingent before Troy and Meriones is his squire). At the most, therefore, the sanction of Atreus, the great Mycenaean king, to their following what was in fact the normal course of succession, would have been needed. Further, the story seems to suggest at first sight that the right to rule in Crete descended from father to son, since Idomeneus was the son of Deucalion. But as we shall immediately see, the royal Cretan line was apparently matrilineal. In fact, we receive a strong hint from Apollodorus (*Epit.* 6.10) that it ran in the female line. While Idomeneus was away at Troy, one Leukos first seduced his wife, Meda, and then killed her and her daughter, who had both taken refuge 'in the temple'. He then detached ten Cretan cities from their allegiance to Idomeneus, and when Idomeneus returned from Troy, drove him out of Crete. We meet once more, then, the theme of seduction of the existing ruler's wife as a preliminary step to obtaining the kingship. Later, there seems to have been a certain resistance by Meda to Leukos' design (or, what is perhaps more likely, two accounts have been conflated), for he then murders her and her daughter. This seems to imply that Leukos could not obtain Meda's agreement to his taking over the kingship, and therefore killed her and her daughter, to whom the right of succession would pass.

If Idomeneus and Meriones were in fact not heirs to the rule of Crete, the statement of Dictys that they held their positions by the command of Atreus becomes immediately comprehensible. As they are designated the rulers of Crete by Atreus after his death, it seems to be implied that in Atreus' own time there were no such rulers, and that he himself was lord of Crete as well as King at Mycenae. This would accord very well with his reputed marriage to Cretan Aërope. His designation of Idomeneus and Meriones as his successors would perhaps have involved approval of their marriages. That there was a special relation of some kind between Idomeneus and the ruler of Mycenae seems to be indicated by *Iliad* 4. 256 f., where Agamemnon reminds Idomeneus of past favour shown him, and Idomeneus reassures him, saying that he would be a faithful *hetairos* to him, as he had 'promised and consented'.

[35] See preceding footnote.

Aërope. For it was only through the female line that they were great-grand-children of Minos.

We may, then, accept it at least provisionally as a fact that the Mycenaean kings, at any rate in the great days of Mycenaean civilisation, came to power through marriage with, or relationship to, the women of certain dynastic clans. This is a suitable opportunity to deal with the question of the so-called Pleisthenidae.

The distribution of the name Pleisthenes[36] over three generations is very striking, and it is not unnatural that in later times it was taken to indicate the existence of a clan of the Pleisthenidae, though the difficulty of reconciling it with the other genealogical traditions is to be noticed. Two statements have, however, been preserved which give a strong indication of the true significance of the name Pleisthenes. The first is by Dictys[37], who says, 'Agamemnon and his brother are sons, not of Atreus, but of Pleisthenes, and as such are considered *ignobiles*.' The second is by a scholiast on Sophocles[38], who says that Aërope was given to Nauplios by her father Katreus, the son of Minos, to take overseas, because she had let herself be seduced by a slave. Nauplios, however, did not do so, but betrothed Aërope to Pleisthenes. If we take these two statements together, it seems a reasonable inference that Pleisthenes and the 'slave' are one and the same.

We may recall that Frazer in *The Golden Bough,* speaking of the Roman kingship, observed, firstly, that there was evidence that the right to the kingship was transmitted in the female line, and that it was actually exercised by foreigners who married the royal princesses. Euripides, we may notice,

---

[36] A man called Pleisthenes, according to Schol. Pind. *Ol.* 1.89 (144), was the brother or half-brother of Atreus and Kleola, daughter of Dias, and, marrying Eriphyle, became father of Agamemnon, Menelaus and Anaxibia. Schol. *Iliad,* 1.7, says that Hesiod called Agamemnon the son of Pleisthenes. Schol. *Iliad,* 2.249, tells us that Porphyry and many others make the Atreidae sons of Pleisthenes. Apollodorus (3.2.2.) says that Katreus gave Aërope and Klymene to Nauplios to sell into foreign lands, Aërope marrying Pleisthenes and becoming mother of Agamemnon and Menelaus, and Klymene marrying Nauplios and bearing Oiax and Palamedes. Schol. Eurip. *Orest.* 4 also describes Pleisthenes as the son of Aërope and Atreus; he married Kleolla *(sic),* daughter of Dias, becoming father of Agamemnon, Menelaus, and Anaxibia (see also Hyginus, *Fab.* 86). Two other accounts make him a son of Thyestes and a son of Menelaos and Helen.

[37] V. 1.

[38] *Ajax* 1297.

shows that he knew the same practice characterized the Greek kingships. Kreousa, daughter of Erechtheus, is addressed:

ὅστις σε γήμας ξένος ἐπεισελθὼν πόλιν
καὶ δῶμα καὶ σὴν παραλαβὼν παγκληρίαν[39]

'(The man) who came as a stranger to the city and married
thee and took thy house and thine inheritance.'

The word 'house' shows that the property descended in the female line. The word παγκληρίαν means 'the inheritance as a whole,' that is, that which should come properly to the principal heir or heiress. Electra uses the same word in the *Choephoroe*[40]. Secondly, Frazer said, it seemed that these men might be of lowly birth, provided that otherwise, for instance physically, they were suitable mates[41]. From this it would follow, as Frazer says, that the male descendants reigned in successive generations over different king-doms. It would seem that, as in the story of Pelops' winning of Hippoda-meia, some sort of contest preceded the bethrothal, and the strong man won the royal bride. Sometimes, however, a bride-price took the place of the contest, so that Aërope and Klymene were said to have been 'sold abroad'. The husbands in this last case, whether Greeks or not, were to the civilised Cretans rough, uncultivated, but forceful people; on the other hand, the higher Minoan culture, and its embodiment in the women of the royal or princely families, attracted the immigrants powerfully. Although Atreus was evidently regarded as a great king, others who married women of the priestly nobility of Crete were looked on by the Cretans as *ignobiles,* and perhaps because of their brief and undistinguished reigns (as was that of Pleisthenes, the father of Agamemnon and Menelaus[42]) were recorded by history only under the anonymity of the word 'Pleisthenes'. A princess who married one could be said to have married one of the lower orders, a ser-vant[43], in modern slang 'a tough' (πλεισθένης).

It is of course likely that such a state of affairs was, as far as the ancient

---

[39] *Ion* 813 f. The same theme reappears with the utmost clarity in 1295—8 and 1304—5.
[40] 486.
[41] *The Golden Bough* (abridged edition), p. 152, pp. 154 f.
[42] Dictys I.1; Schol. Eurip. *Orest.* 4.
[43] According to Schol. Laur. Soph. *Oed. Col.* 1375, Oedipus also was 'of thoroughly low birth' (τελέως ἀγεννῶς) (Kinkel, *Epic. Graec. Frag.,* p. 12). As far as the mixture of race is concerned, notice that, speaking of Medea's children, whom Hera had promised to make immortal, the Scholiast on Pindar, *Ol.* XIII.74, says ἀποθανοῦντας δὲ τούτους τιμῶσι Κορίνθιοι, καλοῦντες μιξοβαρβάρους (Kinkel, *Epic. Graec. Frag.,* p. 189).

Minoan rule itself is concerned, the result of irruption into an ordered world.
The traditions of princesses marrying commoners or slaves imply that the
innovation was not regarded as desirable. It is very likely that the princesses
of the ancient houses felt a real resentment against the brutal intruders: the
story that Agamemnon married Clytaemnestra against her will seems to
reflect something of the kind.

According to Thucydides[44], as we have seen, Atreus became ruler at Mycenae not through a marriage but because he was the brother of the queen,
Nikippe, daughter of Hippodameia. It is a well-known feature of some
matrilineal societies that the brother of the mother, the maternal uncle, not
the husband, is responsible for the protection of the family and the bringing
up of the children. Something like this happened at Thebes: Kreion[45], Jocasta's brother, took (or already had) control of the government and of the
children of Oedipus and Jocasta when the former fled and the latter hanged
herself. Atreus, having been confirmed as the king of Mycenae, will presumably have installed his wife, whether Kleola or Aërope, in the palace.
This story cannot, it would seem, be easily reconciled with that of the
struggle with Thyestes, which centres round his wife, not his sister. Thucydides says that Atreus, by his action, established the supremacy of the Pelopids over the Perseids, a statement which we shall consider in dealing with
the Perseids. One thing at any rate is clear: according to either story, that
which centres round Aërope or that which centres round Nikippe, Atreus
came to power in Mycenae through the operation of a matrilineal rule[46].

Atreus seems to have been a true Tantalid. In spite of the tradition that

---

[44] 1.9.

[45] It may be that ὁ κρείων was the recognized name for a brother or uncle who had
assumed this position. Thucydides' account distinguishes Atreus' first position as regent
for Eurystheus from his later position as *basileus*.

[46] According to Schol. *Iliad*, 2.105, citing Hellanicus, Atreus returned to Pisa after his
father's death with a large army and conquered the country. The implication of this
story might perhaps be that Atreus was not a son of 'Pelops', but a stranger who dispossessed him or his successor by force. Secondly, Atreus is said to have instituted
the funeral games at Olympia in Pelops' memory (Velleius Paterculus, 1.8.2.). There
is a similar story that Pelops had developed the games at Olympia on a larger scale
in memory of the slain suitors (one of whom may have been Myrtilos, whom he himself
had slain). The death of the king Akrisios at the hands of Perseus, his successor,
occurred at funeral games (Apollod. 2.4.4.). Velleius Paterculus' statement taken in
conjunction with Atreus' invasion of Pisa, seems to carry a hint that Atreus slew
'Pelops', even though the invasion is said to have taken place after Pelops' death.

Agamemnon was a son of Atreus, we must give serious consideration to the statement that he was the son of Pleisthenes and Aërope. As the name 'Pleisthenes' is unlikely to have been invented to compete with that of the mighty Atreus for the fatherhood of Agamemnon it seems in principle more probable that Agamemnon's father was Pleisthenes. The passage in the second book of the Iliad (101 ff.) giving the names of the successive holders of the sceptre then in the hand of Agamemnon, does not say that the sceptre passed from father to son. If we may believe the story in the *Ephemeris* of Dictys, Agamemnon was through his mother the grandson of Atreus. As we shall see, there is another account of a Pelopid claiming a kingdom on the ground that his mother's father had ruled there and for this reason we may be inclined to give credence to Dictys. A mistaken belief that Pleisthenes was Atreus' son may have given rise to the story that Atreus had a wife Kleol(l)a. She may really have been the mother of Pleisthenes.

Some evidence that Agamemnon was a Tantalid may be drawn from the fact of common cult hostility: that Agamemnon shared with Atreus and Broteas[47] the hostility of Artemis is at least an indication of similar cult and may imply common clan-membership, for clan and cult undoubtedly went together.

It is assumed that Agamemnon was born of parents resident in Mycenae. There is however a legend[48] that Agamemnon and Menelaus were taken by their nurse, presumably from Mycenae, to Sicyon. Stories about princes who are taken in infancy from a city in which they later ruled to some other place are quite common and should be regarded with suspicion. Their intention is at times plainly to establish an hereditary connection where none had existed, at any rate none which a later age could recognize. Perseus[49] floats as a babe in arms with Danaë across the sea from Argos; Oedipus is exposed as a baby by his Theban parents, found, and brought up in Corinth; Theseus, left as the unborn child of Aigeus in Troezen, finds his father in Athens when he is a grown man; Agamemnon is taken by his nurse from Mycenae to Sicyon; Orestes is brought away by his nurse to Phocis. The story hints therefore that Agamemnon came from Sicyon. There is nothing strange in this. Sicyon was a centre of Pelopid power[50]. It was one of the places which

---

[47] Apollod. *Epit.* 2.2; Schol. Eurip. *Orest.* 4.
[48] Apollod. *Epit.* 2.15.
[49] See below.
[50] The treasury of the Sicyonians at Olympia contained Pelops' sword (Paus. 6.19.3).

contributed men and ships to the contingent led by Agamemnon himself on
the expedition to Troy[51]. T. W. Allen[52] held that Agamemnon's personal
kingdom was based on Mycenae-Corinth-Sicyon. If our supposition is right,
the statement of the scholiast on *Il.* 1.7 that Agamemnon was by clan a
Mycenaean, while not strictly accurate (for he was by clan, no doubt, a
'Pelopid' or 'Tantalid') is, from the point of view of a later age which thought
in terms of cities and kingdoms rather than clans, not wholly untrue. Mycenae was the chief centre of 'Pelopid' power, and is distinguished, not from
Sicyon and other places with 'Pelopid' dynasties, but from Argos[53]. Agamemnon was as much surrounded in Mycenae by his *hetairoi*[54] as he would
have been in Sicyon.

A portion of the combined lineage of the Perseids and Pelopids, as given
by Apollodorus[55], shows in an interesting way both the matrilineality of the
Pelopids and one of the kinds of error which may creep into mythology. In
tabular form, Apollodorus' account may be set out thus:

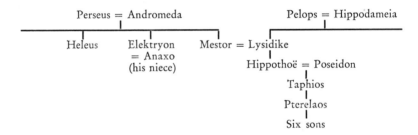

Apollodorus says that when Elektryon was reigning over Mycenae, the
sons of Pterelaos came with some Taphians and demanded the kingdom of
Mestor, their maternal grandfather. Frazer, in his translation and edition of
Apollodorus, observes that, on Apollodorus' showing, Mestor was not the
grandfather but the great-great-grandfather of the sons of Pterelaos. Furthermore, he points out that it is hard to believe that Elektryon was still reigning

---

[51] *Il.* 2.572.

[52] *The Homeric Catalogue of Ships*, p. 73.

[53] Allen, *ibid.*, with map at end.

[54] See M. Miller, 'Greek Kinship Terminology', *J. H. S.* LXXIII (1953). It would be
wrong to assume that in a matrilineal world paternal kinsmen were of no importance.
In fact, as we shall see, the greatest social crisis of early Greek history turned partly
on their rivalry with a man's maternal kinsmen.

[55] 2.4.5—6.

over Mycenae, for, as a son of Perseus, he was a brother of Mestor. To these difficulties we may add another: when the Taphians arrived, not only did they drive off Elektryon's cattle, but Amphitryon, brother of Elektryon's wife, Anaxo, was helped by, among others, Heleus, another son of Perseus, to ravage the Taphians' land in return. Thus everything, except the three generations of sons descended from Hippothoë and Poseidon, points to the visit of the Taphians to Mycenae having taken place in the third generation after Perseus. Frazer nonetheless wishes to seclude the words τοῦ μητροπά-τορος, 'maternal grandfather', as a gloss, apparently accepting the sequence Poseidon-Taphios-Pterelaos. But the considerations just urged point to this word's being correct, and another feature of the passage instead strikes us as odd. In the extensive genealogy which he gives of the intermarriage of Perseids and Pelopids in the two generations after Perseus and 'Pelops', Apollodorus is careful to give in every case, except that of Heleus[56], the names of wives as well as of husbands. Only in naming the descendants of Hippothoë and Poseidon does he fail to give the names of the wives. At the same time he makes nonsense of the stated chronology by providing two generations too many of these descendants. Moreover, the appearance of the god Poseidon *in the middle* of a human family tree is clear evidence that something is amiss.

What has happened is surely quite clear. The succession is matrilineal, for the sons of Pterelaos claim Mycenae from Elektryon as the kingdom of their maternal grandfather: that is, their claim runs through their mother and her mother. Some chronicler who knew nothing of the religion of the Mycenaean world was probably disturbed by the statement that Hippothoë married Poseidon, a god, and also 'Taphios Pterelaos'. He will not have known that in early times a human being could be possessed by a god or at least impersonate him, and so be called, at any rate on certain occasions, by his name. He therefore distinguished Poseidon from Pterelaos. He seems also to have been an ignorant man, for he took Taphios to be a proper name, instead of simply meaning 'a Taphian'. But for 'Taphios' and Pterelaos he could provide no wives (although Pterelaos' sons based their claim on matrilineal

---

[56] Heleus is in any case a somewhat doubtful son of Perseus. If Aegius' emendation of ἐλούσης Ἀργείας in Apollod. 2.4.7 is accepted, he came from Helos in the Argolid. It seems more likely, since we know of no association of Perseus with this place, that he was simply a Perseid by clan, of the generation following Perseus, than that he was a son. The absence of mention of a wife likewise tends to distinguish him from the other sons of Perseus. Alternatively, he may have been a son-in-law.

succession), because only one woman, Hippothoë, was in fact mentioned. Poseidon, 'Taphios', Pterelaos became representatives of separate generations, when in fact they are one and the same man. Through his Pelopid wife and her mother, his sons held themselves justified in claiming Mycenae.

III. The Perseidae

The myth of Perseus is, in its historical aspect, one of the most confused and obscure of all the major Greek myths. Much, as will be seen from the following brief treatment, remains dark, though further research may bring light. Nevertheless, certain important features seem to emerge clearly and firmly.

The relations of the 'Perseids' with the 'Pelopids' play a central part in the earlier history of Mycenae, Tiryns and Argos. It seems that the Perseids arrived in Mycenae after the Pelopid invasion of Greece. Apollodorus[57] tells us that before 'Perseus' came as a grown man to Argos he was requested by Polydektes, king of the island of Seriphos, to contribute to a wedding-gift for Hippodameia, daughter of Oinomaos. It is true that Pelops himself is not mentioned, and that therefore another 'Hippodameia' may be intended, but three of Perseus' sons married daughters of 'Pelops'; their names were Alkaios, Mestor, and Sthenelos. Sthenelos was the husband of Nikippe[58]. The Pelopidae seem therefore already to have had sufficient power in the Peloponnese for Perseus' sons to have cultivated them, once the power of their dynasty was established. It is indeed evident from Thucydides' account that the Pelopids or Tantalids were already well esconced in Mycenae when Atreus became king. This is implied by the position of Nikippe there. Atreus and Nikippe can hardly be the children of a man who was himself a newcomer in Greece and who lived at Pisa. As we have already seen, the name 'Pelops' covers a succession of rulers, and it would seem that this must be true of 'Perseus' too.

It is by no means certain that Mycenae was the seat of Perseus' rule. Apollodorus[59] apparently makes Tiryns the centre of his government, from which place he exercised control over Mideia and Mycenae. Pausanias[60] makes him the founder of Mycenae: if this is true, he must, at least at first, have based his rule on one of the other cities. Apparently he based it on

[57] 2.4.2.   [58] Apollod. 2.4.5.   [59] 2.4.4.   [60] 2.16.3.

Tiryns. By 'founded' we must understand that 'Perseus' established the city in its later form, for the site had long been inhabited in some fashion, and in view of the fact that he is said to have built its Cyclopean walls, we may take it that the fortification of its citadel was carried out later than that of Tiryns, which seems to have been fortified well before Perseus' arrival. There is therefore no disagreement between Pausanias and Apollodorus. It was Perseus who first gave Mycenae a military and political importance. If so, he must have been of an earlier generation than Atreus. Mycenae seems to have been developed by a kind of wary co-operation and rivalry between the Pelopids and the Perseids.

At first, Perseus was, as one would expect of a *protégé* of Athena, strongly hostile to those who cultivated Poseidon and to the dynasty represented by Hippodameia. Medusa, whom he slew, is very closely associated with Poseidon: the god mated with her[61], and after her death the horse Pegasus sprang from her. The monster from which Perseus rescued Andromeda, and which he likewise slew, was sent by Poseidon[62]. In art, Medusa is constantly associated with a horse; indeed, a Boeotian clay pithos of the second half of the seventh century shows Medusa as a centaur-like figure, that is, with a horse's body[63]. The story of Perseus' relations with Polydektes in Seriphos shows that they were enemies. Polydektes tried to exact from Perseus a mark of friendship towards Hippodameia, daughter of Oinomaos[64], in the form of a wedding gift, but while others, at Polydektes' demand, contributed horses, Perseus refused, and said he would bring Medusa's head instead[65]. This is evidently a declaration of hostility towards Hippodameia and Poseidon (and possibly Ares, whose son Oinomaos was), and implies that Medusa is, in Perseus' view, their representative. It looks indeed as though this Hippo-

---

[61] Apollod. 2.3.2. See 2.4.2,3 for the assistance given by Athena to Perseus in the decapitation of Medusa, and notice Apollodorus' remark that 'it is said by some that Medusa was beheaded for Athena's sake', which clearly implies the assertion of the cult of Athena against another cult.

[62] *Id.* 2.4.3.

[63] Louvre, C. A. 795. See J. W. Woodward, *Perseus* (C. U. P., 1937), for this and other representations of Medusa in art. The textual sources for the Perseus legend are also collected in this pleasant book.

[64] How far the myth has been contaminated with that of Pelops at Pisa it is hard to say. See footnote 67.

[65] This, in the context, I take to be the sense of καὶ ἐπὶ τῇ κεφαλῇ τῆς Γοργόνος οὐκ ἀντερεῖν.

dameia and Medusa were identical. The name 'Medusa', of course, simply means 'the woman ruler'. After Perseus has slain Medusa, he returns with the head to Seriphos and turns Polydektes and his companions to stone. There was a local Argive tradition that the head of Medusa was buried in the agora of the city[66].

The story seems to imply that, at the time when Perseus arrived in Argos, the ruling dynasty of the city celebrated the cults of Poseidon and Hippodameia, whom Hesychius equates with Aphrodite. Earlier, it had had a line of Danaid princesses (see § IV) and this line (if interrupted) was restored later. An apparent change of religion suggests at first sight that an interregnum occurred: the Danaids, as we shall see, worshipped a goddess whom we may call Helen-Artemis or, in Argos at least, Hera, and their male deity was Zeus. Yet we find Poseidon fathering Pegasus on Medusa. The stories about Medusa cannot, for the most part, easily be associated with Argos (see footnote 66), but there remains enough of a connection to make it unwise to assert that there was no slain Medusa of Argos, whatever other such 'Medusae' there may have been.

If an interregnum occurred, it would seem that the restoration of the Danaid line was the work of 'Perseus'. The break would then have lasted only one generation and have occurred after the reign of Eurydike and Akrisios. It is noticeable that Akrisios had no successor in the generation that succeeded his own: he is doomed to be killed by his grandson (*i.e.* the apparent interregnum is passed over in silence). His daughter, Danaë, makes no marriage, though there is the story of her pregnancy with Perseus by Zeus or, alternatively, her uncle Proitos. All the evidence, except for the story of Akrisios putting Perseus in a chest with Danaë and setting them adrift on the sea, suggests that Perseus was not descended from the Argive ruler and his consort. Before Perseus reaches the Greek mainland he is associated with Seriphos, 'Libya' and 'Ethiopia'. The story of Danaë's solitary

---

[66] Paus. 2.21.6., where (with the preceding sub-paragraph) it is stated that Medusa led the Libyans in battle and that she died during the campaign. Lucian, *Dial. XIV*, makes Perseus slay Medusa in Libya. Poseidon is also closely associated with Libya (Apollod. 2.1.4.). These are evidently legends which refer to the period before the arrival of Perseus in Greece: Medusa of Argos has been confused with some 'Libyan' or Asiatic figure or figures. This confusion, it may be suspected, arose from these earlier encounters having provided some of the material for the narration of the last ecstatic flights of 'Perseus' as shaman on his arrival in Greece: see Chapter IV.

voyage with the infant Perseus across the sea, however charming it may be, is possibly an invention designed to bridge the gap of the interregnum and to show that the continuity of the line was not broken[67]. At the same time one cannot dismiss it as complete fiction: a daughter of the house may have been banished with her offspring[68]. The offspring, however, cannot have been Perseus, for Perseus did not worship Zeus, by whom, or by whose Danaid representative, Proitos, Danaë was said to have become pregnant.

'Danaë' is, of course, not a personal name, simply meaning, as it does, 'the Danaan woman'. In the latter part of the legend of Perseus and Danaë, Danaë is associated with Andromeda: the hero brings Danaë and Andromeda from Seriphos to Argos[69]. The one name is a racial adjective, the other a proper name. 'Danaë' may have originally described Andromeda, with whom he intended to claim succession to, or refound, the royal Danaid line at Argos. In the same way, we have seen, the Taphian Pterelaos became Taphios and Pterelaos. If so, the fact that she is of the same race as Perseus' traditional mother is certainly significant. Alternatively, Perseus' claim to rule in Argos may well have rested on the fact that his mother was an *émigrée* daughter of Eurydike: the Danaë whom he brought to Greece may indeed have been his mother. The myth may then be right in distinguishing her from Andromeda. Patrilineal in practice (as we shall suggest), Perseus seems in either event to have used matrilineality to advance his position in a dynastic contest for power.

The precise identity of this second Danaë is not a matter of the first importance. The essential facts are: the apparent descent of Perseus from a

[67] Hyginus' account, which makes Oinomaos marry Euarete, daughter of Akrisios, and beget a daughter Hippodameia upon her, must refer to a daughter who was not the heiress to the Argive throne, but a sister of the heiress. The mother of 'Hippodameia', whatever her personal name, must herself have been a 'Hippodameia' or 'Nikippe' or 'Hippomedusa'; there is, however, no mention of Pelops, and Oinomaos was the son of Ares.

[68] For an interpretation, by no means implausible, of this banishment see W. J. Gruffydd, 'Moses in the Light of Comparative Folklore', *Zeitschrift für die Alttestamentliche Wissenschaft*, Vol. 46 (N. S. Vol. 5) (1928). One should not, however, forget that Schol. *Iliad* 14.319 says that, according to Pindar, Proitos slew Danaë. Perseus is also said (Ovid, *Metam.* 5.239) to have killed Proitos (in Argos): it seems more likely that Perseus slew Proitos' consort with Proitos himself. We shall see that such practices existed, but in this case the suggestion is purely speculative. We may in any case suspect that two men named 'Perseus' are involved, the one, conqueror of Tiryns, the other, of Argos.

[69] Apollod. 2.4.4.

Danaid princess; the fact that Poseidon was not a Danaid deity; the patronage of Perseus by Hermes and Athena, who were also no Danaid divinities; the hostility of Perseus to Poseidon and to Hippodameia; the murder of Medusa, who is closely associated with 'Poseidon' and whose head was believed by the Argives to be buried in their *agora;* the apparent gap of one generation between Eurydike and Akrisios and their next recorded successors; the fact that Perseus' life, apart from the story of his extreme infancy, had been spent outside the Greek mainland before he came to Argos; his arrival in Greece with a Danaan princess; and the fact that a matrilineal Danaid line is to be found in Argos after him[70].

The account we have given above is simplified at one critical point. When Perseus cuts off Medusa's head, not only Pegasus, but Chrysaor springs from her body. Both were apparently begotten by 'Poseidon'. Yet Chrysaor is quite certainly the name of a 'Zeus' associated especially with the site of the Carian town Stratonikeia since very early times[71]. The name of the town was originally Chrysaoris, and the sanctuary of Zeus Chrysaoreus became a sanctuary common to all Carians. It was said to have been the first of the towns founded by the Lycians, and we may conclude that the cult was of Lycian origin[72]. The cult is to be associated with the figure of a horse and rider[73], the horse being identified with Pegasus, and also, it seems, with Leukippos. There seems to be an absurdity here: how can Poseidon father Pegasus and a Zeus-like figure?

Laumonier refers to a passage of Pausanias[74] which links by a curious legend the temple of Zeus Osogoa at Mylasa in Caria with that of Poseidon Hippios at Mantinea and the Acropolis of Athens. In his view the link implies a deity anterior to Zeus and the Poseidon of the west and related to both. In Hesiod[75] Chrysaor, that is, a form of Zeus, appears in a chthonic setting, and Laumonier suggests that behind this conjunction may lie a nature in Chrysaor which is at once chthonic and celestial. This view receives support from the name of a Carian Zeus called Zenoposeidon which appears in literary texts and in an inscription from Crete of about 200 B. C. Other-

---

[70] See below, on Clytaemnestra.

[71] A. Laumonier, *Les Cultes Indigènes en Carie* (Paris, 1958), pp. 193 ff.

[72] Laumonier, *op. cit.,* pp. 206 f.

[73] Roscher, *Lexikon d. gr. u. röm. Mythologie, s. v.* Zeus Χρυσαόρειος, p. 669. Laumonier, p. 205, also notices the connection with Pegasus, and, p. 206, with Leukippos.

[74] 8.10.4. Laumonier, *op. cit.,* pp. 124 f.

[75] *Theog.* 280 ff. See Laumonier, *op. cit.,* p. 210.

wise it appears in association with Osogoa. Laumonier attributes the formation of the name 'Zenoposeidon' to the Greek distaste for barbarian words. The deity must have embodied characteristics of celestial Zeus and chthonic Poseidon, and in Greek eyes have been closer to the latter. Surprising as the suggestion may at first sight appear, the Danaid 'Zeus' and the 'Poseidon' who lay with Medusa are thus not improbably one and the same deity. There was in this case no interregnum. Perseus brought a Danaid bride with him[76] in order to justify his claim, but he had no hesitation (if a historical princess lies behind the Argive Medusa) in killing the reigning Danaid queen and her husband, Akrisios (although myth lays the scene of Akrisios' death elsewhere, presumably in order to lend verisimilitude to Perseus' ignorance of the king's identity). Perseus thus established himself and his consort. If this account is essentially the true one (and no one can be certain that it is), 'Medusa' was the queen Eurydike, his supposed grandmother. Perseus' action, then, in slaying a princess of the sacred Danaid dynasty[77] in order to put his own Danaid bride in her place, is a first sign of the patrilineal tendency, which, as will be suggested, distinguished the Perseids.

The sharp division which appears in the Danaid myth, and in myths related to it, between the adherents of a Poseidonian cult and those who worshipped Zeus, Hera, Artemis or Helen seems to have developed as the legends and the cults of Asia Minor came into contact with the Greek world. In the Appendix on Helen we have occasion to remark on the early friendship of goddesses who have associations with Asia Minor and on their later mutual hostility. The Greek mind, in making these divisions, has, it seems, presented us with a more or less distorted view of the cults of early times[78].

Perseus the founder of Mycenae is not, essentially, a religious figure. This view of him is emphasized by his refusal to present horses on the marriage of Hippodameia: it is a rejection of the shamanist world, for the horse which Hippodameia tamed was the spiritual steed of the ecstatic[79]. He goes further: he cuts off the head of the mother of Pegasus. Indeed, he is the very type of the skilful, and fundamentally cynical, politician: when he has cut

---

[76] *i.e.* If the 'Danaë' whom Perseus brought with him was his mother, it is unlikely that his bride Andromeda was of another clan. Moreover, the Danaid line was evidently restored, for the typical names recur.

[77] See § IV below.

[78] See also footnote 136.

[79] See Chapter IV.

off Medusa's head, Athena places it in the middle of her shield. (If Athena's shield was a shaman's mirror, it naturally reflected the visage of her enemy[80]). Having won the political and military victory, however, Perseus was quite willing to come to terms with matrilineal cult: after he had first established his power by aggression against matrilineal Danaids, he apparently arranged marriages for his sons with Tantalid women. Three of his supposed[81] sons married 'daughters' of Pelops.

Of the sons attributed to Perseus, Sthenelos, who married Nikippe, may really have been a descendant. Thucydides says[82] that Atreus, after Eurystheus had gone off to fight the Heraclidae, by making himself regent and then king of Mycenae, established the ascendancy of the Pelopids over the Perseids. The close association of Perseus with Athena seems to mark the Perseids as a patrilineal dynasty. If one bear in mind that Eurystheus was reputedly the son of Sthenelos, one may infer that a possibility had existed of Eurystheus' establishing a male Perseid succession at Mycenae. This would have replaced the matrilineal Pelopid tradition. Atreus, as brother of the Pelopid Nikippe, owed his position as regent to the working of the matrilineal rule. Eurystheus had apparently stood in the way of its operation. If he was really the son of Sthenelos, and if Sthenelos was really the son of 'Perseus', we may say that patrilineal custom seems to have been characteristic of the Perseidae, even if they could not always assert it against Pelopid custom. (It is evident that in the marriages of the other sons the matrilineal rule prevailed.)

That Sthenelos, exceptionally, may have represented a patrilineal tradition, and that he therefore may really have been a Perseid, appears from Book II of the Iliad. We have had occasion to remark, and shall remark again, that names are sometimes, even often, extraordinarily faithful witnesses to clan and cult. One of the leaders of the Argive contingent in the Iliad is named Sthenelos. His father was Kapaneus. Euadne, the wife of Kapaneus, immolated herself on her husband's funeral pyre[83]. This seems

---

[80] See below on the shield of Abas (footnote 93) and Chapter IV.

[81] I say 'supposed' sons, not only on the general ground that the traditions of father-son relationship are not reliable, but because it is, in the case of Perseus' legendary son Alkaios, very difficult to believe that a man with a name containing the element Alk-could have been Perseid and Danaid by descent. See Appendix II. Alkaios may have been a son-in-law of Perseus.

[82] 1.9.

[83] Apollod. 3.7.1.

to show a patrilineal rule[84], in which respect it may be compared to the Indian *suttee*.

A good deal turns upon the patrilineality of Athena. No doubt there has been some, perhaps much, renaming of deities, but it seems unlikely that one goddess alone, of all the goddesses of Mycenaean times, underwent, after the Mycenaean age, so radical a metamorphosis as that from matrilineality to patrilineality. We may infer her to have already been a patrilineal goddess in the Mycenaean age, and the clan of which she was the guardian to have observed a patrilineal rule. She may at some very early stage have been matrilineal, for it is clear that Perseid patrilineality was due to considerations of a political kind. Eurystheus, who had apparently tried to assert his right to the succession against Atreus, seems to have continued in religious matters to observe the matrilineal tradition. This we noticed in connection with his purification of Kopreus, who was his kinsman on his mother's side.

We shall have something more to say of the Perseids in connection with the Danaidae (immediately below) and of Perseus himself in Chapter IV.

IV. The Danaidae

The Danaidae were settled at several centres in Greece, and members of Danaid dynasties are the subject of major myths[85]. There can hardly be any serious doubt that they were matrilineal. This is indicated by the very fact that fifty daughters, and no sons, are attributed to 'Danaos'. Nor is there any suggestion that the first generation after 'Danaos' succeeded to the rule of Argos otherwise than matrilineally. Hypermnestra is queen at Argos as a matter of course: she is the daughter of 'Danaos', and Lynkeus, the alleged son of Aegyptus, only reigns at Argos as her consort[86].

Hypermnestra, however, is said to have had a son Abas, who married Aglaia, 'daughter of Mantineus'. Aglaia and Abas in turn had twin sons, Akrisios and Proitos, who contested the rule of Argos, Akrisios emerging as victor, while Proitos became ruler of Tiryns. Akrisios married Eurydike

---

[84] Which prevailed over Euadne's own matrilineal tradition.

[85] Campbell Bonner's 'A study of the Danaid Myth' in *Harvard Studies in Classical Philology*, XIII (1902), is a valuable and balanced piece of work, but does not touch upon matrilineality or *partheneia*. The folk-lore element in the 'fifty' daughters does not eliminate the suggestion of matrilineal descent.

[86] Apollod. 2.1.5.

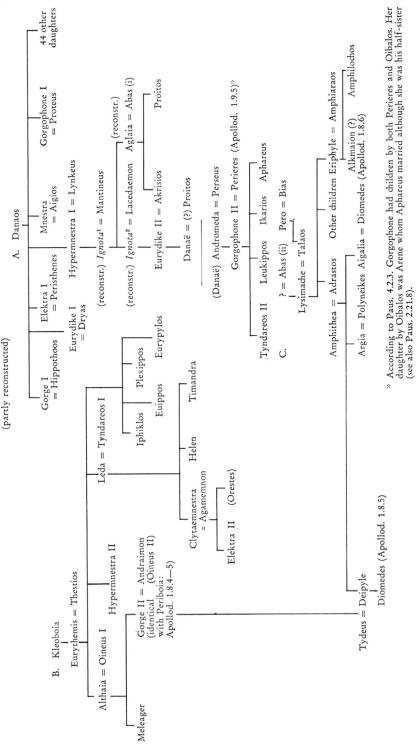

Danaid and Argive Dynasties
(partly reconstructed)

* According to Paus. 4.2.3. Gorgophone had children by both Perieres and Oibalos. Her daughter by Oibalos was Arene whom Aphareus married although she was his half-sister (see also Paus. 2.21.8).

of Argos and their daughter (they had no recorded son) was Danaë. Abas, Aglaia and their sons raise a difficulty, for with them a patrilineal practice seems to be intruded.

If Hypermnestra succeeded to the throne in Argos in her own right, this was either in default of male heirs or as a result of a matrilineal rule. Two general considerations lead one to the view that a matrilineal rule continued to be observed down to 'Danaë'. Firstly, if it be granted for the moment that the first mythical generation of Danaids, that of Hypermnestra and her 'sisters', is in all probability a recollection of matrilineal tradition, then it is extremely difficult to believe that this tradition was not continued in succeeding generations. The growth of warfare and politics may have increased the importance of the male ruler and made the ultimate change to patrilineality inevitable, but the essential elements of inheritance[87], succession, and authority in cult ritual[88] seem in general to have remained in the female line for several generations after the establishment of a new matrilineal house on the Greek mainland. Secondly, the transference of these to the men occasioned, as we shall see, a tremendous crisis in early Greece which has left very clear traces in myth. There is no sign of such a crisis in the accounts of the marriage of Abas and of Akrisios' accession to the throne of his grandmother, real or supposed, and this is a very strong indication that even if they were the son and grandson of Hypermnestra and both lived in Argos they had not become the heirs of Lynkeus.

Neither Pausanias[89] nor Apollodorus[90] suggests that Abas ruled in Argos. We learn only that he married Aglaia, the daughter of Mantineus, and that their children were Akrisios and Proitos. The easiest supposition at first sight is that Abas, under the matrilineal rule[91], left Argos and married the princess of Mantinea, where he then resided. Eurydike, however, is undoubtedly a queen of Argos. She is said to be the daughter of Lacedaemon, or of Lacedaemon and Sparta[92]. This seems to imply (if the latter descent is erroneous, as it surely is, for her daughter was Danaë) a generation at Argos

---

[87] See p. 15.

[88] These matters are treated from another aspect in the next two chapters.

[89] 2.16.2.

[90] 2.2.1.

[91] That a son could not succeed to his father's throne.

[92] Apollod. 2.2.1. gives Eurydike as 'daughter of Lacedaemon'; in 3.10.3. her parents are 'Lacedaemon and Sparta'. Pausanias however does not mention Eurydike among the children of Lacedaemon and Sparta. It may be suspected that Apollodorus includes

between Hypermnestra and Eurydike, a generation in which a daughter of Hypermnestra took as her consort at Argos a prince from Lacedaemon, their daughter being Eurydike, who married a man from Mantinea, Akrisios. If this is what happened, the matrilineality of the Argive line is perfectly clear. The solitary great-granddaughter of Danaos in Argos, 'Danaë', is evidence that the matrilineal Danaid succession had in fact continued. (It is to be noticed that the masculine, 'Danaos', never recurs.)

There is, however, a serious difficulty about Abas. His name shows that he was not a Danaid at all but a member of the tribe of the Abantes. The patrilineal thinking of mythographers probably lies at the root of the trouble. As Akrisios was the son of an Abas who had, as it was thought, married the princess of Mantinea, Abas, as father of a king of Argos, was probably assumed to have been a member of the Danaid dynasty. He was thus turned into the son of Hypermnestra. In reality, however, as one would expect in a matrilineal context, the father of the king, Akrisios, was not a Danaid, but an outsider[93].

Even this suggestion is not wholly satisfactory: the rivalry of the brothers Akrisios and Proitos for Argos suggests that they may have had a claim to the throne and that their maternal grandfather may have been the ruler of

her as a daughter of 'Lacedaemon and Sparta' in 3.10.3. only because she had been given as a daughter of Lacedaemon in 2.2.1.

[93] Schol. Eurip. Or. 965 speaks of Abas as king of the Argives, and Servius on *Aeneid* III, 286, implies the same. Neither of these authorities is to be rated above Apollodorus and Pausanias. Indeed the story in the latter passage is most easily interpreted on matrilineal lines: the handsome youth who receives the consecrated 'arms' of Abas is the new king (see below in this chapter). The absence of any suggestion in Apollodorus and Pausanias that Abas was king in Argos is very striking. The 'shield of Abas' seems to have been really a Danaid shield, for, according to Hyginus, *Fab.* 170, Danaos had consecrated it to 'Juno'. (In all probability the 'shield' was a shamanist mirror, for the mere sight of it put to flight the foes of him who bore it (Servius, *loc. cit.*, and Hyginus, *Fab.* 273). These foes will originally have been assailant spirits, not human enemies: see Chapter IV, on the shield-mirror used by Perseus). As to the association of the name of Abas with both the shield and the Danaid dynasty, which cannot have come about directly through Abas the father of Akrisios, since, if we are right, he had nothing to do with Argos, it is possible that another 'Abas' (i.e. one of the Abantes) of whom there is no longer any record married an Argive princess who has also fallen out of history, and so became ruler of Argos. Thus there is Abas the ancestor of Eriphyle, whose wife's name is not recorded (see table of Danaid and Argive Dynasties: C). This is speculation, of course. What is certain is that Abas was not a Danaid.

Argos[94]. That is to say, their mother, Aglaia, may have been a daughter of the *potnia meter* of Argos, and, not being herself the heiress to the throne, but a sister of the heiress, have left Argos and married an 'Abas' who lived elsewhere, just as the Pelopid Hippothoë married the Taphian Pterelaos (see § II *ad finem*). 'Mantineus' will then not have been the legendary founder of Mantinea but a man from Mantinea who was the consort of her mother, a forgotten queen of Argos. In other words, Aglaia and Abas should exchange their places in the dynastic tree: Aglaia was not a daughter-in-law but a daughter of the queen of Argos, whose son-in-law, Aglaia's husband, was Abas.

This appears to be the most probable solution of the difficulties. Some slight corroboration of it lies in the fact that it places Aglaia, 'the bright one', among the Danaidae, who have cult associations with light and radiance (see below). The line of descent thus restored is shown in the table of Danaid and Argive dynasties on p. 28.

There is further evidence that points to matrilineality. A striking feature of the dynasties marked A and B in the table on p. 28 is that the names of five daughters of Danaos recur in later generations: Gorge, Eurydike, Elektra, Hypermnestra, Gorgophone. Two other names, Mnestra and Clytaemnestra, share a common element with Hypermnestra. In view of the fact that the ending *-m(n)estra* apparently does not otherwise occur at all[95] we may regard these as names peculiar to the Danaidae, while the recurrence of the five distinctive women's names may indicate in this context a tradition of nomenclature transmitted matrilineally. Gorge, Gorgophone, Elektra and the names ending in *-m(n)estra* further suggest a connection with religion: the relationship of Clytaemnestra and Iphigeneia and Elektra as mother and daughters seems to unite cult with matrilineal descent.

It is true that two male names recur, Oineus and Tyndareos. Of these, however, Oineus is certainly not a true personal name, but the name given to the husbands of a line of Danaid princesses in Aetolia in virtue of the office they held as the consorts of the reigning house. This becomes clear from a comparison of two passages of Apollodorus[96]. In one of these, Oineus is said to have had a daughter Gorge, whom Andraimon married;

---

[94] See pp. 50 f.

[95] Kretschmer and Locker, *Rückläufiges Wörterbuch der griechischen Sprache* (Göttingen, 1944), give no names ending in *-m(n)estra*.

[96] 1.8.1. and 1.8.5.

in the other, this Gorge is said to have borne Tydeus to her own father. As
the former passage gives the name of Gorge's husband, it seems clear that
the allegation in the latter is due to the fact that Andraimon, the successor
of 'Oineus', was also known as 'Oineus'[97]. That the name 'Oineus' was
attached to successive holders of the same office is also implied by the story
that Diomedes visited Oineus in his old age and transferred the kingship to
Andraimon[98]: since Oineus the husband of Althaia was at least Diomedes'
great-grandfather[99], more than one 'Oineus' must have preceded Andraimon.
The recurrence of the name Oineus is not likely to be an obstacle to the
inference of matrilineal descent to be drawn from the names of the women.

As to 'Tyndareos', the name, although it conceals an individual (or several
individuals), seems to mean 'a man of the Tyndarid clan'. It may or may
not be a Danaid name. In the case, however, of the Tyndareos said to be
one of the four sons of Gorgophone II, it seems clear that he is to be reckoned
as a Danaid: we have no ground for refusing to admit him as such. When
Tyndareos the father of Helen married Leda, he married another Danaid.
He seems to have been a figure of importance in cult, and his marriage to a
Danaid woman (that is, a woman who represented Leda in cult) suggests
that he may have belonged to an indigenous dynasty, assimilated to the
Danaidae in some way which is no longer clear, with a custom of endogamy
and of an especially sacred character. (Helen's connection with the Leleges
makes her quasi-indigenous.)

The suggestion that there was a tradition of endogamous marriage among
the Tyndaridae is apparently confirmed by Euripides, *Elektra*, 312 f.
Elektra, who in line 60 had called her mother 'the all-destroying Tyndarid',
declares:

$$\mathrm{ἀναίνομαι\ δὲ\ Κάστορ᾽,\ ᾧ\ πρὶν\ ἐς\ θεοὺς}$$
$$\mathrm{ἐλθεῖν\ ἔμ᾽\ ἐμνήστευον,\ οὖσαν\ ἐγγενῆ.}$$

It would appear that this is a tradition which related to earlier Tyndarids
but had become attached to Elektra the daughter of Clytaemnestra. 'Elektra'

---

[97] The story about Periboia and Oineus in Apollod. 1.8.4,5 is obscure. It seems to have
   arisen from a tradition that one bearer of the title Oineus was named Hipponous
   and came from Olenos. This, to later generations, made little sense, for it was supposed
   that there was only one Oineus and that the descent was patrilineal. The patrilineal
   implication of the tale given by Apollodorus simply will not fit into the matrilineal
   tradition of this house. There may, however, be another explanation of the story.

[98] Apollod. 1.8.6.

[99] See table of Danaid and Argive dynasties.

was perhaps a cult-title, hereditary in the Tyndarid clan. In 311 Elektra had declared herself a *parthenos,* and it is at least possible that she was vowed to sacred union with her kinsman, the Διὸς κοῦρος, alone. The myth of the Danaids may describe the attempt of the royal Danaidae to maintain or restore a tradition of *partheneia.* Lynkeus, alone of the sons of Aegyptus, respected the *partheneia* of Hypermnestra[100]. The myth, as we have it, seems to be a fusion of earlier and later elements, in that the sons of Aegyptus are wrongly equated with the kinsmen with whom a true endogamic relationship must once have been observed.

That Helen was a sister of Clytaemnestra, whose daughter was Iphigeneia, tells us that the cult of Helen-Artemis[101] was practised in this dynasty. The children of Leukippos, son of Gorgophone II, point in the same direction: their names were Hilaira and Phoibe and they married the Dioscuri[102]. The cult and representation of Helen-Artemis can, however, only have been a tradition passed on from mother to daughter, possibly in association with a sacred college, and Hilaira and Phoibe must therefore owe their association with the cult to their mother. No wife, however, is mentioned for Leukippos, which in this context is surprising. If one consider also the names of Leukippos' daughters and their marriage to the Dioscuri, the strong probability will be apparent that these figures, and by implication their father, are purely divine. Leukippos had a third daughter, Arsinoë, who became the mother of Asklepios by Apollo. This daughter also seems to belong entirely to the divine world. Why then is 'White Horse', Leukippos, said to be a son of Gorgophone? I would suggest that his parentage by Gorgophone finds a parallel in the parentage of Pegasus by Medusa: he is the Danaid horse of ecstasy, white because the Danaid cult was celestial, as that of Pelopid Poseidon was chthonic[103]. Naturally, he has no wife. He is the father of Hilaira and Phoibe, those heavenly maidens, because only when

---

[100] Apollod. 2.1.5., and several other authorities. A close study of Pindar, *Nem. X,* 49 (93) ff., shows, as I hope to demonstrate elsewhere, that a *Tyndarid* Lynkeus is there almost certainly partially assimilated to, and to be identified with, the true Dioscurus (Polydeukes). I believe that Euripides, in the passage quoted above, is mistaken, inasmuch as it was Polydeukes, not Kastor (who is a chthonic figure), to whom Elektra was related. By Euripides' time this distinction between the Dioscuri was probably no longer fully understood.

[101] See Appendix I.

[102] Apollod. 3.10.3.

[103] See Chapter IV and Laumonier, *op. cit.,* p. 206.

mounted upon him, that is, in ecstasy, can one behold them. There is a Siberian parallel, it would seem, to Hilaira and Phoibe: G. Nioradze[104] describes the vision of a certain shamaness, who saw two maidens, daughters of Aurora *(sic)*, descend to earth from the sky. Their faces were of magical beauty and the glance of their eyes burned like fire. Their long hair waved in the wind, their clothes were of many-coloured skins and in their wide sleeves shone flickering lights. The implications of 'Leukippos', if our interpretation is right, is that Gorgophone was a shamaness.

Pausanias[105] says that the author of the *Cypria* calls Hilaira and Phoibe the daughters of Apollo[106]. They had a shrine at Sparta and were tended by maidens who were consecrated to their service and were called, like the goddesses, Leukippides. It would seem likely that this fact—that both the goddesses and the virgins who served them were called daughters of Leukippos—caused the confusion through which the heavenly hierarchy found a lodging in the dynastic tree of the Danaids. If so, the implication would seem to be that the women who served them were in early times members of a Danaid dynasty or clan of sacred character. This conclusion accords well with what we know of Tyndareos. Leukippos will then have been a brother of Tyndareos in the same sense as Helen was a sister of Clytaemnestra[107]. The suggestion of shining light which we find in the name Phoibe, and which is characteristic of Helen and the Dioscuri in general, is, as we have remarked, also to be found in Aglaia, 'the bright one', whom Abas married.

Something must now be said about the *partheneia* of Hypermnestra. It is undoubtedly relevant that the Tyndarid-Danaid goddess could be identified with the 'virgin' Artemis. Lynkeus was said (surely wrongly) to be a descendant of chthonic Poseidon, and the brides of the Pelopid or Tantalid worshippers of Poseidon seem to have represented a goddess, not of an ascetic character, but of fertility[108]. Lynkeus' respect for the queen's *parthen-*

---

[104] *Der Schamanismus bei den sibirischen Völkern* (Stuttgart, 1925), p. 99.

[105] 3.16.1.

[106] For ambiguity between Zeus and Apollo see footnote 136 and Appendix I.

[107] Herodotus, 2.171, connects Demeter with the Danaidae. There is a hint of a connection between Demeter and Helen in Paus. 10.28.1., where Kleoboia is said to have brought the rites of Demeter from Paros to Thasos: Helen's maternal great-grandmother was a Kleoboia.

[108] See p. 148 and Appendix I *ad* fin., in connection with Niobe. The statement that Lynkeus was a son of Poseidon seems to be due to his erroneous inclusion among the 'sons of

eia would apparently mean that he did not insist on his bride's representing the Poseidonian fertility goddess in cult. The cult of Hera at Argos was, it seems, for its initiates, a mystery religion. Traces of this remained until much later times: Pausanias[109] says that once a year the goddess was bathed in a spring near Nauplia, and that this bathing, which was connected with the mysteries of her cult, rendered her a *parthenos*. We shall speak below[110] of the possible, and indeed in some cases, evident, element of identity in Hera and Artemis and Helen and certain other celestial goddesses.

Physiological virginity may be left on one side as being of only marginal relevance in connection with the Tyndarid-Danaids and the cults of Helen-Artemis and Hera. A possible meaning of *partheneia* in connection with the Tyndarid-Danaid dynasty is that the queen represented the goddess in cult and that the goddess had no spouse. If the goddess were Artemis this would be easy to believe. A second possibility is that the only proper consort of the goddess was her brother: Homer and others tell us that Zeus and Hera were brother and sister[111] as well as husband and wife. It seems that the legends of the birth and childhood of Helen may imply that Apollo and Artemis had also been both brother and sister and husband and wife at some very early stage[112]. Such relationships among the gods may reflect those in the earliest form of the Tyndarid-Danaid dynasty: the queen's consort may originally have been her brother, although the myths seem to have been formed when a wider degree of kinship was permissible to the sacred and royal pair. Elektra, as we have seen, was both *parthenos* and the erstwhile bride of her kinsman, the Dioscurus. We shall return to this topic shortly.

A third possible sense of *partheneia* derives from the nature of the religion itself. The prestige of a cult of the Tyndarid-Danaid kind rests on the access which the sacred dynasty is believed to have to divine powers. The cult is essentially ascetic, connected, as the association of Helen, Phoibe and Aglaia

---

Aegyptus', aided perhaps by the ambiguity of Zeus Chrysaoreus (see above). All the indications make him a 'son of Zeus': hence his respect for the *partheneia* of Hypermnestra.

[109] 2.38.2.

[110] See especially Appendix I.

[111] κασιγνήτην, *Il.* 16.431.

[112] See Appendix I. The possibility depends on the degree of equivalence to be attributed to Artemis and the Aphrodite associated with Apollo. Leda's swan, the father of Helen and her sisters, is undoubtedly Apollo, to whom the bird was sacred.

with light indicates, with ecstatic vision[113]. Any direct association with
fertility is extraneous to the true sense of the cult and can only be an interpretation attached to it by those who stood outside its inner circle. The
association of Artemis with Eileithyia is no evidence of an original fertility
cult, but only of the status of the goddess as, in philosophical language, the
First Cause[114]. Artemis has no children, but even the ascription of divine
children to a deity is no evidence whatever of a fertility cult. It frequently
indicates only cultural change. In any case, although utilitarian reasons,
as well as fear, may have accounted for much of the attachment of the
vulgar to ritual, they form no part of the essence of a religion of this
character. It was perhaps in some measure because of the very limited com-
municability of a cult's inner meaning that the secrecy of the initiate became
so common a feature of ancient religion in its higher aspects. The seclusion
of the practising ascetic who undergoes a rigorous training was probably also
a factor which led to the same development. These qualities and characteristics are likely to mark a sacred dynasty, at any rate in its formative
generations.

One must admit that it is not easy, if one accept the myth as it stands, to
see how the endogamous Tyndaridae could have become fused with the
ruling dynasty of the apparently exogamous Danaidae. It becomes easier if
one assume that the story of the sons of Aegyptus was added later to the
Danaid myth, as E. Meyer suggested. The visit to Rhodes *en route* for
Greece may then point to an origin in south-western Asia Minor. Certainly
Helen at one time had a temple in Rhodes. Moreover, the Leleges of Laconia,
with whom she was connected[115] seem to have had very close Carian associations. It is significant that Tyndareos celebrated the cult of Zeus, while
Hera was already the goddess of Argos when the Danaids settled there[116].

[113] The proof of this must await another occasion.

[114] Frazer was a Utilitarian and apparently unable to conceive of mystical experience as
a religious fact. The transcendental element in religion was therefore entirely neglected
in *The Golden Bough*, with such absurd results (uncritically accepted by some writers
of to-day) as the description of the devotion of a *gallus* to Cybele as an aspect of a
fertility-cult. However beastly the devices of the heathen may have been, the cause
of the world's existence is exalted far above the self-regarding purposes of men. Of
course the popular conceptions of these ascetic cults were doubtless often very far
removed from any understanding of their true nature.

[115] See Appendix I in connection with Niobe. On the connection of Carians and Leleges
see Laumonier, *op. cit.*, pp. 17 ff.

[116] See footnote 122. It is not clear to me that the *association* of 'Zeus' and 'Hera' is

The Zeus of the early Peloponnese (or rather Apia[117]) had close connections with south-western Asia Minor. Proitos, brother of Akrisios, married into a Lycian ruling house which supported him with military force in Tiryns. This suggests an earlier connection between his own house and the Lycian dynasty. He may have represented Zeus in cult, for while one tradition makes Danaë pregnant by Zeus, another makes her so by Proitos. Both he and Akrisios were sons of Aglaia. Zeus himself in the Iliad[118], filled with grief at the impending doom of Sarpedon, who is especially dear to him, debates with Hera whether to remove him from the battle and set him down in Lycia. There is thus evidence connecting the cults of Zeus, Hera and Helen, which already existed in the Peloponnese when 'Danaos' arrived, with Lycia and Caria[119]. Proitos' connection with Lycia tends to reinforce the presumption of dynastic relationships implied by the community of cults. As we have remarked, for the Greeks Hera was traditionally the sister as well as the spouse of Zeus. The marriages of the Danaidae with an endogamous dynasty already established in the Peloponnese are then not difficult to understand: if the relationship of spouse and consort was no longer that of sister and brother, it may well have been a marriage of kin within a sacred dynastic clan. The pressure from the adherents of the cults of Poseidon and of Athena will perhaps have strengthened the inclination to maintain or revive the endogamous custom.

The Danaidae, then, were characterized by a distinctive cult, of which their royal women, formerly perhaps in association with their brothers, at one time almost certainly with their kinsmen, were the bearers.

---

generally pre-Hellenic in mainland Caria. See however H. Opperman, *Zeus Panamaros* (Giessen, 1924), pp. 86 and 88 ff., for a divine pair called Zeus and Hera at Panamara. For Hera as autochthonous on Samos see Laumonier, *op. cit.*, pp. 705 f.

[117] See Appendix I in connection with Niobe.

[118] 16.436 f.

[119] I do not wish to enter into the disputes about the meaning of Zeus 'Lykeios'; see however Appendix I in connection with Niobe for further evidence of an early Peloponnesian Zeus. From the relationship of Zeus and Hera as brother and sister, referred to just below, one would be wise not to draw firm conclusions. It may be nothing more than a logical consequence of the fact that they are the children of Kronos, and their relationship to Kronos nothing more than simple succession. It may thus be simply 'theological' schematization, reflecting no social usage. At the same time one may wonder why, if this was so, Homer, in the passage from the Iliad cited above, drew express attention to the double relationship of the two deities. In any case the other hints of endogamy remain.

A difficult problem is raised by the fact the association of Athena with the Danaidae did not begin with Perseus. Danaos builds his ship on Athena's advice[120] and, breaking his voyage at Rhodes, sets up a statue of Lindian Athena there. After the Danaidae have murdered their husbands, they are purified by Athena and Hermes[121]. It would certainly seem on this evidence that the Danaidae brought the cult of Athena with them. Yet she was not a Danaid goddess. It is quite impossible that the patrilineal Athena should have been the goddess of matrilineal Danaidae. In any case, the Danaid goddess was Helen-Artemis.

When the Danaidae arrived in Argos, the goddess of the country is said to have been Hera[122]. The constant association of Hera with Argos, and that of Helen and Artemis with the Danaidae, suggest that the name Hera is one of a number of names, such as Niobe and Artemis and Helen, which denoted female divinities who in earlier times had been substantially identical. The extensive identity to be found in Helen, Artemis, and a certain Aphrodite distinctly indicates (as we shall remark) that this was so[123]. However that may be, the local cult was very powerful: Argos was always known as the city of Hera, not of Athena. Perseus, moreover, whose goddess was Athena, seems to have been unable or unwilling to maintain himself in Argos, if we may judge by the story of the exchange of cities with Megapenthes. Whether the Danaidae already cultivated Helen or not when they arrived in Greece, they certainly cultivated a goddess who closely resembled her, and they were able to make Argos a great centre of their clan its cult. To goddesses of the kind of Helen, Artemis, the celestial Aphrodite and Hera, Athena has no apparent relation.

The only way in which the problem of the connection of Athena with the Danaidae seems soluble is to suppose that the connection of the Danaidae with the 'Perseidae' goes back to times before 'Perseus', and that when the Danaids arrived they were accompanied by male 'Perseids'[124] or at least adherents of Athena and Hermes. This would not be surprising, for the Danaidae, apart from the Tyndarid dynasty, were certainly not always endogamic in Greece and the association of Perseus and Danaë shows that they were under pressure to contract exogamic marriages.

---

[120] Apollod. 2.1.4.
[121] Apollod. 2.1.5.
[122] Paus. 2.15.5 and Apollod. 2.1.4. with Heyne's emendation of Ἀθηνᾶς (Frazer *ad loc.*).
[123] See Appendix I.
[124] That is to say, members of a clan of which Perseus later was a member.

This first wave of 'proto-Perseids', then, may have been attacked by another immigrant people, represented by the 'sons of Aegyptus'[125] soon after their arrival. The slaughter of the 'sons of Aegyptus' did not, as the Medusa myth suggests, relieve the Danaids of the pressure of Poseidon- and Hippodameia-worshipping suitors until Perseus on his arrival re-established the Danaidae in Argos. A further consideration suggests that our interpretation is sound. When Perseus sets out to kill Medusa, he is guided on the first stage of his enterprise, the visit to the Phorkides, by Hermes and Athena. He goes on to the next stage with Athena, and apparently without Hermes but wearing winged sandals. It is suggested that Perseus on this second stage is thought of as an embodiment of Hermes, who, it seems, was the male deity associated with Athena in early Perseid cult. At any rate, the two divinities are intimately connected with him. Now we have noticed that, in the first period of Danaid settlement in Greece, it is Athena and Hermes who purify the Danaidae after the murder of their husbands[126]. This seems to be an unmistakable indication of the presence of 'proto-Perseids'. We may suppose that the reputed large-scale nocturnal attack on the 'sons of Aegyptus' was carried out by their rivals, the menfolk of the proto-Perseid clan with which we believe the Danaidae to have arrived in Greece. We may further take it that it was these proto-Perseid men rather than the Danaid women who received purification, and that they received it at the hands of the representatives of their own patron deities. It is, after all, more likely that the attack on the 'sons of Aegyptus' was carried out by their male rivals than by their brides[127]. The reason why the guilt was attributed to the women is, one may think, the same as that for which the death of Agamemnon was attributed to Clytaemnestra, a reason which is put forward in Chapter II. We need not assume, indeed, that the story of the murder of

[125] It may well be that, as E. Meyer thought (see Campbell Bonner, loc. cit., pp. 138 ff.), the story of the 'sons of Aegyptus' is a later addition to the myth. The references to Perseus' contests with worshippers of Poseidon, however, show that there were opponents and rivals who, even if they did not come from Egypt, had at least a religion of a similar kind. Belus was the son of Poseidon (Apollod. 2.1.4).

[126] Apollod. 2.1.5.

[127] The hostility between Poseidon and Athena appears even at this early stage, if the 'sons of Aegyptus' represent Poseidon-worshipping rivals of the Perseids (though probably not from Egypt: if Belos is Baal, their origin is sufficiently indicated). Aegyptus was the son of Belos, and Belos was the son of Poseidon (Apollod. 2.1.4). Athena and Perseus were, as we have seen, hostile to Poseidon from the moment of their arrival in Greece, and, as it appears, before this.

the bridegrooms implies a large-scale, simultaneous assault at all. The myth
in its earliest form may only have indicated a general practice of Danaid
princesses: they killed their husbands, as the Tyndarid Clytaemnestra was
(falsely, as we shall suggest) believed to have done.

The dynasty marked 'C' in the table of Danaid and Argive dynasties
raises another difficulty. There is no indication, apart from its association
with Argos, that it was a Danaid line at all. That Eriphyle should have had
a son with the name Alkmaion, in which the constituent *Alk-* seems to point
to one of the clans associated with Ares or Poseidon[128], makes it very difficult to believe that she was one of the Danaids associated with the Perseidae
or the Tyndaridae. On the other hand, the attribution of Alkmaion to her
as a son may be without historical foundation. Alkmaion, in early life, may
have had no connection with Argos at all, the relationship having been
invented to explain a misunderstood tradition that he slew the *potnia meter*
in Argos, who was taken to have been his own mother. Less debatable
evidence is the fact that the characteristic Danaid names do not appear in
this dynasty. Thirdly, there is some reason to think that Eriphyle herself
was connected either with a Pelopid dynasty[129], or, more probably, with
the cult of Ares and Aphrodite[130].

Yet Clytaemnestra lives in Argos and is an incontestable Tyndarid-
Danaid. Clytaemnestra's mother seems to be connected, not with Argos, but
with Aetolia[131]. It would seem that the Danaid rule in Argos had again been
interrupted, perhaps after Gorgophone II, and another dynasty held sway
there for two, possibly three, generations, until Alcmaeon brought it to an
end. Clytaemnestra seems to have been the first of the restored Danaids at
Argos. Her mother was Leda, whose sister was Althaia, the wife of Oineus (I)
of Aetolia and mother of Meleager. (See dynastic table of the Danaidae).
It seems that Clytaemnestra may well have come from Aetolia and it is not
unlikely that Agamemnon himself brought her to Argos by arrangement

---

[128] See Appendix II.
[129] Herodotus, 5.67, says that Adrastos of Argos had a shrine at Sicyon, because he
was the son of the daughter of Polybus, King of Sicyon, and had inherited the kingdom. If so, then Eriphyle must have been a daughter of Polybus. As we have seen,
Sicyon seems to have been a centre of Pelopid power. It is therefore possible that
Eriphyle was regarded as a Pelopid.
[130] See below in this chapter.
[131] Apollod. 1.7.10.

with the heads of the Danaid royal line. Apollodorus[132] tells us that Agamemnon, before he married Clytaemnestra, visited Oineus in Aetolia,
together with Menelaos[133]. Tyndareos, the husband of Leda and father of
Clytaemnestra, 'brought them (sc. Agamemnon and Menelaos) back again.'
They expelled Thyestes (presumably from Mycenae) and married Clytaemnestra and Helen respectively. Clytaemnestra was already married, it
would seem to another 'Pelopid', Tantalus[134], whom Agamemnon slew,
together with their infant child, before himself marrying Clytaemnestra.
Agamemnon thus came to power with the help of the Danaidae, the condition of which help was apparently the restoration of the Danaid line,
represented by Clytaemnestra, to Argos.

This temporary alliance of the Tantalidae with the Danaids brought no
fundamental reconciliation of the two clans: the hostility of Artemis continued to pursue Agamemnon as it had pursued Atreus, no doubt because,
unlike Lynkeus, he refused to recognise his wife's cult. Indeed, we must
recognise that this period, the late Mycenaean age, was characterized by an
almost chaotic violence, in which the protagonists were seldom the women,
who were the axes around which the whole society turned, but the men, who
sought the power and prestige which association with these women brought.
The women indeed played, at least at times, a moderating part in the centre
of the conflict. This we may see in Apollodorus' words about Eriphyle: 'the
decision as between the arguments of Polynices and those of Amphiaraus
lay with her, because once, when a difference arose between him (Amphiaraus) and Adrastus, he had made it up with him and sworn to let Eriphyle
decide any future dispute he might have with Adrastus'[135]. We may perhaps
see the same *rôle*, and its importance, implied in the name of Eriphyle's
mother, Lysimache.

---

[132] *Epit.* 2.15–16.

[133] This cannot have been the Oineus who was the husband of Althaia, though he may
have been the husband of her daughter, Gorge, the mother of Tydeus. There is a
discrepancy between the generations: Clytaemnestra would appear to be a contemporary of Gorge, yet Tydeus, son of Gorge, was apparently a generation earlier
than Agamemnon. This is probably due to there having been yet another 'Oineus'
after the father of Tydeus, though it should be remembered that the 'Oineus' for
whom Diomedes arranged a successor was said to be an old man (Apollod. 1.8.6).

[134] One may hazard the guess that this Tantalus and the Oineus whom Agamamnon
visited were one and the same man, and that Agamemnon visited Aetolia in order
to carry off Clytaemnestra.

[135] Frazer's translation.

The male Danaid deity was Zeus[136] and 'Tyndareos' celebrated and apparently represented him in cult[137]. We have seen some reason to suspect that an endogamous marriage custom persisted in the Tyndarid dynasty, at any rate for cult purposes, although at times the Danaidae were apparently exogamous, probably perforce. The exogamous marriages of the Danaidae with the Perseids or 'proto-Perseids' resulted in the appearance of a new deity, Athena[138], who was associated with the male Perseids with whom they intermarried. Athena thus had to be related to the Tyndarid-Danaid Zeus, although there was no true clan relationship, and this situation may be represented by the story that Athena sprang fully armed from the head of Zeus, which clearly indicates that there is no blood-relationship between the two, and that Athena is the later deity from the point of view of the Zeus-worshippers.

V. The Athenian Royal Line

The ancient Athenian royal line was clearly matrilineal: from Erechtheus to Theseus, not a single ruler was born in Athens[139]. It will repay us to tell the familiar story of Theseus, as given by Plutarch, in some detail.

Aigeus, on a journey to Athens, stopped at Troezen, the city of 'holy Pittheus'[140], where he associated with Pittheus' daughter, Aithra. On leaving Aithra, he hid his sword and sandals under a large stone, and told her that, if a son should be born to her who, on growing to man's estate, should be able to lift the stone and remove from beneath it what he had left there, she was to send the young man to him, with the sword and sandals. A son

---

[136] See however Appendix I for ambiguity as between Zeus and Apollo. Also Laumonier, *op. cit.*, p. 122: 'Les Zeus anatoliens ne se distinguent pas toujours nettement d'Apollon.'

[137] Apollod. 3.10.7.

[138] One must, however, bear in mind the possibility of a renaming of deities quite apart from the substitutions which are so clearly visible in the Homeric poems. It is hard to associate the Athena of Athens with the Perseid Athena because the Perseids do not appear to have been connected with Athens.

[139] J. Töpffer, *Attische Genealogie* (Berlin, 1889), p. 162: 'Es ist eine wenig beachtete, aber merkwürdige Thatsache, daß die traditionelle athenische Stadt- und Königsgeschichte in der Zeit zwischen Erechtheus ... und dem ἔπηλυς Theseus von keinem eingeborenen Landeskönige weiß.'

[140] Eurip., *Hippol.* 11, calls Hippolytus ἁγνοῦ Πιτθέως παιδεύματα.

was born, and named Theseus: he duly recovered the tokens from under the stone and was despatched to Athens. When he arrived there, he found public affairs disturbed by factions, and disorder in the house of Aigeus. Medea was living with Aigeus, and had undertaken to cure him of his childlessness by means of drugs. She discovered who Theseus was, but Aigeus, who was an old man and feared everyone because of the disturbed state of society, did not recognise him. She suggested to Aigeus that he should invite Theseus to a feast, with the intention of poisoning him. Theseus came, but did not tell his name: instead, when at the table, he drew his sword[141] 'as if to cut some meat', to give his father an opportunity of recognising him. Aigeus recognised the sword at once, upset the cup of poison, looked closely at his son and embraced him. He then introduced Theseus as his son and heir to a meeting of the citizens.

One clan, however, the Pallantidae, viewed Theseus with great disfavour. They had expected to inherit the kingdom on the death of Aigeus without issue. Indeed, they had been angered that Aigeus, who was merely an adopted child of Pandion and not related by blood to Erechtheus at all, should have obtained the kingdom. Now Theseus, who was also a stranger and a foreigner, was to inherit. There was a battle between Theseus and his supporters and the Pallantidae, in which Theseus was victorious.

The time now arrived when the tribute of seven youths and seven maidens was due from the Athenians to Minos in Crete. The people began to abuse Aigeus, whom they regarded as responsible for the calamitous surrender of their children while at the same time making a man who was a foreigner and a bastard the heir to his kingdom. Theseus then offered to go with the children to Crete, and there try to slay the Minotaur, the monster whose victims they were intended to be. This he did, successfully.

Because of Theseus' omission to replace the ship's black sail by a white one on the return journey, Aigeus assumed Theseus to have been killed and, in his despair, threw himself over a cliff and died. When Theseus arrived at the harbour, he performed the sacrifice which he had vowed to the gods if he returned safe, and sent off a herald to the city with the news of his safe return. The herald met many who were lamenting the death of the king, and others who were glad at the news of the safe return. They congratulated him and wished to crown him with garlands, which he received, but placed on his herald's staff. He then returned to the seashore, where, finding that

---

[141] μάχαιραν, *Thes. XII.*

Theseus had not completed his libations, he waited outside the temple, not wishing to disturb the sacrifice. When the libation was finished, he announced the death of Aigeus, whereupon they all hastened up to the city with loud lamentations. To this day, therefore, says Plutarch, people declare that at the Oschophoria it is not the herald that is crowned but his staff, and that at the libations the bystanders cry out 'Eleleu, Iou, Iou,' of which cries the first is used by men in haste, or raising the paean for battle, while the second is used by persons in surprise and trouble[142].

The real course of events is here thinly disguised. The story of Aithra and the sword of Aigeus is a wholly unpersuasive attempt to represent Theseus as the natural heir of Aigeus. The same pattern appears here as we have seen in other cases of accession to a kingdom descending in the female line. Theseus is not recognised by the old king when he arrives, just as, in Pindar's version of the story, it is made clear that Pelias did not recognise Jason[143]. A clan who support a rival claimant object to Theseus as a stranger and a foreigner, which he quite plainly was. This objection is mentioned twice. Moreover, it is expressly stated that Aigeus too had been a stranger and intruder[144]. The old king is ailing and unable to control affairs, and impotence is perhaps a sign that he is no longer fit to be king. Indeed Aigeus is afraid of Theseus and tries to poison him at the banquet to which, at Medea's instance, he is invited. We shall take notice later of the meal that in several cases precedes the killing of a king. Theseus draws his sword, and it is a reasonable presumption that the 'recognition' of the sword by Aigeus is a substitute for the king's death. The story thus seems to contain reminiscences of the deaths of two kings, for there is the account of Aigeus' death by falling down a cliff. This is combined with a prolonged sacrificial ritual carried out by Theseus on the seashore (as was the sacrifice at which Jason and Pelias spoke of the Golden Fleece, and Pelias plainly saw that his successor stood before him). When the sacrifice is finished, the herald announces the

---

[142] Except for a few slight alterations the wording of this account follows Stewart and Long's translation of the *Lives*.

[143] Pind. *Pyth.* IV, 86: τὸν μὲν [*sc.* Jason] οὐ γίνωσκον and 97 ff. (Pelias addresses Jason when he appears before him):

ποίαν γαῖαν, ὦ ξεῖν', εὔχεαι
πατρίδ' ἔμμεν; καὶ τίς ἀνθρώπων σε χαμαιγενέων πολιᾶς
ἐξανῆκεν γαστρός; ἐχθίστοιτι μὴ ψεύδεσιν
καταμιάναις εἰπὲ γένναν.

[144] *Vita Thes.*, XIII, XVII.

king's death. It is to be remarked that there seem to be two parties, for while some lament the old king's death, others welcome Theseus. That there was a tradition that Theseus had brought about his predecessor's death is clear from the absurd story of his having forgotten to hoist the white sail, thereby causing Aigeus to commit suicide through grief. It has obviously been invented in order to reduce the degree of Theseus' responsibility, if not to exculpate him. 'Theseus' is, no doubt, a composite figure, and the stories of two kings' deaths, one by the sword and one by being hurled from a cliff, seem to have been combined.

There are, however, two unusual features of this legend. The first is that after the first meeting of Theseus and Aigeus there is no further mention of Medea[145]. The second is that there is a close connection of Theseus with the Delphic Apollo[146]. These two features are reciprocally interdependent and are signs of the change from the Mycenaean world to the Apolline cult of archaic Greece. Theseus is supposed to have founded the Athenian state by unifying Attica and centralising its government through the act known as the συνοίϰισις. This act was decisive for the future of the clans: they were doomed, and with them the matrilineal kingship. The state was beginning to arise. Medea perished, and Delphi began to take her place.

VI. Laïos and Oedipus

There is another cycle of myths of which we must take some brief notice in its connection with the same kind of practices. This is the Theban cycle. The Theban stories need a far fuller treatment than that which we can give them here, but the similarity of feature in the myth of Oedipus is so striking that the nature of the events which gave rise to them can only have been essentially the same.

Oedipus is said in Sophocles' *Oedipus Tyrannus* to have come to the throne of Thebes in the following circumstances. He was exposed as a baby because of a prophecy that Laïos would die at the hands of his son. Found by a servant of Laïos, he was given to a shepherd, who gave him to Polybus and Merope of Corinth. This couple brought him up as their child. So far,

[145] Apollod. 1.9.28 and *Epit.* 1.6. give two different accounts of Theseus' expulsion of Medea.

[146] V, XIV, XVIII.

then, we notice two *motifs* which should be familiar to us: firstly, there is
the prophecy, which reminds us of the prophecies that Oinomaos would die
if his daughter Hippodameia were to wed, and that the king Akrisios would
be killed by the son of his daughter Danaë. Secondly, there is once more the
childhood and youth of the future ruler spent in some distant place. This
was part of the legend of Perseus, of Theseus, and of Jason too, who, it will
be remembered, before he challenged Pelias, lived in the countryside. Pelops
himself also came to Oinomaos' kingdom from a distance, Agamemnon was
taken by his nurse to Sicyon, and Orestes' 'return' belongs to the same
category.

When Oedipus meets his father on the road, neither, of course, recognizes
the other, just as Pelias, according to Pindar, had never seen Jason before,
and as Aigeus failed to recognize Theseus. There was a quarrel, and Oedipus
killed Laïos.

When Oedipus arrived in Thebes, he found the people in great distress.
Similarly, public affairs at Athens were in a state of disorder, because of
the age and infirmity of Aigeus, when Theseus arrived there. At Athens, it
was Theseus' deliverance of the people from the Minotaur's demands which
finally won him the throne: at Thebes, Oedipus saved the people from the
ravages of the Sphinx. What these ravages were is not clear. There may have
been an outbreak of some plague. What seems clear is the diagnosis of the
cause of the trouble which Oedipus pronounced when he answered the
Sphinx's riddle: his answer, in effect, pointed out that the king was an old
man, and the fact that the Sphinx set the riddle seems to imply that his age
was connected with the people's affliction. When Oedipus had given his
answer, their sufferings came to an end. Oedipus, we know, killed the king
and reigned in his stead. That, according to the story, he had killed the
king unwittingly before arriving in Thebes can hardly be other than a later
attempt to conceal the truth[147].

Oedipus, we may surely say, was not Laïos' son, any more than Pelops
was the son of Oinomaos, Aegisthus of Agamemnon, Pelias of Aison, Jason
of Pelias, or Theseus of Aigeus. In the cases of Theseus and Oedipus, a fictitious story of their birth has been prefixed to the true account in order to

---

[147] It should be noticed that the answer Oedipus gives to the riddle is quite inconsistent
with the story of his meeting and quarrel with the king when the latter was driving
in a chariot on a road outside Thebes. This story implied that the king was still
a vigorous man. See also below, on the gifts given to Oedipus' 'father'.

give it a patrilineal form. A consequence of this was the story that Oedipus married his mother. Oedipus of course did not marry his mother: he married Laïos' widow, and only by so doing could he become king. It follows that the story of the self-blinding is almost certainly a later invention.

VII. The King's Curse, the Sacrificial Meal and the Succession

The succession to the kingship is, at times, connected with a curse and on occasion with a sacrifice and with a meal. The curse may perhaps, like the sacrifice, and, it would seem, the meal, be part of a ritual.

When Aison killed himself at a sacrifice and Pelias became king in his place, Aison's wife cursed Pelias. Plutarch tells us[148] that before Theseus embarked for the island of Skyros, where he was thrown from a cliff and killed, he solemnly uttered curses upon the Athenians and that the place where he took ship was called the place of cursing. Plutarch also mentions a story that Theseus' death occurred after a meal. The accounts of the curse called down upon Eteokles and Polyneikes by Oedipus connect it with, on the one hand, the partaking of wine, on the other, with a sacrifice. The story is told in a surviving fragment of the *Thebaid:*

'But the fair-haired Polyneikes, of divine race, first put before Oedipus a fine silver table that had belonged to Cadmus of god-like mind, and then he filled a fine cup of gold with sweet wine. But when he (*sc.* Oedipus) noticed lying before him the costly gifts that had been given to his own father, his spirit was filled with great evil, and he forthwith called down dire curses upon both his sons, and the Erinys of the gods heard him. He cursed them with the prayer that they should never divide their inheritance from him in friendship, but that there should ever be wars and battle between them[149].'

It is clear that the drinking of wine is here a ritual act, and that the presents given to Oedipus' father are traditional ceremonial objects. (The usual story of Laïos' death seems thus to be contradicted.) Oedipus recognises their implication, which is such as to cause him to utter his curse upon Eteokles and Polyneikes. It is further a reasonable inference that the implication was one that involved the ownership of his property, whatever else

[148] *Vita Thes.* XXXV.   [149] Kinkel, *Epic. Graec. Frag.*, p. 11.

it may have involved. The explanation given by the scholiast on the Laurentian manuscript of the *Oedipus Coloneus*[150] is as follows. The adherents of Eteokles and Polyneikes had by custom sent to their father Oedipus, as his share of each sacrifice, the shoulder. On one occasion, however, 'whether from carelessness or for some other reason', they sent him the hip. Oedipus was 'a small-minded man of thoroughly low birth', and, thinking he had been slighted, cursed them. We may set aside the scholiast's attempt to find a subjective explanation of Oedipus' wrath, and may draw the conclusion that Oedipus was enraged because on this occasion he was not given the portion which was due to him as king: his deposition is implied. This deposition takes place in a ritual of the drinking of wine and of sacrifice. What happened then to Oedipus we do not know: we have only the separate story of his self-blinding. Nevertheless, it is possibly significant that before Apsyrtos was slain before the shrine of Artemis, he was offered splendid traditional presents (which included the robe of Hypsipyle).

We come to the Pelopidae. The story of Tantalus' offering of Pelops to the gods is not connected with any mention of a curse. This is natural, for Pelops was not slain. The first curse is delivered by Oinomaos upon Myrtilos, his charioteer, as he is dying after the accident to his chariot which enabled Pelops to win the race for the hand of Hippodameia. He cursed him with the wish that he, Myrtilos, might perish by the hand of Pelops[151]. Why should Pelops have been expected to kill Myrtilos?

According to one version of the story[152], Pelops, when he saw the heads of the unsuccessful suitors nailed over the door of Oinomaos' house, feeling that he might have been rash to seek Hippodameia's hand, offered Myrtilos half the kingdom if he would help him to win the race. Apollodorus[153] says that after the race, when Pelops, Hippodameia, and Myrtilos were on a journey, the last tried to rape Hippodameia. Pelops threw him into the sea, and as he fell, he uttered curses against the clan of Pelops. If we combine the wording of Oinomaos' curse with the attempted rape, Pelops' offer of half the kingdom with the improbability of a charioteer endangering himself as well as his master in order to let a competitor win a race (even if bribed), and with the curses uttered by Myrtilos in his turn, we may reasonably conclude that Myrtilos was the actual successor of 'Oinomaos' and

---

[150] 1375; Kinkel, p. 12.   [152] Hyginus, *Fab.* 84.
[151] Apollod. *Epit.* 2.7.   [153] *Epit.* 2.8.

predecessor of 'Pelops'. According to tradition, Pelops killed both him and Oinomaos[154]. Pelops then, as one statement has it, instituted the Olympic games in Oinomaos' memory, according to another, in that of the dead suitors. That is to say, they were funeral games. We are not told how Pelops died[155].

The next curse is that pronounced by Pelops on his sons on account of the murder of Chrysippos, his son by another wife[156]. There then follows that pronounced by Thyestes on the Pelopidae[157] when Atreus, after the cannibalistic feast, showed him the severed hands and feet of his children. Aeschylus makes Cassandra call it the πρώταρχον ἄτην, the original evil deed, which brought the Erinyes, having drunk of human blood, to brood over the palace[158]. (The next evil deed, the sacrifice of Iphigeneia, is, according to Aeschylus, unaccompanied by curses, for Iphigeneia was gagged to prevent her uttering them. In any case, it has nothing to do with the succession).

In three of the examples we have quoted, Theseus, Oinomaos, and Myrtilos, the curses uttered have immediately preceded the death of him who uttered them. In the case of Aison, his wife spoke the curses on Pelias after her husband's death, as did Thyestes after the death of his children. The deaths of Aison and Thyestes' children occur in connection with a sacrifice which is explicitly mentioned. So, it can hardly be denied, does that of Aigeus in Plutarch's narrative. There is also a tradition that Thyestes himself was killed after a banquet[159]. Hyginus says that Atreus was killed at a sacrifice on the seashore. Pelias meets Jason, his successor, at a sacrifice.

---

[154] Apollod. *Epit.* 2.7. Confusion may have arisen because 'Oinomaos' was not a proper name but a cult-title, or at least a popular descriptive name. Thus Myrtilos may also have been named 'Oinomaos' aftere taking over the cult functions of his predecessor. This is, of course, speculation, but 'Oineus' provides a parallel.

[155] But see footnote 27.

[156] That Chrysippos, said to have been the son of Pelops by a previous marriage, was really one of the succession of rulers hidden under the name 'Pelops' seems very probable.

[157] *Agam.* 1600.

[158] *Agam.* 1191 f.

[159] Schol. Eurip. *Orest.* 812, apparently basing his account on Sophocles' *Atreus* or *Mycenaeae* (Wagner, *Aesch. et Soph. perdit. fab. frag.* s. Soph. *Atreus [Mycen.]*). The scholion is omitted by Schwartz, apparently following Nauck, but is given in Jebb and Pearson, *Fragments of Sophocles*, I, p. 92. It certainly raises difficulties, but it is not clear that the tradition is to be rejected out of hand.

Oedipus' pronunciation of curses on his successors is connected both with a sacrifice and with, apparently, a further ritual act, which involved the drinking of wine. His actual fate is not mentioned. A ritual of sacrifice, meal and cursing seems to have gone together with an enforced death. In Chapter II we shall see further evidence.

The matrilineal dynasties evidently became, on occasion at least, centres of savage competition among the more ambitious men of the time, succession to the kingship, as the tale of the suitors for Hippodameia seems to suggest, being decided by brute force. There are signs, however, that a male descendant was not without claim to a throne if he was a ruler's daughter's son. Thus the sons of Pterelaos the Taphian, as we have seen, claimed the succession as the grandsons of their mother's father. Sometimes, apparently, the father was too powerful to be dispossessed by the daughter's husband and was succeeded by her son. Polybus of Sicyon, dying, as it is said, without a son, left his kingdom to his daughter's son, Adrastus[160]. Akrisios was told 'by an oracle' that he would be killed by his daughter's son. Agamemnon, whose father was, we think, 'Pleisthenes', may have had a claim to the succession at Mycenae as the grandson of Atreus through his mother. Certainly, as we saw, he was one of those children of Atreus' daughters to whom, according to Dictys, Atreus left his possessions in Crete[161]. This may indeed be the sense of 'Atreides': the ending of the stem in -id, as has often been pointed out, implies female descent. 'Atreides' may therefore mean 'matrilineally descended from Atreus', and so by custom 'Atreus' daughter's son.' Jason is 'Aisonides', and he is separated by an intervening generation from Aison, namely that in which Pelias was the ruler. 'Aisonides' may likewise really mean 'Aison's daughter's son.' Aegisthus, whom the Odyssey[162] calls 'Thyestiades', was the son of Thyestes's daughter[163]. The instances in which brothers are rivals for a throne (Akrisios and Proitos[164]; the sons of Pterelaos, who are not stated to be rivals, but, being six

---

[160] Herodot. 5.67.

[161] See p. 12 f.

[162] 4.518.

[163] Apollod. *Epit*. 14. We may disregard the story that Aegisthus was the issue of a union between Thyestes and his daughter: it seems plainly to be due to a misunderstanding of 'Thyestiades' as meaning 'son of Thyestes'.

[164] But only if their mother had been a daughter of the πότνια μήτηρ of Argos. Aglaia might have been a daughter of an Argive queen who had married a 'Mantineus' and sister to the heiress to the throne, leaving Argos to marry and live with an 'Abas'. See § IV of this chapter.

in number, could not sit on one throne; Atreus and Thyestes) suggest that these male generations in the dynastic families concerned may have held that they were entitled to claim particular thrones, without there being any rule to determine which brother was the heir. It thus seems that, while the successor to a ruler might well be unrelated to him, and was certainly never his son, in the next generation the throne was commonly claimed by a son of the first ruler's daughter and that this relationship is the meaning of the ending -ίδης (-άδης)[165]. Orestes, however, while he may have been Agamemnon's grandson (Ἀγαμεμνονίδης), as Agamemnon had been the grandson of Atreus, by matrilineal descent, observed, it seems, the un-Pelopid cult of Ares, as presumably his father (whoever he may have been) had done. He was a leader of the attack upon the matrilineal world.

VIII. The Assault on the Matrilineal Order

The matrilineal world was brought to an end by a number of murderous assaults upon the heart of that world, the *potnia meter* herself. The opposition to the *potnia meter* seems to have been closely connected with the cult of Ares. The first appearance of this anti-matrilineal movement of which we have any record is to be found in the story of Meleager.

Meleager was the son of Oineus, who seems to have represented and embodied Ares[166], and of the Tyndarid Althaea. He had been fighting for the Aetolians (whose distinctive deity was Ares) against the Kouretes in defence of Calydon[167]. As long as he was fighting for the Aetolians, all went well for them. But he had killed a maternal kinsman (κασίγνητος) of his mother Althaea, and was incensed with her because she had cursed him. In his anger at his mother, Meleager turned to the arms of his wife, Kleopatra, and fought no more for the Aetolians. The fight then started to go against the Aetolians and they were in great danger. Oineus, the old father, came to beseech Meleager to fight and so did his maternal

---

[165] The custom extended far beyond the borders of Greece: see W. J. Gruffydd, 'Moses in the light of Comparative Folklore', *Zeitschrift für die Alttestamentliche Wissenschaft*, Vol. 46 (1928).

[166] This seems to be the meaning of Apollod. 1.8.2.

[167] *Il.* 9.529 ff. In 532 the Kouretes are apparently inspired by Ares. There is no evident reason why both sides should not, in this region, have cultivated Ares.

kinswomen (κασίγνηται) and his mother (πότνια μήτηρ). Then his paternal kinsmen (ἑταῖροι)[168] 'who were much the dearest to him', also came,
but still he would not fight[169]. Only when his wife entreated him did he
yield. Meleager's wife has a patrilineal name. Meleager himself does his
father the service of slaying a boar which is ravaging his vineyards. The
boar was sent by Artemis, who is often to be equated with the Danaid
Helen[170], the goddess of his mother's clan. He likes his paternal kinsmen
much better than his maternal relations. Indeed, he kills one of the latter.
The story in the Iliad thus strongly emphasizes the patrilineal inclinations
of Meleager.

That these inclinations were not simply a personal vagary, but that,
on the contrary, there really was a conflict between the patrilineal and the
matrilineal principles in early Greece appears from the legends of Eriphyle and of Alcmaeon. In Argos, the relations of Eriphyle with her
brother, Adrastos, and her husband, Amphiaraos, reveal a world verging
on the matriarchal. Apollodorus says[171], 'Polynices gave her the necklace,
and begged her to persuade Amphiaraus to go to the war: for the decision
lay with her, because once, when a difference arose between him and
Adrastus, he had made it up with him and sworn to let Eriphyle decide any
future disputes he might have with Adrastus.' Even in Argos, however,
matrilineality did not go uncontested. Amphiaraos was (it is said) a prophet of Apollo[172], and he showed marked signs of hostility to Eriphyle.
He was opposed to the campaign against Thebes, and bade Alcmaeon take
vengeance on Eriphyle. The acceptance of the necklace and robe[173] by
Eriphyle at the hands of Polyneikes clearly symbolizes the acceptance of
cult office. The cult seems to have been that of Ares and Aphrodite, for

---

[168] See footnote 2.

[169] On the significance of this further refusal see footnote 196 and § IX of this chapter.

[170] See Appendix I.

[171] 3.6.2. Frazer's translation.

[172] This is, however, highly improbable. His disappearance into a chasm with his horses
suggests chthonic religion. Delphic influence has converted the early opponents of
matrilineality, Amphiaraos and Orestes, into agents of Apollo. W. K. C. Guthrie,
The Greeks and their Gods, p. 219, sees Amphiaraos as a local underworld spirit.
This does not explain the part he plays in the myth: the priestly prince and the
'underworld spirit' for whom (presumably) he spoke may have been known by the
same name. The problem goes beyond the limits of our present context.

[173] *Ibid.* 3.6.2; 3.7.2.

Pausanias[174] records, between Argos and Mantinea, a double temple of Ares and Aphrodite which was said to have been founded by Polyneikes and the Argive chieftains on their way to Thebes. The temple will, of course, have been a later one, but its association with Polyneikes in the context of the legend may point to an old tradition that he upheld the joint cult of Ares and Aphrodite. Moreover, the robe was that which Cadmus gave to Harmonia, daughter of Ares and Aphrodite. It seems likely that the enmity felt by Amphiaraos for Eriphyle, and his hostility to the expedition to Thebes, was due to dynastic cult rivalry between Amphiaraos and Polyneikes and to the anti-matrilineality of the former.

The attitude of Meleager, son of Ares (Oineus), seems to reflect a disturbance of a normal state of equilibrium (represented perhaps by Harmonia) in the joint cult of Ares and Aphrodite. The sexes must have been delicately balanced in the cult, so that neither predominated: though 'Harmonia' and Eriphyle each was offered, and wore, the robe and necklace of office, each received them at the hands of a man, of Cadmus and of Polyneikes[175] respectively. Such a state of balance, of mutual counterpoise, implies common understanding and acceptance of the religion as a harmonious whole. If one partner begins to behave erratically, the disintegration of the religion as a whole cannot be prevented, and, conversely, the erratic behaviour of one partner is a sign of the impending dissolution of the cult-community.

Alcmaeon killed Eriphyle, the *Potnia Meter* of Argos (whether she was or was not his mother). Her Erinyes visited him, and he went mad. He fled first to Arcadia, to Oïkles, who was his paternal grandfather, and then to Phegeus in Psophis. Alcmaeon's relations with Phegeus, who purified him, are most illuminating, and so indeed are events in Psophis altogether. Pausanias has something to tell us of the history of Psophis and its rulers[176]. The original name of Psophis was Erymanthos. It was renamed Phegia after King Phegeus. When Echephron and Promachos, who were the sons of Herakles and Psophis, daughter of the Sicilian king Eryx, arrived there, its name was changed once more, this time to Psophis. It seems reasonable to see in the latter change the result of the establishment of a matrilineal dynasty. By implication, the former dynasty will have been patrilineal,

---

[174] 2.25.1.

[175] Polyneikes' quest for a new queen in Thebes was presumably due to Jocasta's suicide.

[176] 8.24.4.

a conclusion which is confirmed by the sequel. It was, Pausanias tells us, while the city was called Phegia that the Greeks sailed to Troy[177]. The Phegians, however, did not take part in the expedition. The reason for their abstention was that the kings of Phegia hated the leaders of the Argives: many of the Argive leaders were related to Alcmaeon, and had taken part in the expedition to Thebes.

It would appear, then, that the rulers of Phegia sympathized with the new Theban line which Alcmaeon and the other Epigoni sought to displace. Polyneikes had evidently (in view of his offer to Eriphyle of the symbols of robe and necklace) favoured the old matrilineal line at Thebes and its double cult of Ares and Aphrodite.

The attitude of Phegeus towards Alcmaeon seems, then, to have been determined by sympathy for the *régime* at Thebes which is traditionally associated with the name of Eteokles. It would appear that Aeschylus, to judge by the *Seven against Thebes,* regarded Eteokles as representative of a strongly masculine tradition and of the Olympian gods. 'May I never', exclaims the Theban leader, 'in foul times or in fair have women for my associates: in victory they have an intolerable pride; when they are afraid they are still worse for home and city.' 'Things outside the house are a man's concern, not for women to think about. Stay indoors and do no harm'[178]. It is not for women to call on the gods, to sacrifice and consult the victims when enemies threaten; that is a business for men. Thus public religion is a masculine affair, and we find that Aeschylus makes, on the one hand, the Argive challenger, Hippomedon, bear as an emblem on his shield the likeness of Typhon, 'the hateful body of a chthonic demon'[179]. Round the edge of the shield are wrought twined snakes[180]. The Theban champion, Hyperbios, however, carries on his shield a representation of Zeus grasping the thunderbolt[181]. If we bear in mind the other tradition which Sophocles emphasized in the *Antigone*[182], we cannot fail to see that

---

[177] It had therefore lost its pre-Greek name, with the ending in *-nthos,* before the expedition to Troy.

[178] *Septem* 187–90; 200 f.

[179] 522 f.

[180] 495 ff.

[181] 510 ff.

[182] *Cf.* 466 f. Antigone says she could not have borne to have left τὸν ἐξ ἐμῆς μητρὸς θανόντ' unburied. Yet Polyneikes was supposed to have been equally her father's son. For Kreion, Polyneikes is the son of Oedipus (193 and 199). Antigone acknowledges

a contrast both between man and woman, and between Olympian and 'chthonic', is intended.

If Phegeus disapproved of Alcmaeon and all that he stood for, and yet allowed Alcmaeon to wed his daughter (as we shall see that he did), it seems clear that Alcmaeon was present in Psophis, or Phegia, as an aggressor, and had support perhaps from local adherents of the matrilineal ruling house also. Apollodorus' statement that Alcmaeon 'fled' to Phegeus is therefore probably a euphemism. Yet in spite of Alcmaeon's apparent championship of a cult in which woman plays so important a part as Aphrodite must have done in the joint cult she enjoyed with Ares, we have the story of his murder of the *potnia meter* at Argos to explain. Let us, however, first follow Pausanias' narrative.

In Phegia-Psophis Alcmaeon married Phegeus' daughter, Arsinoë, and 'gave her the necklace and the robe'. After a while, however, 'the ground became barren because of him', and in an oracle he was bidden go to Achelous[183]. Before arriving at the home of Achelous he visited that very important consultant in things religious and dynastic, Oineus of Calydon. He eventually reached Achelous, who again purified him and gave him his daughter, Callirrhoë, in marriage. Callirrhoë, however, insisted on having the necklace and the robe, saying that she would not live with him without them. Alcmaeon therefore returned to Psophis and told Phegeus that it had been foretold that he would be freed of his madness when he had brought the robe and necklace to Delphi and had dedicated them. Phegeus believed him and gave them to him. But when he discovered that Alcmaeon was only taking the emblems to Callirrhoë, he ordered his sons to kill him, and they did so. The sons of Phegeus then sent their sister, Arsinoë, as a slave to Tegea (or, according to another version, 'shut her up in a box', presumably a sarcophagus), and set off for Delphi to dedicate the robe and necklace there. This, according to Pausanias[184], they did; accord-

---

the power of Zeus to bring suffering (2 f.), but 'those below' weigh more heavily in her own decisions (74 ff.).

[183] The names 'Achelous' and 'Callirrhoë' should not necessarily lead one to deny that human beings are intended by them. Poseidon, who in the form and name of the river Enipeus was beloved by Tyro, may well have been a representative of the god who lived by that river. Pterelaos of Taphos was also known as 'Poseidon' (as we have seen). Behind 'Achelous', as behind 'Enipeus' (Apollod. 1.9.8) probably stands a representative of a god.

[184] 8.24.4; 9.41.2.

ing to Apollodorus[185] they were killed on the way there by Alcmaeon's
sons by Callirrhoë, and these sons made the dedication at Delphi instead
of them.

We shall not attempt to disentangle the complications of the tale as a
chronicle of the deeds of Alcmaeon. It seems, indeed, that traditions about
several heroes of that name are attributed to a single figure. The story has,
however, certain features which are closely relevant to our theme. Alcmaeon, if we put aside for the moment his murder of Eriphyle, plays a
consistent part; before Thebes he champions the joint cult, apparently of
Ares and Aphrodite, which Polyneikes and Eriphyle had represented. The
daughter of Phegeus accepts the emblems of what seems to be the same
cult from him, and he tries to establish the same relationship with, and
rôle for, the daughter of Achelous. Throughout, Phegeus is inimical to Alcmaeon's designs, and the story of the end of Arsinoë at the hands of her
father and brothers, connected as it is with the dedication of her robe and
necklace at Delphi, shows that Phegeus' and his sons' hostility is to the
cult tradition with which Alcmaeon was associated and to dynastic matrilineality[186]. This is consistent with their reputed hostility to Polyneikes
and the Argive chieftains, and with Aeschylus' delineation of Eteokles,
their opponent, as a strongly patriarchal figure. They were apparently
successful for the time being and put an end to the matrilineal line at
Phegia-Psophis. In order to do so, they seem to have murdered the *potnia
meter* there, Arsinoë, or at least exiled her. As we have seen, the matrilineal line was apparently later restored and the city renamed Psophis. As
to Alcmaeon's murder of Eriphyle, the legend that she was his mother
arose, as we have suggested, from a later misunderstanding of a statement
that he killed the *potnia meter* at Argos. The history of the times is pene-
trated through and through with the clash of patrilineal and matrilineal as
the old religious dynasties were broken, swept away, and re-established.
Unfortunately, Delphic influence has distorted the traditions.

That Alcmaeon the 'Matricide' also was a representative of Ares is an
uncertain but probable conclusion from the regular association of parti-

---

[185] 3.7.5. This tradition points, with its chronological difficulty, to some corruption of
the legend.

[186] The Alcmaeon who, with the Epigoni, took Thebes is said to have sent part of the
spoils to Delphi (Paus. 7.3.1; 9.33.1. Apollod. 3.3.4.). Clearly, this is an Apolline
addition, which flatly contradicts the story given above.

cular names with particular dynasties and, seemingly, with particular cults[187]. The murderous reputation of Ares needs explanation. Inconstancy and infidelity are attributed to the god in the "Diomedeia" of the Iliad. It may be that this characteristic was due to a disturbance of the harmony of male and female within the cult. Representatives of Ares are perhaps to be found on either side in the great struggle. It is of course possible that one and the same representative of Ares supported now the one cause, now the other, as opportunity and personal advantage suggested: the self-aggrandisement of the freebooter is in any case apparent in these violent renegades (if renegades they were) from the joint cult. It seems, however, more likely that a man who has broken loose from a joint cult, that is, has upset the balance between male and female in his cult and done violence thereby to the latter element, should continue as an increasingly bitter foe of women in dynastic positions than return to the cult to which he has done such injury. It may, on the other hand, have been the practice for the protagonist of Ares to kill both his predecessors, male and female. It certainly seems that the representative of Ares, on acquiring a kingdom, not infrequently slew both the king and the queen. Not only do the stories of Orestes and Alcmaeon suggest this, but, as we shall see in Chapter III, it is apparently hinted at in the song of Demodocus in the *Odyssey*. The new ruler brought no consort with him, and must have married the daughter. Polyneikes and Eriphyle were a special case, for the old Theban line had apparently been wiped out.

There was an Orestes who was one of the sons of Perimede and of Achelous[188], whose daughter Callirrhoë (though perhaps in another generation) we have just seen reason to associate with the cult of Ares and Aphrodite[189]. The hint is admittedly a somewhat slight one, but in view of the

---

[187] One must admit that names compounded with *Alk-* are more commonly associated with the cult of Poseidon, but the frequent attribution of *alke* in the Iliad to the Ajaxes, who seem to be undeniable Ares-worshippers, gives some further support to the view that there is a connection between names beginning with *Alk-* and the cult of Ares. For the connection of the Ajaxes, *alke* and Ares, cf. *Iliad*, 7.164 and 8.262, (Αἴαντες, θοῦρον ἐπιειμένοι ἀλκήν), 7.200 (Ajax σεύατ' ἔπειθ' οἷός τε πελώριος ἔρχεται Ἄρης), 8.79 (Ἄιαντες ... θεράποντες Ἄρηος), 10.228 (Αἴαντε δύω, θεράποντες Ἄρηος), 13.47 f. (Αἴαντε ... ἀλκῆς μνησαμένω), 13.197 (Αἴαντε, μεμαότε θούριδος ἀλκῆς). In 13.47 f. the words are put in the mouth of Poseidon, but, as the phrase is purely conventional, this may not be significant.

[188] Apollod 1.7.3.

[189] The brother of this Orestes was Hippodamas, whose daughter married Porthaon.

association of particular names with certain dynasties and cult-communities, we may find a clue here to the religious affiliations of the Orestes of
the Oresteia. In the passage in the Iliad where Ares is made to kill his
closest followers[190], he kills πλήξιππον 'Ορέστην[191]. This Orestes, then, also
seems to have been an adherent of the cult of Ares. The tradition connecting the Orestes who killed Clytaemnestra with Ares is found in the *Choephoroe*[192] (if the passage is taken literally) and in Sophocles' *Elektra*[193].
This religious orientation would provide a precise parallel to the story of
Alcmaeon[194].

The conclusion to which these considerations seem to point is that, at the
time with which we are dealing, it was mainly the women of a royal house
who were consistently devoted to a particular cult and to maintaining
dynastic connections[195]. The more determined and ruthless of the men,
especially in the cult of Ares, were prepared to take the extreme step of
destroying the gynaecocratic order so that they might establish their own
power. They thus cut across all cult loyalties, for they indirectly did violence to their own cult as well as to the matrilineal cults they destroyed.

Their sons were Oineus and Alkathoos (Apollod. I.7.10.; Schol. Pind. *Ol.* 1.114).
The connection of Oineus with Ares has already been mentioned, while Alkathoos
married Hippodameia (*Iliad*, 13.428 f. This passage places Alkathoos among the
Trojans, as he is in 12.93, but he seems to be an importation from a Greek context).

[190] 'Trechos, the Aetolian spearman' is clearly intended to be a servant of Aetolian Ares,
and Oinomaos was a son of Ares. In 5.842 f. Ares kills Periphas, 'much the noblest
of the Aetolians', who were peculiarly his people. It is part of the design by which
the god is portrayed as ἀλλοπρόσαλλος (5.831).

[191] 5.705.

[192] 938.

[193] 1385.

[194] There is little doubt that the tradition which lays Orestes under the behest of the
Delphic Apollo, and associates Alcmaeon with Delphi is a relatively late one. There
has been a foreshortening of events. If we are right in seeing Orestes and Alcmaeon
as representatives of Ares they cannot also be emissaries of Apollo. Indeed, Apollo
and Ares have virtually no contact with each other in Greek mythology, and the
Iliad carefully removes Ares from the scene before introducing Apollo as the
associate and protector of Aphrodite (see Appendix I). The destruction of the old
religion and the clan world was at least in part the work of Ares. It was a purely
negative achievement and the foundations of a new order were laid by Apollo, Athena
and Zeus. See below.

[195] We should perhaps remember that in Late Mycenaean times only the palace at
Mycenae shows signs of a strongly religious outlook. The houses of the wealthier
families round about the palace no longer show marks of religious pre-occupation.

They shattered the old society at the same time as they annihilated its religion. Such men were Alcmaeon of Argos and Orestes[196].

The first step towards ending the bloody tradition of the times appeared to a later age to have been the ending of matrilineal succession and female supremacy in the clan. As long as succession descended in the female line, there was bound to be fierce rivalry for the kingship of the more powerful realms. Those very rivals, whose struggle for power destroyed the old world, were held to be the founders of a new order. So the Chorus in the *Choephoroe* tell Orestes, just before he kills his mother, that, when Clytaemnestra calls out to him, 'Child', he is to cry out in answer, 'Of my father'[197]. It seemed that salvation was to lie in substituting paternal for maternal ascendency.

Indeed, from its opening line, the patriarchal note of the *Choephoroe* is heard. Zeus and Apollo are to be Orestes' supporters[198]. At his father's tomb, Orestes invokes Zeus[199], and, though speaking for Elektra too, makes the whole relationship with Zeus centre upon the male line: 'If thou let perish these offspring of my father, the ritual slaughterer who greatly honoured thee, where shalt thou find another such hand to give thee thy rich due? Nor, shouldst thou destroy the eagles' brood, couldst thou send back persuasive signs to mortal men. If this ruling stock should wither away utterly, it will no longer help at the altars on the days when the cattle are

---

[196] A clear hint of the society which was to follow is contained in the story of Meleager in the Iliad. Even though he much prefers his father's kinsmen to his mother's, he rejects their solicitations: only at the urgency of his patrilineally-named wife, Kleopatra, does he consent to fight. That is to say, the world of the clan is abandoned in favour of the individual patrilineal household of man and wife. (This is not the only presentation of the theme in Greek myth: see below on the legend of Alcestis.) The propagandist, or educational, use to which the Homeric poems were put comes out clearly in certain passages; the contests and agonies of more than one generation, and their approved resolution, are compressed into the story of the persuasion of Meleager. Aeschylus, in Periclean Athens, found another solution: all feuds were to cease in the reconciliation and absorption of every rival in the united, uniform (*Eum.* 984 ff.) and aggressively militant (*ibid.* 864 f.) city of which all were members.

[197] *Choeph.* 828 f. Of course, Orestes is meant to imply that a mother who could murder her husband, his father, was no longer a mother in his eyes, but the injunction of the Chorus in the *Choephoroe* is certainly to be seen also in the context of the conflict of patrilineal and matrilineal which Bachofen found in the *Eumenides,* as indeed is the whole play.

[198] *Ibid.* 18 f.

[199] *Ibid.* 246–63.

sacrificed.' Throughout the last two plays of the Oresteia the co-operation of Zeus and Apollo in the cause of Orestes is evident. Bachofen pointed out long ago that the patrilineal and matrilineal principles were at strife with each other in the last play of the trilogy. The Pythian prophetess is quite explicit:

'Loxias is the prophet of his father, Zeus.'

And Apollo himself says: 'I never spoke on my prophetic throne, about man or woman or city, one word which was not commanded me by Zeus, the father of the Olympians[200]. Finally, there are Athena's words quoted at the head of this chapter. The Olympian gods are the gods of the rising masculine tradition.

IX. The Founding of a New Order

The attack on the matrilineal clans destroyed the power of the clan world itself, and with it its religion. It was the task of the rising cult of Apollo to form a new society of individual households, headed by a man and consisting essentially of himself, his wife and his children.

Fragments of the history of these events are preserved in myth, perhaps most clearly in the story of Alcestis. In order to understand the legend of Alcestis we must remember that certain cult-communities were distinguished by what we might call heraldic beasts[201]. Notable among these

---

[200] *Eum.* 19; 616 ff.

[201] G. H. Chase, 'The Shield Devices of the Greeks' in *Harvard Studies in Classical Philology*, XIII (1902), p. 82, makes it clear that it is vain to seek in archaic and classical Greek art for a consistent relationship between shield devices and particular heroic and divine persons. Athena, for instance, bears on her shield sixty-two different devices. Animal emblems, in particular the Gorgoneion, griffin, winged boar, winged horse and winged lion, in Chase's view probably originally referred to religious cults (p. 84), but the monuments—for the most part of course vases—show no satisfactory examples of devices which refer to family or descent. This hereditary aspect of emblems he recognises however in the literary tradition and cites, *inter alia*, Eurip. *Phoen.* 1106 ff., where Parthenopaios is spoken of as bearing as a device on his shield a picture of Atalanta shooting with her bow and arrows at the Aetolian boar. The emblem is described as οἰκεῖον because Atalanta was the mother of Parthenopaios (p. 72). This reveals matrilineal descent of the right to the device. As cult and dynasty went together in pre-Olympian Greece, Chase's belief that certain devices based on animal forms in the monuments refer to religious cults is

were the boar of Artemis and the lion, which seems to have symbolized certain cults of Aphrodite, apparently those connected with Ares and Poseidon. Thus, when Polyneikes arrived in Argos he went to the palace by night and there engaged in a fight with Tydeus. Tydeus was the son of Oineus and of a Danaid woman[202], whose clan celebrated the cult of Artemis. He belonged to the matrilineal tradition and his symbol was therefore the boar (of Artemis). Polyneikes, on the other hand, was, it seems, an adherent of the Theban Aphrodite and of Ares. His symbol was the lion[203]. Adrastus parts Tydeus and Polyneikes and 'remembering the words of a certain seer who told him to yoke his daughters in marriage to a boar and a lion, he accepted them both as bridegrooms, because they had on their shields, the one the forepart of a boar, the other, the forepart of a lion'[204]. According to Euripides[205], the advice on the marriage of Adrastus' daughters was given by Apollo.

Having thus seen this aspect of 'lion' and 'boar' in the world of clan and cult, we may turn to the story of Alcestis and of the part played in it by Apollo, as it is related by Apollodorus[206]:

'When Admetus reigned over Pherae, Apollo served him as a thrall, while Admetus wooed Alcestis, daughter of Pelias. Now Pelias had promised to give his daughter to him who should yoke a lion and a boar to a car, and Apollo yoked them and gave them to Admetus, who brought them to Pelias and so obtained Alcestis. But in offering a sacrifice at his marriage, he forgot to sacrifice to Artemis; therefore when he opened the marriage chamber he found it full of coiled snakes. Apollo bade him appease the goddess and obtained as a favour of the Fates that when Admetus should be about to die, he might be released from death if someone should choose voluntarily to die for him. And when the day of his death came neither his mother nor his father would die for him, but Alcestis died in his stead.'

Apollo had apparently only recently acquired influence over Admetus,

reinforced by his conclusion, drawn from literature, that they also had a significance for 'family and descent'.

[202] See table of Danaid and Argive dynasties.
[203] See Schol. Eurip. *Phoen.* 409, 411. *Cf.* the lion of Cybele.
[204] Apollod. 3.6.1. Frazer's translation.
[205] *Phoen.* 409.
[206] 1.9.15. Frazer's translation.

for Zeus had sent him to serve a mortal for a year[207]. The lion we have just noticed as an emblem of a clan-cult which recognised the overlordship of Ares and perhaps Poseidon in association with a particular Aphrodite[208]. Pelias was a son of Poseidon, and his wife, Anaxibia, was a Pelopid[209]; that is, she was a representative of the cult of this Aphrodite. The story of Meleager shows, as we have seen, that hostility between the clan-cult of Ares-Aphrodite and the worshippers of Artemis prevailed even within what later times saw as a single family; the boar was sent to ravage Oineus' vineyards because Oineus, who represented Ares (and Dionysus as Wine God), had, like Admetus, 'forgotten' to sacrifice to Artemis, the goddess of his wife's clan. It is implied that Admetus was (of course, through his mother), a member of the cult-community of Artemis. He was, however, allying himself in marriage with the Aphrodite who was Artemis' traditional enemy. The hostility of Artemis to the Pelopidae is, of course, notorious. All the elements of discord were present, but through Apollo they were fused into a single unity. Apollo was no god of love, and his contribution to the marriage of Admetus and Alcestis was not the love that compels self-sacrifice. We may see this element in the story but it was not the work of Apollo. The significance of the story of Alcestis' sacrifice, so far as it concerns the god, is that the tie with the patrilineal or matrilineal clan was now loosened: neither father nor mother would die for Admetus. His wife, however, would[210]: the day of the individual family household and its affections had dawned, and it looked down upon the husband as lord and the wife as his devoted helpmeet[211]. The old enmity between the clan-cults was at an end: the lion and the boar were yoked. Under the

---

[207] *Ibid.* 3.10.4. This tradition, and that which associates Apollo (and Poseidon) with the building of the walls of Troy, after which he was defrauded of his wage by Laomedon, as also his hostility to the ancient clans, suggest that Apollo arrived in some parts of Greece as the god of certain immigrants of relatively humble station (who may have contained bards and reciters among their number). He 'came up in the world', as it seems, at least in some places.

[208] See also Appendix I.

[209] See table of Pelopid descent in § II above.

[210] For a possible interpretation of Alcestis' giving up her life for her husband see M. Eliade, *Le Chamanisme et les techniques archaïques de l'Extase* (Paris, 1951), pp. 199 f., where the ransoming of the soul of a sick man (among the Buryats) from the Lord of the Underworld by offering him another living soul in exchange is described. See, however, footnote 214 below.

[211] See footnote 196 for the same features in the Iliad's version of the story of Meleager.

auspices of Apollo, the chthonic or fertile Aphrodite[212] and the deities that went with her were reconciled with Artemis. It was in the name of Apollo that religion was severed from dynasty and blood-relationship. Apollo was undoubtedly one of the powers that completed the destruction of the clan-world, but he was also one of the formative agents that brought the household family into being, and performed the union of man and wife through Aphrodite Pandemos under the auspices of Zeus and Hera.

The social revolution is summed up in five lines of Aeschylus' *Eumenides*[213], where the Chorus, having declared that it is a graver thing to slay one of kindred blood, as Orestes slew his mother, than for a wife to slay a husband, receive from Apollo the reply: 'You dishonour and set at nought the oaths of Hera Teleia and of Zeus. With these words Kypria has been flung away without honour.' That is, marriage is dishonoured. Indeed, at the close of the argument between the Erinyes and Apollo, the former remind Apollo that he did the same in the house of Pheres (*i. e.* for Admetus) as he is now doing for Orestes[214].

The destruction of the clans began, as we have noticed, without Apollo's aid, apparently through an upheaval in the cult community of Ares, a god of great importance whom later times somewhat misrepresented. There is no mention of Apollo in the story of Meleager, which reflects, as we have already noted[215], the same change as that which lies behind the story of Admetus. Meleager would not fight when his mother's kinsmen besought him, nor even for his father's kin, although they were 'much the dearest' to him. Only when his wife with the patrilineally-sounding name, Kleopatra, turned to him and herself made the request did he consent.

---

[212] See Appendix I.

[213] 211–15.

[214] 723 f. The Erinyes are made to elaborate on this and say that Apollo persuaded the fates to make a mortal immortal, that is to say, he put men beyond the power of the old gods and the clans. This is an inversion of the truth: only under the old religion could a man be made immortal.

The saving of Admetus by his wife's sacrifice may refer to the conception that at the installation of a new shaman, a number of his kin must perish. This fate his true kindred, his parents, had refused. His wife's acceptance of the sacrifice then looks forward to the shamanism of the archaic age. Admetus was, I suspect, suffering from the 'shaman sickness'. (See H. Findeisen, *Schamanentum* [Stuttgart, 1957], Chapters IV and V). Mere personal misfortune is seldom, if ever, reflected in myth, which generally retains only that which had meaning for past times.

[215] Footnote 196.

The religious revolution was probably profounder than the social change, deep indeed as this went, but that earlier world has been fairly well concealed. In the remaining essays of this book we shall attempt to recover some small fragments of it and in doing so may be able occasionally to point to some of the devices, as well as the misunderstandings, by which the true nature of the elder tradition has been hidden from us.

CHAPTER II

The Death of Agamemnon

The earliest accounts that we have of the killing of Agamemnon are to be found in the Odyssey. The story of Agamemnon's death and of the vengeance which Orestes took for it is indeed closely related to the structure of the Odyssey itself. At the very beginning of the poem[1] Zeus is introduced as *Father of Gods and Men.* He is found reflecting on Aegisthus, who was killed by Orestes, son of Agamemnon. He speaks his thoughts aloud to the immortals, and remarks upon the way in which men blame the gods for the evils that come upon them, when these are really the consequences of their own folly. Just so had Aegisthus killed Agamemnon on his return, and wrongfully married his wife, when he had known it was sheer doom for him to do so. Zeus had sent a warning to him not to kill Agamemnon nor to marry his wife, for if he did, punishment would come to him from Orestes when he had grown up. But Aegisthus had not heeded the warning, and now he had paid for his neglect. The Father of Gods and Men thus makes his principles clear at the beginning of the poem, and the poet his patrilineal outlook.

Athena replies to him. The absence, return, and fate of Agamemnon have apparently brought the missing Odysseus to her mind. Aegisthus, she says, had met a fitting end, but she is now worried because Odysseus had not yet returned home. She intends to go to Ithaca and persuade Telemachus to take some action about the suitors and seek news of his father. In 1.294 ff. she tells Telemachus that after he has returned from his voyage of enquiry he is to plan how to kill the suitors. He is no longer a child: does he not know the fame which Orestes got for himself when he killed Aegisthus, who slew his father? Telemachus and Orestes, the suitors and Aegisthus, we see, correspond in her thought[2].

---

[1] 1.29 ff.

[2] This has also been noticed by H. Hommel in 'Aigisthos und die Freier', *Studium Generale,* 8, 1955, pp. 237 ff. I am grateful to Professor W. Marg, of the Johannes Gutenberg University, Mainz, for drawing my attention to this article.

Telemachus, arrived at the palace of Nestor, is told news of the Greek
leaders returned home from Troy. Nestor ends his recital[3] by speaking
of Aegisthus' killing of Agamemnon, and of how Aegisthus paid for his
deed at the hands of Agamemnon's fine son. Nestor concludes with a broad
hint, remarking that Telemachus is big and strong. Telemachus takes it up,
and says he wishes the gods would give him enough strength to take vengeance upon the suitors for the insults they had offered him, but he fears
the gods have not designed such fortune for his father and himself.

A little later[4] Athena returns to the same comparison. She speaks in the
guise of Mentor. Mentor says that he would rather return home, even if it
cost much toil, (and live) than be destroyed on his own hearth, as Agamemnon was by the guile of Aegisthus and his wife. This is the first
suggestion that Clytaemnestra was also involved in Agamemnon's death.
Telemachus turns to Nestor and asks how Agamemnon died.

Nestor says that while the other Greeks had been at Troy, Aegisthus
had charmed Agamemnon's wife with words. At first she had refused the
shameful deed, for she had a noble mind, but after Aegisthus had removed
the minstrel who had been left with her to protect her, she went willingly
to his home. (Thus the Odyssey here makes Clyaemnestra leave her home
and go to live with Aegisthus). After he had killed Agamemnon, Aegisthus
lived for seven years in Mycenae and subjected the people under him[5]. In
the eighth year Orestes came back from Athens and killed the man who had
killed his father and gave a funeral feast to the Argives for 'the weak
Aegisthus and his hateful mother'[6]. Nestor warns Telemachus not to leave
his home unguarded as Agamemnon had done.

Telemachus leaves Nestor and travels to Lacedaemon, to visit Menelaus. Menelaus also tells him the story of Agamemnon's end[7]. It is not
stated where the event takes place. Aegisthus arranged that twenty men
should wait in hiding, then invited Agamemnon to a meal. When Agamemnon had dined, he killed him, as one would slaughter an ox at the crib.
None of the followers of either Agamemnon or Aegisthus was left: they
were slain in the palace. Menelaus makes no mention of Clytaemnestra.
His last action before leaving the island of Pharos, where he himself had

---

[3] 3.193 ff.   [4] 3.234 ff.   [5] 3.304 f.

[6] This is the only indication in Homer that Orestes killed Clytaemnestra.

[7] 4.524 ff.

learned of Agamemnon's death from Proteus, was to erect a memorial to Agamemnon.

In the eleventh book, the shade of Agamemnon himself tells Odysseus the tale[8]. He and his companions had been killed in the house of Aegisthus[9] by Aegisthus and his baleful wife. He had been killed after dining. Clytaemnestra herself killed Cassandra, the daughter of Priam, on top of Agamemnon's body. Agamemnon lay dying, pierced by the sword, and Clytaemnestra left him without drawing down his eyelids or closing his mouth. There is nothing more terrible and more shameless than the woman who could devise such things in her heart. She has heaped disgrace upon herself and upon all women in time to come, even those whose deeds are good. When Odysseus hears this, he exclaims that wide-browed Zeus has indeed shown terrible hatred towards the seed of Atreus from the beginning because of the devices of woman: many had suffered because of Helen, and Clytaemnestra had worked treachery towards Agamemnon from afar. Finally, in the last book, Agamemnon's shade speaks again of the fate he suffered at the hands of Aegisthus and his baleful wife[10], and compares Clytaemnestra's evil fame with the good report that Penelope will have with future generations[11]. These are his last words.

Now it is sometimes inferred from these passages that there are two different traditions about the death of Agamemnon in the Odyssey, one in which the blame rests wholly with Aegisthus, another in which Clytaemnestra's responsibility for it is almost as great. This is not so. It is quite apparent when the accounts are considered in their several places in the poem, that Homer emphasises first one party, then the other, in relating the murder, according to the requirements of the story of the Odyssey itself. At the beginning, from the introduction of the theme by Zeus and Athena to Menelaus' narrative in Book IV, the aim of all concerned with Telemachus' difficulties is to get him to take Orestes' conduct as his model. He is to behave as the son of his father should behave: as Orestes killed his father's murderer, so he is to aim at killing the suitors who are seeking to take away Odysseus' kingdom and his wife. The guilt of Clytaemnestra is not relevant to this purpose, and by complicating the situation could only weaken the force of the example held up to Telemachus. Moreover, Penelope is to be a model of wifely faithfulness. As long as the attention of

---

[8] 405 ff.   [9] 388 f.   [10] 96 f.   [11] 196 ff.

Homer's audience is concentrated on Telemachus (that is, for the first four books), so long almost the whole weight of the guilt falls upon Aegisthus.

Nevertheless, women can be forced into situations, and so into alliances, that they do not wish, and Telemachus has to be warned of the dangers of the situation. Athena in 3.235 just mentions, without attaching any epithet to Clytaemnestra, that Agamemnon perished through her guile as well as that of Aegisthus. It is very lightly touched on. Nestor expands the story, but in doing so explains that Clytaemnestra was bewitched by Aegisthus' words, and that she at first rejected Aegisthus' proposals, because she had a noble mind. Enough has been said: when Menelaus in his turn relates what Proteus told him, he does not mention Clytaemnestra at all. When the story of Agamemnon's death is told the next time, in the eleventh book, it is told to Odysseus alone; the effect on Telemachus has not to be considered, and Clytaemnestra appears in her most heartless and treacherous aspect. In the final book[12]—where our attention is directed upon the triumph of Odysseus—Agamemnon's shade makes the reason clear: it is to point the contrast with the faithfulness of Penelope to her lord during the long years of his absence.

It is thus extremely difficult to guess what the original story may have been upon which Homer was drawing; he is seen to alter the balance, to suppress and emphasise elements in it, as it suits his purpose in telling the story to Telemachus and Odysseus. Any interpretation of the story of Agamemnon's death which is based on evidence drawn from the Odyssey must be treated with the greatest caution. In particular, one can clearly not assume that there is any element in the story as told by Aeschylus which was not already known to Homer. Homer only tells as much of it as he needs and wishes to tell for the purposes of the Odyssey.

The Odyssey, in the form in which we now have it, was composed under strong Olympian, and, in certain places, especially Apolline, influence, and it is inevitable that a story so closely bound up with the theme and action of the whole poem as is that of Agamemnon's death and Orestes' vengeance should come under these influences as well. It is certain that later poets who treated the theme also wrote under the same influence. There was an epic poem, whether the *Nostoi* or the Ἀτρειδῶν κάθοδος, attributed

12 192 ff.

dubiously to Agias of Troezen[13], in which Orestes is accompanied by Pylades when he takes vengeance on Aegisthus and Clytaemnestra. This suggests that Orestes, in this poem, took refuge not at Athens, as in the Odyssey, but at Krisa in Phokis, where Pylades' father, Strophios, was the ruler. But Krisa comes within the circle of Delphi, and the change may therefore be due to a wish to associate Delphi with Orestes' vengeance. In the lyric poets this suspected influence becomes unmistakable. Stesichoros, taking his *Oresteia* from that of a poet called Xanthos[14], whose work has wholly perished, makes Apollo give Orestes a bow with which to defend himself against the Erinyes. Stesichoros indeed, if one may judge from the contents of another poem attributed to him[15], found the espousal of the cause of the Olympian religion against chthonic, or at any rate older, beliefs to be a partnership after his heart. He also placed the scene of Agamemnon's death in Lacedaemon, as did Simonides and Pindar too[16]. This seems to have been due to a desire to support the Dorian claim to hegemony with a basis in history[17].

We see therefore that both epic and lyric poets made a practice of associating persons and actions that are intimately involved in the Oresteia legend with different places as religious or political considerations required. We have therefore a good *a priori* reason for treating the statement in the Odyssey that Clytaemnestra went to Aegisthus' house with reserve. If she did so, it would be evidence of a patrilineal rule (unless she were only the sister of the heiress). But there is reason to think that the rule in Clytae-

---

[13] See Proclus in Kinkel, *Epic. Graec. Frag.*, pp. 52 f.

[14] Athen. XII, 512 f., quoted Bergk, *Lyrici Graeci*, Stesich. *Fr.* 57.

[15] Aelian, *Hist. Anim.* XVII, 37, Bergk, *loc. cit.*, fr. 66. Bergk mentions that the attribution to Stesichoros has been questioned, but the fact that a poem of this character has been attributed to him at all is significant.

[16] Schol. E u r i p. *Orest.* 46.

[17] Vürtheim, *Stesichoros' Fragmente und Biographie* (Leyden, 1919), in commenting on this, points out that it was on the advice of Delphi that the bones of Orestes were moved from Tegea to Sparta, and that Orestes himself had left Mycenae for Arcadia on the instructions of the oracle (Paus 8.5.3). T. W. Allen, *The Homeric Catalogue of Ships* (Oxford, 1921), pp. 67 f., apparently unaware of Vürtheim's observations, says that Homer nowhere tells us where Agamemnon was killed and sees no reason why the lyric poets should not be right. His remark that this would explain Telemachus' question, 'Where was Menelaus?' in *Od.* 3.249 overlooks both the fact that *Od.* 4.562 implies that Menelaus' home was in the Argolid and that Menelaus heard of Agamemnon's death while he was trying to return from Egypt to Greece.

mnestra's home was matrilineal. We know that on this subject the author of
the Odyssey held very strong views[18]. Moreover, Aeschylus himself did not
follow the Odyssey in this matter. There was at least another tradition
about it, and we are for these reasons justified in refusing to regard the
statement of the Odyssey as carrying any considerable authority.

We know nothing of Stesichoros' account of Agamemnon's death. The
fact, however, that Apollo gave a bow to Orestes for his defence against
the Erinyes seems to imply, not only that Orestes killed Clytaemnestra,
but that he had regarded her as bearing a principal share of the guilt for
Agamemnon's death. Pindar[19] seems to have regarded Clytaemnestra as
more culpable than Aegisthus; she it is who stabs Agamemnon, and the
poet merely mentions that Orestes 'laid Aegisthus in death' when he killed
his mother. Pindar, too, represents her as killing Cassandra with Agamemnon, and he seems to have the same conception of Clytaemnestra as has
Aeschylus: the nurse rescues Orestes from her guile and her strong (κρατερᾶν)
hands. The same idea of Clytaemnestra as a formidable woman seems to
lie behind the words. But it is in the highest degree remarkable that Pindar
does not know why she killed Agamemnon. He asks whether it was because of her grievous anger at the sacrifice of Iphigeneia, or because she
was led astray by desire for Aegisthus. Aeschylus makes vengeance for the
sacrifice of her daughter one of her motives, and we learn from him that
she loved Aegisthus, but Pindar does not know if these were in fact the
springs of her action. This shows that there was no definite tradition on
the subject. The Iliad indeed, if we may equate Iphianassa with Iphigeneia,
denies by implication that the sacrifice of Iphigeneia ever took place, for it
represents Agamemnon as naming her as one of his three daughters living
at home[20]. This, however, is not conclusive evidence that there was no old
tradition on this subject, for it is possible that Homer deliberately introduces Iphianassa into the statement in order to dissociate Agamemnon from
the sacrifice by implying that it never took place. We may perhaps view
the change of name to Iphianassa as due not to a different tradition but to
design[21]. We can therefore not conclude that the story of the sacrifice of

---

[18] Homer's attitude has already been made clear in our remarks on his treatment of the
story of Agamemnon and Orestes in relation to the situation of Telemachus, but further
evidence will be found in Chapter III.

[19] *Pyth.* XI. 17 (25).

[20] 9.145,287.

[21] Cf. Anticleia-Eurycleia, Telemachus-(Telegonus) in the Odyssey. See Chapter III.

Iphigeneia was attached to Agamemnon in post-Homeric times. Nevertheless, we notice, and it is a highly significant fact, that Pindar did not
know why Clytaemnestra killed Agamemnon.

What then of the actual slaying? Was it, as the account given by Menelaus to Telemachus would have it[22], a surprise attack upon Agamemnon,
feasting with his followers, by Aegisthus and his men? It is difficult to
reconcile this version with the story that makes Clytaemnestra Agamemnon's slayer, or, as in the eleventh book of the Odyssey, the slayer of
Cassandra upon the body of the dying Agamemnon, even though this last
account attempts to do so. Pindar takes no notice of it, nor does Aeschylus. The tradition that Clytaemnestra played one of the principal parts in
Agamemnon's death is old and strong, but only Agamemnon's shade in
the *Nekyia* tries to make it appear that she played an active part in the
battle in the hall, and that this was the scene of both Agamemnon's and
Cassandra's death. If he really met his death in a battle of armed men, it
is wholly incredible that this fact should be nowhere else reflected in the
literature that deals with him, and that, on the contrary, another, and
superficially less probable story, which Aeschylus followed, should have
been current, and that this should show certain features which are irreconcilable with the Odyssey's narrative.

Nevertheless, it is not unlikely that there was some battle between the
followers of Agamemnon and those of Aegisthus. So much may well lie
behind the story told by Agamemnon's ghost. It was, however, not the
occasion of his and Cassandra's death, and it is this occasion that is the
origin of the tradition that the lyric poets and the dramatists knew. The
reason for making their death occur in the battle in the hall is, I suggest,
that the true story of Agamemnon's end was one which Olympian Homer
wished to conceal. The same aversion to it is to be inferred from its rarity
as a subject of Greek art, while the death of Aegisthus is commonly depicted. It has yet to be shown that there is any resemblance between the
death of Pelias at the hands of Jason and Medea and that of Agamemnon
at the hands of Aegisthus and Clytaemnestra, but if we may assume for
the moment that there is a certain similarity, we shall be able to understand more readily the story of Agamemnon's end in the *Nekyia*. The
Argonauts seized the citadel of Iolkos[23] before Pelias perished at the

---

[22] *Od.* 4.524 ff.   [23] Diod. Sic. 4.50,52.

ceremony ostensibly designed to renew his life: Aegisthus' followers may
have seized the palace at Argos before Agamemnon met his end. Two
separate, but of course related, events may thus have been fused into one
in the eleventh book of the Odyssey, and this, I believe, is what happened.

We now turn to Aeschylus' presentation of the story. Here, likewise,
the evidence cannot be dissociated fully from Aeschylus' construction of the
Agamemnon. With the arrival of Agamemnon from Troy at the palace in
Argos there opens the strangest scene in the Oresteia. The king is met by
Clytaemnestra who welcomes him in a long speech. The manner of her
speech and its substance displease him; there is something inappropriate,
even disturbing, about it. At the end, she bids him not touch the ground
with his foot as he descends from the chariot. She urges the servant girls to
hurry forward and spread, as she has already told them, cloths upon the
ground for him to walk upon: 'Let there be at once a way strewn with
purple, so that the right course of things[24] may lead to a house one had
not looked to see'[25].

Agamemnon comments on the length of her speech and says that he finds
something unfitting to the occasion in what she has said. It would have
come better from someone else. 'And for the rest' he says, 'do not treat me
with this womanish luxury. Do not mouth and shriek at me, and bow your-
self to the ground, as though I were a barbarian. And do not strew the path
with clothing: it is unlucky. With this, one should do honour to gods. I am
a human being and simply cannot walk on many-coloured finery without
fear. I tell you, do reverence to me as a man, not as a god. Fame speaks
without carpets and many-coloured cloths'[26]. But Clytaemnestra persuades
him. She gets him to admit that Priam would certainly have walked on
purple had he been victor, and tells him that he need not fear unfavourable
comment from the people. Agamemnon is struck by her persistence, and
remarks that it is not a woman's part to desire contest. In the end he
yields. Yet, having yielded, he continues to express his dislike of walking
on the cloths. He hopes that no god's jealous anger be aroused: he fears
that by trampling on purple and costly cloths he may be destroying the
house.

---

[24] δίχη. The English 'justice' is not a satisfactory translation: it has too strong a moral
   tone. δίχη means rather 'the way things go', either by convention or by the necessity
   of some law or symmetry in things.

[25] *Agam.* 906 ff.

[26] 916 ff.

More than a third of this scene between Agamemnon and Clytaemnestra, reckoning from the moment of his entry, and that the final and most important part, is taken up with the argument about walking on the carpets. This argument must, therefore, have an especial significance. The purpose of the scene, looked at from a theatrical and external point of view, seems generally to be taken to be twofold. Firstly, it is to emphasize the insincerity of Clytaemnestra's welcome by grotesquely caricaturing the reception which a loving consort would give a king on his return victorious from war. Secondly, by the dramatic irony of the manner of his entrance to the palace, to impart a sinister atmosphere to the end of the scene. Clytaemnestra's words and behaviour are taken to be the result of cold calculation: she is supposed to be acting a part to disguise her purpose. She has nerves of steel; her hatred of Agamemnon is a cold implacable determination to avenge. This I believe to be very largely a misconception.

The long speech which Clytaemnestra makes, in front of the assembled citizens and in reply to Agamemnon's speech at his entrance, is distasteful to the king, as we have already noticed, and ends with the words: 'Now, dear one, I beg you, come down from this chariot. Do not put your foot upon the ground, O King, the sacker of Troy. Women, what are you waiting for? You were told to spread the ground along the way with tapestries. Let there be at once a path strewn with purple. So let the right course of things lead to a house one had not looked to see. And all the rest a mind that has not slept will order rightly, with the gods and destiny.'

The strictly dramatic function of the speech is to indicate that the climax has not yet been reached. Up to now, the whole movement of the play has been towards the moment of Agamemnon's arrival. Now he has come, and we are made aware of deeper waters moving onward. If one reads the speech bearing in mind its length, its matter, and the manner of its delivery —which Agamemnon calls βόαμα, 'shouting' or 'shrieking'—, the wide-open mouth (προσχάνης) and the prostration on the ground at the end of it, one must become aware that Clytaemnestra is only partly acting and only partly in control of herself. The very fact that Agamemnon finds her manner strange shows this. The tension of the speech begins to rise sharply towards its climax from 'The fountains of my tears are dried up'[27], the ἀμφί σοι πάθη ὁρῶσα[28] refers, for her, to her past experiences of Aga-

---

[27] 887.   [28] 893 f.

memnon or perhaps to her intention, not to events at Troy, and she cannot
have spoken them without emotion; the accumulated images of praise and
thankfulness in lines 896–901 are the beginning of the climax. She regains
control of herself, defending the exaggeration of her words in three lines[29]
but she has revealed something of her inner tension, and her enunciation of

$$\mu\grave{\eta} \; \chi\alpha\mu\alpha\grave{\iota} \; \tau\iota\vartheta\epsilon\grave{\iota}\varsigma$$
$$\tau\grave{o}\nu \; \sigma\grave{o}\nu \; \pi\acute{o}\delta', \; \grave{\omega}\nu\alpha\xi, \; \H{\iota}\lambda\acute{\iota}o\upsilon \; \pi o\varrho\vartheta\acute{\eta}\tau o\varrho\alpha$$

must be taut with suppressed urgency.

It must be taut with urgency because now begins the argument to persuade
Agamemnon not to set foot upon the ground but to walk upon the costly
cloths. It is a contest of wills, and Clytaemnestra, having a clear purpose,
wins it. We see that she has imposed upon Agamemnon a *rôle* of some kind
which he does not like at all. What is the part which she is determined to make
him play?

When Clytaemnestra desires him to walk from the chariot on purple
tapestries, he replies that he is a mortal and fears to do so: 'I say do reverence
to me as a man, not as a god'[30]. Three lines above he says, 'With these (cloths)
one has to honour gods.' Why does she want him to walk on the carpets into
the house? The obvious answer is that she does so in order to excite the φθόνος
of the gods against him. But this would seem to be unnecessary, for he is
already doomed. Certainly, even so, it is good to ensure that the gods are
against one's enemies, but there is a further objection: Agamemnon recognises
this danger, and is unwilling to tread on the carpets, an attitude of which the
gods would surely take notice. If the object is to show *hybris* in Agamemnon,
the device fails of it. Aeschylus should have made Agamemnon a vainglorious
conqueror, if we are to be convinced. But this he is not. We are, I think,
bound to consider the possibility that the incident of the carpets is not
Aeschylus' invention, but part of a legend about Agamemnon's death of
which we no longer have any other trace, a piece of the legend which was felt
by Aeschylus to be a significant element of the story, even if he did not fully
understand it himself.

If this be accepted as a possibility, we must ask what its significance may
be. The answer to this question is, I believe, supplied by Sir James Frazer[31]:
'It will be well to begin by noticing two of those rules or taboos by which, as

[29] 902–4.   [30] 925.

[31] *The Golden Bough* (abgd. edn.), pp. 593 ff.

we have seen, the life of divine kings or priests is regulated. The first of the rules to which I would call the reader's attention is that the divine personage may not touch the ground with his foot.' Frazer goes on to give many examples of this rule. In Mexico, he says Montezuma 'never set foot on the ground; he was always carried on the shoulders of noblemen, and if he lighted anywhere they laid rich tapestry for him to walk upon. For the Mikado of Japan to touch the ground with his foot was a shameful degradation; indeed, in the sixteenth century, it was enough to deprive him of his office. Outside his palace he was carried on men's shoulders; within it he walked on exquisitely wrought mats... Within his palace the King of Persia walked on carpets on which no one else might tread; outside of it he was never seen on foot but only in a chariot or on horseback.'

After mentioning other examples, Frazer gives what he thinks to be the explanation of this rule: 'Apparently holiness, magical virtue, taboo, or whatever we may call that mysterious quality which is supposed to pervade sacred or tabooed persons, is conceived by the primitive philosopher as a physical substance or fluid with which the sacred man is charged just as a Leyden jar is charged with electricity: and exactly as the electricity in the jar can be discharged by contact with a good conductor, so the holiness or magical virtue in the man can be discharged and drained away by contact with the earth, which on this theory serves as an excellent conductor for the magical fluid. Hence... the sacred or tabooed personage must be carefully prevented from touching the ground...' Except for Frazer's attribution of the practice to the conceptions of 'the primitive philosopher' when in fact one may believe it to have arisen from a genuine but rare experience[32] of very unusual people, the explanation sounds convincing.

Whatever the truth about the significance of the carpets may be, one effect of Agamemnon's resistance to Clytaemnestra's invitation is clear: he has told us that they are appropriate to a sacred purpose and occasion[33]. They

[32] One may think of Jesus 'perceiving that virtue had gone out of him' when a woman touched him in the crowd. *Cf.* also E. R. Dodds, *The Greeks and the Irrational*, pp. 8 ff., on *menos*, and especially note 47, p. 22, on the possession by kings in very early times of a special *menos*.

[33] Prof. E. Fraenkel's comments on 931–4 in his edition of the *Agamemnon* should be carefully considered. Prof. Fraenkel accepts both Kennedy's view of 933 as a question and his paraphrase of it: 'Would you in some fearful crisis have vowed that you would do this thing I am now inviting you to do?' That is to say, Clytaemnestra asks Agamemnon why he should regard walking on the cloths as something dangerous, if not impious, when it is precisely what he might have vowed to do if he had prayed to the gods

signify to us that what is now about to take place has to do with the gods.
Once Agamemnon has consented, a kind of calm comes over Clytaemnestra.
The final nine lines of her speech (966 ff.) glow with an unearthly exaltation[34].
She follows the uneasy Agamemnon into the palace.

In the lyric song which ensues, the Chorus express a sense of acute appre-
hension that possesses them. As they end it, Clytaemnestra comes out of the
palace alone. She addresses Cassandra, who during the whole of the preceding
scene has been standing silent in Agamemnon's chariot:

'Do thou come in too, Cassandra I mean, for Zeus has appointed thee to
share, with good will to the house, in the pouring of purifying water, standing
beside the altar of the house together with many slaves.'

Cassandra is being told that she must be present at, and take part in, a
sacrifice. The sheep stand ready for slaughter[35]. The carpet scene, then, has
led directly to preparations for a sacrifice. It is most important for the understanding of the play that this should be well observed.

When the queen has gone, Cassandra bursts into lamentation and invoca-
tions to Apollo, who had condemned her to so cruel a fate, and passes on to
declare her vision of things past, now happening, and to come. The House of

---

to deliver him from peril, grant him victory, and bring him safely back. Prof. Fraenkel,
however, does not, it seems to me, press the point right home. Surely no ancient Greek,
or any one else, ever vowed, if the gods granted him salvation and success, to walk on
carpets or cloths. Such a vow makes no sense. What must have been promised to the
gods was a great sacrifice, and the walking on cloths must have been a ritual act which
was recognised as preliminary to a sacrifice of quite unusual importance. This interpretation, however, does not by itself explain why Agamemnon should have shrunk
from walking on the cloths. In 934, with ἐξεῖπεν for ἐξεῖπον, he implies that he would
only have made such a vow if someone with understanding of such matters had declared
it to be a proper action. The explanation, I believe, is to be found in Aeschylus'
insistence, through the mouth of Agamemnon himself, that the king was not a god.
This insistence suggests that a tradition existed that Agamemnon *was*, ritually and
ceremonially at least, divine, a tradition which Aeschylus is concerned to contradict
in his presentation of the king, and which is at the same time the explanation of the
story of the carpets.

[34] Consider, for the whole of the scene just ended, the implications of G. Thomson's
article, 'Mystical Allusions in the Oresteia', *JHS* Vol. 55 (1935). See also the interpretation of θύουσαν Ἅιδου μητέρα in footnote 39. It is, however, to be noticed that
the nature of this religous condition seems to vary between mystical vision and possession of a Dionysiac type.

[35] 1056 f. The appropriateness of ἑστίας μεσομφάλου to the plan of a Mycenaean megaron
will be noticed.

the Atreidae is hateful to the gods: it is a bowl for catching the blood of a man, and the floors reek with blood. The word σφαγεῖον (1092), translated 'bowl for catching the blood', is exclusively used in connection with sacrifice. The slaughtered children of Thyestes come before her eyes, served as baked meats to their father. Here again the word σφαγάς, used of the children's end, is the word for ritual slaughter (though not exclusively so: see below). She sees Clytaemnestra pouring the purificatory water over her husband[36]. She sees 'a net of Hades'—it is Agamemnon's wife: 'Let insatiable faction cry out loud for the stoning sacrifice (θύματος) for the clan'[37]. That is, a deed is being done, because of insatiable faction, which calls for a φαρμακός for the clan, a scapegoat to be stoned to death. Clytaemnestra wraps her husband in robes and strikes with a 'black-horned engine'; he falls into the basin filled with water[38]. The λουτροῖσι of 1109 are no surprise to us, for we have been prepared for the purificatory water by the mention of χερνίβων at the forthcoming sacrifice in 1037.

Cassandra's vision changes: she sees the Erinyes brooding on the house; she tells again of the slaughtered children of Thyestes, and then returns to Clytaemnestra. What is she to call her? A snake, a Scylla, a (Maenad) mother of death raging in ecstasy (θύουσαν Ἅιδου μητέρα), breathing truceless war upon those near to her[39]?

---

[36] *Agam.* 1108 f.

[37] The view that γένει must stand for the Erinyes mentioned in the reply of the Chorus is mistaken. Firstly, there has been no talk of Erinyes. Secondly it is στάσις ἀκόρετος that suggests the Erinyes to the Chorus, not γένει. Thirdly, the Chorus have failed to understand Cassandra throughout, and they fail again now.

[38] *Agam.* 1126 ff.

[39] *Ibid.* 1233 ff. It is not impossible that θύουσαν (1235), in view of the use of θύος, θύειν, ἐπιθύειν and σφάζειν referred to below, and in view of the dramatic situation, means 'sacrificing'. If the generally-accepted and more probable view that it means 'raging' (θύω [2]) is maintained, we must nevertheless notice the precise meaning of 'raging' here. The uses of θύω (2) up to and including the time of Aeschylus almost invariably contain the idea of violent movement. The one possible exception quoted by Liddell and Scott (Jones) is in *Il.* 1. 342: ἦ γὰρ ὅ γ' ὀλοιῇσι φρεσὶ θύει. But this is not by any means a certain exception, and analogy from all other instances quoted by LSJ prior to Apollonius Rhodius and Callimachus (excluding, of course, the passage under consideration) shows that it is most unlikely to be so. In the passage from the Iliad, θύει is contrasted with the capacity to *think*: οὐδέ τι οἶδε νοῆσαι ἅμα πρόσσω καὶ ὀπίσσω (343). The meaning is not adequately expressed by 'rages': it means rather 'rushes besotted onward with baleful mind' (and does not know how to think before and after). The physical movement is, of course, here only spoken of figuratively.

[Continued on p.78]

Cassandra cries out again to Apollo, and hurls away the emblems of prophecy, her staff and necklace. She knows that her own end has come; to flee has no purpose[40]. The smell of sacrifice is like a breath from the tomb[41], she dies a slave: 'Alas for human life. If one prospers, it is like a shadow; if one is unfortunate, the stroke of a wet sponge wipes the picture out. And that I grieve for much more than what awaits me now.' Cassandra disappears into the palace[42]. The Chorus intone the verses beginning

> Every man desires insatiably
> To fare well in life;
> Nobody warns him with a pointed finger,
> 'Enter not that room.'

In this case a certain parallel is offered by the English phrase in which we speak metaphorically of someone 'rushing on his doom'. The English phrase, however, does not give the full meaning of the Greek word, which is strongly contrasted with rational deliberation. A mental condition is thus also implied. The other examples quoted of θύειν used of persons clearly contain the idea of movement, as reference to the contexts will show (ἔγχεϊ θύειν, *Il.* 11.180; κασιγνήτα μένει θύοισα, Pind. *Pyth.* 3.33), but also, I think, suggest a state of fury. The remaining twelve instances cited of the use of the word in and before the time of Aeschylus all refer to the movements of the elements, wind and sea. It is quite clear that here θύουσαν must contain this idea of physical movement. It is, however, also noticeable that, except in one instance, in which the word is used of the wind without qualification ([θύουσιν] θυίουσιν ἄῆται, Hes. *Erg.* 621), this verb, in all sixteen instances from the fifth century and earlier is qualified by an adverb or by an noun in the dative case. This makes Aeschylus' naked phrase all the more striking, and suggests that the verb, when used absolutely, had a special meaning, so that, if it were used figuratively, some qualification was needed. The Hesiodic instance above is then a strong poetic figure: it is not vague 'raging'. Hesychius gives us the needed information. Against θύει he has μαίνεται · ἀπέρχεται · ἐνθουσίᾳ. The meaning of θύουσαν then is 'raging in ecstasy', 'possessed'. The movement and state of mind which gave the word this sense was that of the Maenads, the θυιάδες. Here the exceptional absolute use of the word means real possession. Clytaemnestra is being compared to a Maenad mother who brings death to her φίλοις as Agaue did to Pentheus, or the daughters of Proitos, who in Bacchic fury tore to pieces the child of one of their number. The word μητέρα, in itself inappropriate to her relationship with Agamemnon, is thus explained. A further element prompting the comparison may be the dismemberment of the victim: see below, including footnote 50. This interpretation coheres well with Clytaemnestra's strange manner when she makes her speech of welcome to Agamemnon (p. 72).

[40] *Ibid.* 1301.   [41] *Ibid.* 1310 f.   [42] *Ibid.* 1327 ff.

As they end it, the first cry of the stricken Agamemnon sounds from the palace.

Agamemnon's murder takes place within the framework of a ritual; he is slain in ordered ceremony at a sacrifice[43]. The setting is not irrelevant to the murder, and Aeschylus, as we shall immediately see, makes both the Chorus and Clytaemnestra speak of the killing as a sacrifice. When he does so, it is clearly intended that Clytaemnestra's part in the action should be seen to have a religious aspect; she orders the ceremony, from the spreading of carpets for the royal victim to the pouring of water over him and his envelopment in a robe. When she comes out of the palace after the slayings, the Chorus ask the Queen what ill thing brought her to perform the *sacrifice* (θύος)[44]. She replies that this man had sacrificed (ἔθυσεν) his own daughter to be a spell to bind the Thracian winds[45]. A few lines later she exclaims, 'By the justice for my child fulfilled (τέλειον), by Ate and Erinyes, to whom I slaughtered (ἔσφαξα) this man here ...'[46] The verb σφάζειν, although it can be used to mean simply 'kill', is the special word used for ritual slaughter. τέλειον then has precision and point, for it carries with it the idea of *fitting* fulfilment. 'Do not', says Clytaemnestra, 'think me the wife of Agamemnon: the ancient, piercing avenger, taking on the likeness of the wife of this corpse, exacted payment for Atreus, the savage feaster, and made an *adult sacrifice* for the young ones slain[47].' The 'young ones slain' were sacrificed: this was a sacrifice too, but of a grown man and a woman. Clytaemnestra is

---

[43] The question whether the murderer was originally Aegisthus or Clytaemnestra is touched on below.

[44] *Ibid.* 1409. Hesychius, referring specifically to this line, gives θύος · ἱερὸν θῦμα.

[45] *Ibid.* 1417 f.

[46] *Ibid.* 1432 f. For the association of Erinys and Ate, see *Il.* 19.86 ff. For some light on the meaning of Ate here, see Professor E. R. Dodds on Ate, *The Greeks and the Irrational,* pp. 3 ff. For the triad Dike, Erinyes, Ate, cf. Dodds, *op. cit.,* p. 8, on *moira-Erinys-ate.* The Ate to whom Clytaemnestra slaughtered Agamemnon may be, or may at least include, the spirit that possessed her in her ecstasy.

[47] *Agam.* 1498 ff. The theme may reappear in the *Choephoroe,* 405 f.: Electra, in the *kommos* at Agamemnon's tomb, cries:

> 'O earth and sovereign powers of those below,
> Ye curses of the sacrificed (ἀραὶ τεθυμένων),
> Behold.'

Obviously, this, uttered over Agamemnon's tomb by one loyal to him, cannot possibly refer to Iphigeneia: it refers to Agamemnon and those of his forebears who suffered the same fate, and perhaps to Cassandra also. τεθυμένων is, however, an emendation and is therefore uncertain.

seen not only to have ordered the whole 'sacrifice' but in doing so to have been moved by a power stronger than herself.

Hesychius, as we have just noted (see footnote 44), took the θύος of Agamemnon and Cassandra to mean their sacrifice. Indeed, Clytaemnestra's reply justifying it by the sacrifice of Iphigeneia, is pointless unless this is what it means. In the passages we have just quoted[48] Aeschylus uses the words θυσία, θύος, θύειν and ἐπιθύειν of Agamemnon's death. (This is, therefore, apart from the other passages in which he describes or suggests what was happening without using these words.) We have already noted the use of σφαγεῖον (1092), and ἔσφαξα (1433). To these we may add the 'chopping block' (ἐπίξηνον, 1277) which Cassandra says awaits her, the προσφάγματι of 1278[49]. We may now understand why Cassandra calls out (1125), 'Keep the bull from the cow'—for the bull's protection. Why did Aeschylus use this image when it involves an apparent reversal of the natural order? It contains, one may suggest, the idea of the sacrificial bull, Agamemnon, who is to be kept from the priestess, his mate. But she strikes with the pole-axe (μελαγκέρῳ μηχανήματι), her 'horn'. The immediate prelude to this scene played by Cassandra was the carpet scene, and the religious significance of the carpets we noticed to have been clearly pointed out by Agamemnon himself. This sacrifice has been taken to be one of thanksgiving for a safe return after victory. It is nowhere stated or suggested in the text that this is so. Agamemnon himself never refers to such a sacrifice. Nor do we receive any indication that the sacrifice is over before Agamemnon's cry is heard. On the contrary, shortly before Cassandra leaves the stage to pass into the palace, she exclaims that the house breathes death and dripping blood and the Chorus reply that this is the smell of sacrifice within (1309 f.). Surely this is a clear reminder that the sacrifice is not over. Earlier (1298), the Chorus had compared Cassandra to a heifer going to the altar. Certainly the Chorus frequently do not realise in this scene the full meaning of what is being said. But here they have at least accepted the fact that she has been talking about her death. In any case, the words are a reminder to the audience of the theme of sacrifice, which has never been allowed to retire far into the background. Thus every indication points to the sacrifice as being in progress when the water is seen by Cassandra to be poured over Agamemnon by his wife (1109).

Finally, there are the words of Aegisthus, 1598—1603, in which he sees

---

[48] *Agam.* 1235, 1310, 1409, 1504, and perhaps *Choeph.* 405.
[49] On ἐπίξηνον see below, including footnote 50.

the prayer of Thyestes, that all the Pleisthenidae should perish just as his children perished, fulfilled in the death of Agamemnon. That Aeschylus held Thyestes' children to have been sacrificed is clearly implied by 151. The context of Thyestes' οὕτως (1602) makes it clear that he is referring to the dismemberment of the children's bodies. In this sense, too, we are to understand the ἐπίξηνον of 1277: it is not, as Professor Fraenkel thinks, grotesque humiliation, but a form of funeral practice that is implied. As the word does not mean an executioner's block (see Fraenkel *ad loc.*), no other interpretation seems to explain it. Dismemberment of corpses is practised to this day in some parts of the world, *e. g.* Tibet, and according to J. Wiesner was common in the Mediterranean hinterland in the Early and Middle Helladic periods. Wiesner does not mention it in connection with the Late Helladic period. (For references see footnote 50).

In 1107 ff. Clytaemnestra is said to have 'made Agamemnon shine' by bathing him (λουτροῖσι φαιδρύνασα). When he was struck, he fell into a basin of water. Now Agamemnon is not the only ruler whose death is preceded by his being bathed by women. Minos, according to Apollodorus[50] and others, when at the court of Kokalos at Kamikos in Sicily, was destroyed by Kokalos' daughters. 'Some say he perished because boiling water was poured over him'. The word used of Clytaemnestra's bathing of Agamemnon, φαιδρύνασα, is possibly a significant one. Medea is said to have conspired with Jason to take vengeance on Pelias by cutting him up and boiling him on the plea of restoring his youth after the ceremony. She was helped in this by Pelias' daughters. Medea is also said to have 'boiled Jason and made him young'. About Jason's father, Aison, the author of the *Nostoi* says:

[50] *Epit.* 1.15. The expression translated 'destroyed', ἔκλυτος ἐγένετο, is a strange one. If sound, it would seem to mean 'loosed', 'allowed to fall asunder'. It may therefore mean 'dismembered'. (Frazer, however, suggests that the meaning of the phrase is 'was relaxed', but doubts the text. See his notes in the Loeb translation). The only hints that Agamemnon met the same end are in (a) the οὕτως of 1602 (b) the ἐπίξηνον of 1277 (c) the ἐμασχαλίσθη of *Choeph.* 439, on which see footnote 59. Aeschylus does not develop the allusions: the bodies are of course shown covered upon the stage. The interpretation of οὕτως suggested here assumes, of course, that 1601 is syntactically a parenthesis, οὕτως ὀλέσθαι following on ἐπεύχεται; that is to say, it is a deliberate prayer rather than a vague general imprecation uttered in an outburst of wrath. The precise form of the μόρον ἄφερτον is indicated. Wiesner's statements about dismemberment will be found in *Grab und Jenseits* (Berlin, 1938), pp. 108 f. and 113, while footnote 1 on p. 120, *ibid.*, may bear on ἔκλυτος ἐγένετο above.

Αὐτίκα δ᾽ Αἴσονα θῆκε φίλον κόϱον ἡβώοντα,
γῆϱας ἀποξύσασ᾽ εἰδυίῃσι πϱαπίδεσσι,
φάϱμακα πολλ᾽ ἕψουσ᾽ ἐνὶ χϱυσείοισι λέβησιν[51].

I suggest that this rejuvenation is really immortalisation. At any rate in the case of Aison the initiation rite seems to be excluded by the word γῆϱας. The word φαιδϱύνασα may refer to the making of the hero, in this case Agamemnon, young and glorious, that is, immortal. Diodorus Siculus[52] says that when Minos was bathing, Kokalos kept him too long in the hot water and thus killed him; the body he gave back to the Cretans, giving as an explanation of his death that he had 'slipped down on to the bath, and, falling into the hot water, had died'. The implication that the way in which Agamemnon met his end was in fact a widely-spread ritual is extremely strong[53]. Not only the coincident details but the emphasis given to Clytaemnestra's *rôle* as mistress of the sacrifice which embraced Agamemnon's death are explicable only if they are seen as remnants of ancient tradition. Nor is there anything singular about this: Aison died at a sacrifice[54] when Pelias succeeded him. Pelias is challenged by Jason, whom Pelias recognizes as intending to kill him, at a sacrifice[55]. The death of Aigeus seems to be associated with a sacrifice performed by Theseus on the seashore[56] and Atreus himself is said to have been killed also while sacrificing on the seashore[57]. The sacrifice at which Agamemnon died was surely not the invention of Aeschylus[58]. Indeed, we saw in Chapter I, § VII, that there was ample evidence that a sacrifice or sacrificial meal preceded the death of the old ruler.

[51] Argum. Eurip. *Med.*

[52] 4.79.

[53] Diodorus continues, *loc. cit.;* 'The comrades of Minos buried the body of the king with magnificent ceremonies, and, constructing a double tomb, in its hidden part they placed the bones, and in that which lay open to gaze they made a shrine of Aphrodite.' (Loeb translation, modified).

[54] Apollod. 1.9.27.

[55] *Ibid.* 1.9.16.

[56] Plutarch, *Vita Thes.* XXII. In Plutarch's account there is no connection between the sacrifice and Aigeus' death except their proximity in time, but consideration of the sequence of events, and especially of the fact that the herald does not announce the death until the sacrifice is over, leads one to think that the original story was a different one.

[57] Hyginus (Schmidt), *Fab.* LXXXVIII, Atreus.

[58] The extraordinary belief exists that the theme of sacrifice in the *Agamemnon* is merely metaphor. The purpose of the 'metaphor' (in scale and elaboration far surpassing any other metaphor in tragedy, ancient or modern) escapes me. There is nothing in the

In the Odyssey Agamemnon is said to have been killed at, or immediately after, a banquet. In the account of Minos' death, Kokalos is said to have 'entertained' him just before he died. Apollodorus' word ἐξένισεν, 'entertained', cannot, in this particular context, have a general meaning such as 'was hospitable towards': it must refer to some specific act of hospitality. This would naturally suggest the offering of a meal, possible of presents, to Minos. According to Plutarch, some said that Theseus was thrown from a cliff 'after dinner'. A report in Apollodorus (2.7.7.) is particularly significant, for it makes the religious background of such meals apparent: Herakles 'killed Laogoras, king of the Dryopes, with his children, as he was dining in a precinct of Apollo'. The tradition in the Odyssey of the banquet given by Aegisthus to Agamemnon and his followers may therefore have originated in this part of the sacrificial ritual. The ritual bathing of Agamemnon would then have been something that the composer of the Odyssey found it better to omit than to disguise[59].

The reader may now be inclined to say, 'Very well: let us admit that, as far as Aeschylus' play is concerned, Agamemnon seems to have died at the sacrifice. That is not to say that the ritual itself was intended to centre round his death as something intimately bound up with its religious purpose. It was simply the occasion of his death; Clytaemnestra tricked him.' I think that the dramatic development which we have already considered, from the laying of carpets to the preparations for, and performance of, a sacrifice;

play to suggest that it is metaphor, and it is worth noticing that F. R. Earp, *The Style of Aeschylus* (Cambridge, 1948), in the list of metaphors and similes in the *Agamemnon* (pp. 134—142), adduces not a single word with the meaning 'sacrifice', whether as noun or as verb. LSJ quote a 'metaphorical' use of θύω in *Agam.* 137 (noting that the context is lyrical), but in my view this is not metaphorical. It is a semi-mystical use of the word: the sacrifice is seen in the portent of the two eagles tearing the hare, and θυομένοισι should be translated 'sacrificing'. The dark insight of the seer becomes more concrete in the θυσίαν of 151, and wholly so in the θυσίας παρθενίου θ' αἵματος of 214.

[59] The ritual death and, as I suggest, immortalisation seem to have been carried out in the following stages: firstly, a ritual meal, possibly accompanied by the presentation of gifts (see Chap. I, § VII); then, bathing, and the putting on of a robe; slaughter, or sometimes suicide, the body falling into a bath; boiling and dismemberment, at least of the feet and hands. In this connection we should perhaps understand the ἐμασχα-λίσθη of *Choeph.* 439, and the severed hand and feet of Thyestes' children shown to their father. I regret having to present the reader with these matters in this repellent and, as it were, mechanical way. For μασχαλισμός Wiesner, *op. cit.*, p. 111, footnote 3, quotes Kroll, *RE* 14, 1930, 2060 f.

the express and repeated naming of his death as a sacrifice; Clytaemnestra's
ecstasy; and Aegisthus' probable acceptance of his death, as we have noticed,
as the fulfilment of Thyestes' prayer that the 'intolerable fate' should be laid
upon the Pleisthenidae that they should die the same death as his children
died (1598—1603), are themselves enough to show the inadequacy of such
a view. Nevertheless, we can contest this objection on its own ground.

Clytaemnestra is, no doubt, held to have got Agamemnon at a disad-
vantage by suddenly enveloping him in the robe with which Orestes afterwards makes so much play. Let us look at this robe.

Aeschylus himself speaks of it in various terms. In the *Agamemnon*[60] he
says that Clytaemnestra caught Agamemnon ἐν πέπλοισι, 'in robes', and
struck him. A little later, Clytaemnestra says,

> ὡς μήτε φεύγειν μήτ' ἀμύνεσθαι μόρον,
> ἄπειρον ἀμφίβληστρον, ὥσπερ ἰχθύων,
> περιστιχίζω, πλοῦτον εἵματος κακόν.

That is, she wraps him in an endless wrapper, like a fish-net, 'an evil wealth
of weaving'. In the *Choephoroe*[61] Electra also uses the word ἀμφίβληστρον.
Later in the *Choephoroe*, after he has murdered his mother and Aegisthus,
Orestes holds the stage, with the robe in his hand, and speaks at length about
it to the Chorus[62]. At first he describes it as a μηχάνημα, a device, a δεσμός,
a bond to fetter his father's hands and feet. What, he asks, is he to call it?
'A snare for a beast, or a pall reaching over the feet of a corpse upon a bier?'
No, rather is it both, a snare, a net, and a robe that reaches to the feet. For
some reason, we notice, Orestes wishes to emphasize both aspects of the
garment. He asks the servants to stand near in a circle and stretch it out, to
show the covering of a man. It bears him witness, this cloth (φᾶρος) that
Aegisthus' sword dyed it: the stain of blood works together with time to
obliterate the many colours of the robe (πολλὰς βαφὰς ... τοῦ ποικίλματος).
The robe is woven (ὕφασμα). In the *Eumenides*[63] it is a φᾶρος and again
an endless robe (ἀτέρμων πέπλος), cunningly worked (δαίδαλος), in which
Clytaemnestra binds and slays her husband.

Euripides[64] also says that Clytaemnestra wrapped Agamemnon round in
an 'endless piece of woven cloth' (ἀπείρῳ ... ὑφάσματι). The scholiast on
this line says, 'Clytaemnestra wove a tunic (χιτών) which had no opening
for the hands or the head, so that Agamemnon could not defend himself

---

[60] 1126; 1381 ff.   [61] 492 f.   [62] 980—1015.
[63] 634 f.   [64] *Orestes* 25.

against his murderers.' He then realises that ἄπειρος, 'endless', would be an
odd word to use of a shaped garment like a *chiton* (even so strange a *chiton*
as this) and suggests another interpretation of ἄπειρος, deriving it from
περάω, to penetrate or pass through. It then would mean, he says, that
Agamemnon was not able to put his head or hands through it[65]. The
scholiast has apparently tried to reconcile two traditions, one that the
garment was a tunic or chiton, the other, that it was an 'endless' piece
of cloth. Aeschylus, too, we notice, had called it 'endless', ἀτέρμων. But
by 'endless' Aeschylus apparently means 'without a particular beginning
or end', 'without a top or bottom', for he several times compares it to
a net. That is to say, by 'endless', he means 'not shaped', 'not tailored'.
This scholiast on Euripides' *Orestes*, then, had heard of two traditions
about the robe, and did not really know what it was like. From Aeschylus
we learn that it reached over the feet[66], that it was 'cunningly worked',
δαίδαλος, and that it was of many colours[67]. He also calls it a πέπλος,
which was a woman's garment. Now there is one most valuable piece
of literary evidence about it, namely, that of Apollodorus, who says
that Clytaemnestra gave Agamemnon a tunic without sleeves (χιτῶνα ἄχειρα)
and without a neck (ἀτράχηλον)[68] and killed him when he was putting it on.
We do not know the date of the work attributed to Apollodorus or, of
course, of the scholion. 'Apollodorus' may belong to the first or second
centuries of the Christian era; he is first mentioned in the ninth[69]. The scholiast may be either earlier or later than 'Apollodorus'; the important point is
that, in default of information, he is (if it be the same hand) given to
inventing explanations, as we have seen. Apollodorus, on the other hand,
we know to have used good authorities and to have reproduced them, where
we are able to compare the originals, faithfully. He appears to be quite
undisturbed by inconsistencies in the stories he relates (although he is not

---

[65] Seneca, *Agamemnon,* 898 f., takes a similar view of it: *exitum manibus negant
caputque laxi et invii claudunt sinus.* He, like Homer, represents the slaying of
Agamemnon as taking place at a banquet, but presents him as first wearing the robe
of Priam at the feast (as part of his spoils), but then taking it and the ornaments
off as *cultus hostiles,* at Clytaemnestra's suggestion. He then puts on the robe she has
woven. This seems at least to support a tradition that there were two robes, and that the
second was the woven one.

[66] *Choeph.* 984, 986.

[67] *Ibid.* 1013.

[68] 2.6.23.

[69] See Frazer's Introduction to his edition and translation (Loeb).

above rationalising a theogony). For these reasons, we should (since we are
not dealing with divine genealogy) prefer Apollodorus to the scholiast on the
Orestes.

Now we must observe that Apollodorus and the scholiast do not say the
same thing. Apollodorus says that the tunic which Clytaemnestra gave (notice
'gave') Agamemnon was without sleeves or neck. This is not what the scholiast
says. The scholiast says that it had no opening for the hands and the head.
I suggest that the scholiast, or the account which he reproduces, has either
misunderstood the tradition which Apollodorus quite exactly repeats or is
following a different one. What is meant by a tunic 'without sleeves or a
neck'? More than one possible meaning of it occurs to one. But most fortunately, not merely for the understanding of this point, but for confirmation
of our interpretation of the crisis of the *Agamemnon* as taking place in a
religious ceremony, we have an astonishing visible representation of what
may be meant on the Hagia Triada sarcophagus.

The two long panels of the sarcophagus show religious ritual scenes, probably parts of a single ceremony. The right-hand half of one of the panels[70]
shows three male servers, two of whom carry sacrificial victims in their arms,
and the third a boat. They are facing the right-hand end of the panel, looking
towards a male figure, rather smaller than any other of the human figures
depicted, which is standing alone before a building with which he is clearly
meant to be associated. The building forms the end of the panel. Of this last
figure Nilsson says that he is 'the deified dead man appearing to the eye of
the imagination'[71]. To this we have only to add that the deified dead man is,
it would seem, the former ruler in the palace, represented as in the prime of
life.

[70] Plate I.
[71] In *The Minoan-Mycenaean Religion*, 2nd. Ed., p. 438, Nilsson, after comparing the
fragments of paintings from the walls of the Hagia Triada palace with certain of the
scenes on the sarcophagus, writes: 'This comparison establishes the fact that the
libation and probably also the animal sacrifice are parts of the divine cult; on the
other hand all analogies and all customs of other peoples would indicate that the
paintings on the sarcophagos must refer to the deceased who was laid in it. I see
only one way out of this dilemma, and that is to suppose that the dead man was
deified and consequently worshipped in the forms of the divine cult.' N.'s deduction
of the deification (or rather, immortalisation) of the ruler seems to be justified.
It does not, however, seem to justify in turn his further conclusion of a cult of the dead,
or worship of the deceased ruler. This may have been a Mycenaean custom (N. sees
evidence that the dead man was a Mycenaean, not a Minoan), but the scene allows
only a deduction about the nature of the one ceremony, not of a continuing cult.

In this panel, the figure on the right, the deified dead man, is wearing a ceremonial robe. (Cretan men normally wore a loin cloth or a kind of skirt, even in cult ritual, the upper part of the body being bare[72].) The male priests or servers have loin-cloths of the same material as the robe, which Nilsson holds from other representations to be an animal's skin, and the priestess's robe is also made of it. The female server, however, wears a robe made apparently of a woven material.

All the robes are worn very low on the shoulders and this is particularly noticeable in the case of the male figure on the right, whom we take with Nilsson to be the dead man. The upper part of the chest, the upper part of the shoulders and the back just below the neck are visible. It would be perfectly natural to call such a garment 'neckless', as indeed it is: this characteristic would be even more strongly noticeable if, as seems virtually certain, the robe was open in front. The other element in Apollodorus' description is equally clearly shown here: the robe has no sleeves. The man's hands and arms are not visible at all; they are concealed beneath the robe. On the other hand, the robes worn by the priestess, the lyre-player, and the girl-server have normal sleeves. The male servers have the upper part of the body bare.

One may ask why this robe has no sleeves. It is not a loose-fitting garment like a cape, and the dress of the others here, and evidence elsewhere, show that, if the upper body were clothed, sleeves were normal in dress for cult occasions. It may be suggested that the reason why there were no sleeves may perhaps have been that the arms beneath the robe were bound. This would very easily explain the tradition which Aeschylus followed when he called the robe 'a contrivance that bound' or 'fettered'. However this may be, one thing is quite evident: the wearer of this robe can only have played a passive *rôle* in any ceremony in which he took part.

Nilsson's interpretation of the Hagia Triada sarcophagus supposes the ritual depicted on it to have taken place after the death of the figure wearing the robe. Professor Matz[73], whose study is a valuable contribution to the interpretation of the sarcophagus, not only makes the same supposition, but takes the ritual to be one of conjuration of the dead, who here appears in response to the ritual. It is, fortunately, not our business to interpret the

---

[72] The so-called cuirass, used in cult, seems to have had more likeness to a covered framework than a vestment.

[73] F. Matz, *Göttererscheinung und Kultbild im minoischen Kreta* (Akad. d. Wissenschaft u. d. Literatur, Abhandlungen d. Geistes- und Sozialwissenschaftlichen Klasse, 1958, Nr. 7), pp. 18 (398) ff.

scenes depicted, but we must point out that the view that the ritual takes place after the death of the robed figure has led to a description of the figure as 'mummy-like'. This description cannot by any possible argument be justified, for it simply has no resemblance to a mummy whatever. The only grounds given for the description are, firstly, that its position in front of a piece of building is reminiscent of that of the mummy in Egyptian funeral scenes, set up before its tomb, and, secondly, that the arms are not visible. These are not adequate reasons for describing as mummy-like a figure which is in no way like a mummy. It is quite obvious that, whether the figure be conceived as alive or as a spirit visible to the inner eye, he is dressed in a ritual garment which he wore while still alive.

We have seen that in two striking points the robe corresponds to that which Agamemnon was wearing at his death. In certain other respects, however, it does not so correspond. Firstly, the robe on the sarcophagus is an animal's pelt, apparently a sheepskin, whereas the robe Clytaemnestra placed upon Agamemnon is, as we have seen, said to have been woven. Further, it was apparently longer, and covered the feet, and it is described as 'endless'. It is wrapped round the body as this robe is not. What kind of cloth covering for the body could be so described? It may be that this 'robe' is nothing else than a winding-sheet. There are, then, *two* robes, and tradition, while preserving their characteristics, has merged them in a single garment. There is, to my mind, little doubt that the neckless and sleeveless garment worn by Agamemnon at his death was very like the garment shown on the sarcophagus. The other 'robe' may have been that in which his body was wrapped after he had been slain. The account in Seneca's *Agamemnon*[74] is valuable, for it must be based, directly or indirectly, on a Greek original, and the description of a change of robes is not a detail which would seem likely to have been invented; it is too cumbersome. If one tries to imagine something of the course of the grim ceremony, one will, I think, be bound to admit that it is unlikely that it would have concluded with the maimed body of the dead king lying uncovered to the view in his ceremonial robe. Indeed, it could not have been dismembered in the robe. The ceremony will have ended with his body wrapped in the 'cunningly-worked' woven fabric.

In Seneca's description, the second robe is said to have been that woven by Clytaemnestra. It is called 'endless' by Aeschylus seemingly because it is not a fashioned garment, and because the ends of the long cloth which was

---

[74] 898 ff.

wrapped round the body were not visible, being tucked in somewhere. (The word περιστιχίζω, which Clytaemnestra uses in one passage[75], means 'to surround in rows' or 'lines': this would seem to be meant to describe the parallel lines made by the edges of the strip of cloth as it was wound round the body. It does not fit the use she makes of the robe, and it seems likely that the word was borrowed from an earlier narrative, the reason for its use not being properly understood.)

This view has, to support it, the close parallel afforded by the cloth woven by Penelope for Laertes, inasmuch as the latter was certainly woven in anticipation of the death of Laertes[76]. The view of either robe as one of the principal means of making a sudden and unexpected attack on Agamemnon was, we should notice, not that of the account which Apollodorus had before him: if it had been, he would not have written that Clytaemnestra *gave* it to him. Finally, it is important to observe that language extremely close to that of Aeschylus is used by Sophocles in describing a robe worn by the victim at a human sacrifice. In his lost drama *Polyxena* the line occurred:

χιτών σ'ἄπειρος ἐνδυτήριος κακῶν,[77]

'An endless robe with which thou dost put on thy sufferings'.

Agamemnon's robe was not unique, though this last passage does not make the problem easier.

The tradition that Clytaemnestra drew a cloth over Agamemnon's head before he was killed, is, in spite of the view advanced above, an ancient one. This is proved by the clay plaque of the seventh century B. C. from Gortyn in Crete found by Professor Doro Levi[78]. In the scene depicted, Clytaem-

---

[75] *Agam.* 1383.   [76] *Od.* 2.97 ff.; 19.142 ff.; 24.132 ff.

[77] Soph. *Frag.* 483 (Nauck), 526 (Pearson). E. A. J. Ahrens gives it as fr. (190). Another possible meaning of ἄπειρος is, in effect, 'seamless', i. e., the robe was a single circular piece of cloth, in which a hole was cut in the centre so that it might be passed over the head. This, however, would imply a loom of very great width, much larger than any that would have been in normal use.

The reason why the robe worn at the ceremony was of sheepskin while the second was woven was, I suggest, that the former was a traditional garment, preserved for ceremonial use and worn by a succession of rulers, while the second may have been the shroud in which the body was buried. The second robe had therefore to be woven afresh for each interment. *Cf.* for the former the traditional robe given by Medea and Jason to Apsyrtos before his ritual death, Ap. Rhod. IV, 423 ff.

[78] Plate II. Professor Levi's description of the plaque is to be found in the *Annuario della Scuola Archeologica di Atene*, XXXIII—XXXIV (N. S. XVII—XVIII), 1955—6, pp. 275 ff.

nestra is, as Professor Levi rightly suggests, shown beginning to pass the cloth
over the seated Agamemnon's head. The manner of the work is in no way
realistic: it is, on the contrary, stylized and symbolical. This shows us that
the tradition about Clytaemnestra's action was old and firm. Now we must
at this point remember that the evidence we have reviewed shows fairly
conclusively that the death of Agamemnon took place in an ordered ritual.
It excludes the surprise attack by Clytaemnestra and Aegisthus with the aid
of a cloth suddenly flung over the king. Further, the probability that the first
robe worn by Agamemnon resembled that shown on the Hagia Triada sarcophagus appears to be strong. Yet the Gortyn plaque evidently points to a
tradition that Agamemnon was enveloped in a cloth passed over his head
before he was slain. If this happened, then it too must have been a part of
the ceremony. The cloth may have been that used later as a winding-sheet.

Explanation can, at present, only be speculative. There is some evidence[79]
that the Tantalid kings may have been, formally and ritually, shamans.
Quite certainly they looked back to a great shaman as the founder of their
line. Now one of the commonest outward features of shamanism is a mask
or 'cap of darkness' or a cloth placed over the face for a part of the act of
shamanising. This is done because the shaman 'is supposed to penetrate into
the spirit-world with his inner sight'[80]. The shaman may even be completely
enveloped in the cloth. Miss Czaplicka actually saw this happen in the case
of a famous Samoyed shaman named Bokkobushka, who shamanised in her
presence: '(The shaman) seated himself crosslegged on the ground, while his
assistant ... threw over him a cloth, which completely concealed him from
view. After some moments of silence, broken only by the crackling of the
driftwood fire in the centre of the *chum*, a low sound of chanting arose
from the cone-shaped bundle that was all we could see of Bokkobushka.'[81]
'First we had divination, and then prophecy. The shaman now threw off his
cloth, and began the third stage of his shamanising — a contest with the
spirits of disease.'[82]

In some cases, a shaman had his wife for his assistant. Is it possible that
Clytaemnestra ritually performed certain acts as the assistant of Agamemnon, the great shaman, and that one of these was to cover him with the

---

[79] Which appears later in this book, Chap. IV.

[80] M. A. Czaplicka, *Aboriginal Siberia* (Oxford, 1914), p. 226. See also p. 203.

[81] *My Siberian Year*, p. 200.

[82] *Ibid.*, p. 201.

enveloping cloth? It may perhaps have been so. It is certainly conceivable also that on the occasion of his death he was killed while in communication with the spirit-world beneath his cloth. This would perhaps be thought to assure him of a lasting place in that world: in dying in communication with spirits he might well have been held to pass through the portal of immortality[83]. An alternative hypothesis is that the enveloping cloth may have served as blindfolding before execution. In some such way, we suggest, arose the legend of the queen's murderous device. Certainly, the tradition that makes Clytaemnestra a murderess is fairly old; on the plaque from Gortyn, Clytaemnestra is apparently holding Agamemnon's raised right arm by the wrist as if to prevent him thrusting the cloth back from his head. Clytaemnestra's attitude of mind is, however, irrelevant, if, as we suggest, the cloth of divination would in any case have been used in the ceremony. It may be that the cloth beneath which contact had been made with the spirit-world was also the king's winding-sheet, as we have already suggested. At any rate, it seems clear that there were at least two robes, or a robe and an enveloping cloth, and that one or both of them was handed to Agamemnon by Clytaemnestra in the course of an ordered ritual.

There is a possibility that there was a third 'robe'. The word ἀμφίβληστρον, 'net', is used in *Agamemnon* 1382 and *Choephoroe* 492 to describe the robe which Agamemnon wore at his death. This word, which Aeschylus does not seem to use metaphorically, may in fact refer to a net wrapped round Agamemnon's naked body beneath the sheepskin robe, binding him 'with fetters not of bronze'[84]. Network has a religious significance, as Professor Marinatos

---

[83] For a similar reason Hamlet refrains from killing the King, Claudius, while he is at his prayers.

[84] *Choeph.* 493. The net, if net it was, may however have been placed round the body after death. *Cf.* Wiesner, *Grab und Jenseits,* p. 105: 'Auf eine Fesselung der Leiche deutet nicht nur die starke Krümmung verschiedener Skelette, sondern auch die Sarg- und Gefässbestattung. Die Enge des Tonsarges oder des Pithos bedingte meist ein Zusammenschnüren der Leiche, die oft so gewaltsam war, dass die Knie das Kinn berührten.' This practice, while characteristic of the Early and Middle (p. 111) Helladic periods, became rare on the mainland in the Late Helladic age (pp. 114 f.). Although one must make allowance for possibly conservative royal practice, this fact, and the apparent decline of mutilation as a practice in the LH period (see p. 81 above), may point to the origin of some detail of the story of Agamemnon's death in the Early or Middle Helladic age. Nevertheless, as we have remarked, the necessarily passive *rôle* of the standing figure on the H. T. sarcophagus suggests a possible fettering below the robe, *i.e.,* in life. There remains, however, the mutilation.

points out in reference to the LM I rhyton, in the form of a bull covered all over with a painted network, which was found on the island of Psyra[85], and as one can see from the fact that omphaloi at Delphi and elsewhere were often covered with a net or have a network pattern carved upon them[86].

We must not fail to recognise the support for our interpretation of Agamemnon's death given by its association with that of Cassandra. Cassandra, a royal figure, is also so unmistakably a religious one that one would in any case be inclined to suspect her death to have a connection with cult. How Cassandra's death is related to that of Agamemnon remains obscure, but that it was traditionally held to have taken place in an ordered ceremony seems to be suggested by her words in Euripides' *Troades*,

[85] *Kreta und das Mykenische Hellas*, Pl. 90. I am much indebted to Mr. J. Boardman of the Ashmolean Museum, Oxford, for pointing out to me the possibility of a connection between ἀμφίβληστρον in Aeschylus' Oresteia and the network on this bull. For a net *(agrenon)* worn by priests, persons of sacred calling, and, sometimes, deities, see A. Laumonier, *Les Cultes Indigènes en Carie*, pp. 80 ff. The classical *agrenon* so worn covers only the upper half of the body. Laumonier discusses also a network which covers the lower half of the body only. See also, in connection with the network on omphaloi, *I. Kings*, Chap. 7, vv. 17, 18, 20 and 41 for the network on the capitals of the two pillars which were set up in the porch of Solomon's temple. For Mesopotamian parallels see H. Frankfort, *Cylinder Seals* (London, 1939), p. 19 and Pls. III d, V c and XXI i.

[86] The reading of the Medicean manuscript at *Choeph.* 492 may be extremely significant: (ἀμφίβληστρον) ᾧ σ' ἐκαίνισαν, 'with which they made thee new'. If correct, it confirms the view that the object of the ritual in which Agamemnon died was to ensure his immortality. If ἐνοσφίσθης (491) means 'thou wast slain', it is impossible that ἐκαίνισαν (492) could refer to the putting on of a robe: it must refer to something that happened after the slaying. ἐνοσφίσθης may, however, mean approximately 'wast sent on thy way', 'received thy *envoi'*: in this case it need not refer to the final act. Conington's emendation forces him to emend 493 also (and to use a meaningless γ' in doing so). I would suggest that the Medicean reading be preserved in both lines. 492 remains, however, somewhat suspect: μέμνησο followed by the genitive in 491 and by the accusative in 492 is odd.

It may be asked: did Aeschylus know that σ' ἐκαίνισαν meant 'they made thee new (i.e. immortal)'? The proper answer to this is that the question may not be necessary. Aeschylus may be using an expression which was retained in sources of which he made use: whether he understood it in a particular sense or not is a separate question. We have already seen reason to think that the carpet scene and the presentation of the king's death as taking place at a sacrifice are taken from sources which retained very old traditions, and this reproduction of his sources extends, apparently, to single words, if our surmise about περιστιχίζω (*Agam.* 1383) is correct. I suggest that σ' ἐκαίνισαν has a similar origin.

πέλεκυν οὐχ ὑμνήσομεν,

ὃς ἐς τράχηλον τὸν ἐμὸν εἶσι χάτέρων (361 f.),

for this shows that the manner of her (and, here, Agamemnon's) death was beheading with an axe. The tradition that Clytaemnestra's weapon was an axe appears also in Sophocles, *Electra* 99, and Euripides, *Hecuba* 1279 and *Electra* 279. The religious setting of this execution is unmistakably shown on a Greek *kylix* (as it apparently is, a description being lacking and only the painting inside the bowl being shown) found at Comacchio in Northern Italy[87]. The painting shows Clytaemnestra on the point of killing Cassandra with a double axe: Cassandra flees to an altar; behind Cassandra is a tree, on the left a tripod. A shrine is thus intended as the scene.

The deaths of rulers such as Aison, Pelias, Jason, Aigeus, Atreus and, apparently, Theseus, are probably not to be regarded as human sacrifices. They take place *at* a sacrifice, but the purpose of the ritual was probably to secure the immortality of the king after death as a divine being. The slaying, the murder, was unconnected with this purpose, and under the matrilineal system was enforced, if not committed, by the intruding successor. Such too was the death of Agamemnon. It is true that Aeschylus and Pindar make Clytaemnestra the murderess, but here, as we shall see in more detail later, the Odyssey seems to reflect the older tradition when it makes Aegisthus the slayer of Agamemnon. In any case, the killing of Agamemnon has two aspects: it is a murder, but it takes place in a ritual of immortalisation performed by Clytaemnestra, and is presented by Aeschylus as an act of sacrifice carried out in a state of religious exaltation. This is further strongly suggested by the sense of a certain sacramental quality in the scenes leading up to the king's death, particularly in that in which he is persuaded to descend from his chariot and walk on purple carpets into the house. Throughout this scene we become increasingly aware of Clytaemnestra's attitude to the impending event, and we catch a glimpse of the light in which it appears to her in its last lines:

πολλῶν πατησμὸν δ᾽ εἱμάτων ἂν ηὐξάμην,

δόμοισι προυνεχθέντος ἐν χρηστηρίοις,

ψυχῆς κόμιστρα τῆσδε μηχανωμένη.

---

[87] *Jahrbuch des Deutschen Archäolog. Instit.* 43 (1928), Archäolog. Anzeiger, column 132. The sword seems to have been replaced by the axe in the course of the fifth century: a bronze relief from the Heraion at Argos shows Clytaemnestra killing Cassandra with a sword. The relief is in mid–7th. century style (Hampe, *Frühe griechische Sagenbilder in Böotien*, pl. 41; *AJA* 43 (1939), p. 416, fig. 6.).

ῥίζης γὰρ οὔσης φυλλὰς ἵκετ᾽ ἐς δόμους,
σκιὰν ὑπερτείνασα σειρίου κυνός.
καὶ σοῦ μολόντος δωματῖτιν ἑστίαν,
θάλπος μὲν ἐν χείμωνι σημαίνεις μόλον.
ὅταν δὲ τεύχῃ Ζεὺς ἀπ᾽ ὄμφακος πικρᾶς
οἶνον, τότ᾽ ἤδη ψῦχος ἐν δόμοις πέλει,
ἀνδρὸς τελείου δῶμ᾽ ἐπιστρωφωμένου.
Ζεῦ, Ζεῦ τέλειε, τὰς ἐμὰς εὐχὰς τέλει ·
μέλοι δέ τοι σοὶ τῶνπερ ἂν μέλλῃς τελεῖν.[88]

'I should have dedicated much linen to be trodden on, had it been so told me in the house of prophecy, when I contrived the conveyance of this soul. For as long as the root is there, the leaf comes to the house and spreads its shade between it and the scorching days of the dog-star. And thou hast come to the household hearth, and hast thereby signified that warmth is come in winter. But when from the sour grape Zeus makes wine, then it is already chill in the house and just then the perfect man (that is, the man who is mature or fit for the purpose) is visiting the house. Zeus, Zeus Perfecter (*i.e.* Zeus who brings things to pass), perfect my vows: do thou give heed to that which thou wilt bring to perfection.'

These lines can perhaps be made more easily comprehensible in the following terms. The whole passage is lifted above the level of ordinary dramatic irony. Clytaemnestra, for all the double meaning of the words she uses, is expressing something of the innermost significance of the deed she intends. To begin with, one should not overlook the phrase 'when I contrived the conveyance of this soul'. If Hermes Psychagogos were speaking instead of Clytaemnestra, no one would dispute its meaning. If we are right in seeing the sacrificial ritual as a process of immortalisation, then we may read it, spoken by Clytaemnestra, in a like sense. Indeed, this interpretation fits the Greek wording extremely well. It also fits in with our belief in the background of shamanism: a prime duty of the shaman is to convey souls. The 'root' may be the matrilineal house or family itself, the dynasty represented by the present generation: the leaf that comes to it is certainly the man who becomes its head, here Agamemnon. He is thought of as a vine growing against the house. In the summer, he shades the house from the scorching heat. But when it grows cool, the shade of the vine is no longer needed. But, also, this cooler season, the autumn, is the time when the grapes are picked,

---

[88] *Agam.* 963 ff.

and from these once-sour grapes Zeus makes wine. The perfect, the fitting man, is just then in the house: he has protected the house, he has finished his work, he has returned to the household hearth[89]. As Zeus in due time makes wine from the grape, so now he must bring to pass something that has been

[89] τέλειος here means both 'fitting' or 'perfect' and 'mature' or 'ripe'. For the latter meaning cf. Aesch. fr. 44, line 7, where τέλειος is used of the fruit of trees and means 'ripe', 'brought to perfection'. The chief difficulty in these lines seems to lie in 968—9. When Agamemnon is said to have come to the hearth of the house, is his return from Troy referred to, or his original marriage to Clytaemnestra? It would seem that the present tense in σημαίνεις indicates that the former is meant. In this case, the meaning is that Agamemnon's return is a false sign of the coming warmth, for it is winter; and it is when it has already become cold in the house that wine is made from the grapes. Otherwise, 968—9 are to be taken as a general statement with a loose sequence of tense: 'whenever thou hast come... thou hast signified the coming of warmth.' This makes the parallel with the image of 966—7 much closer, and there is correspondence 2 : 2, 2 : 2 in 966—9, 970—3. This may be the true interpretation. Schneidewin, Wilamowitz, Mazon, Denniston and Page, Fraenkel, all apparently fail to understand the point of 970 f., namely that the time when the grapes are picked is no longer a hot time of the year. It is already getting cool, and the shade of the vine over the house is not needed any more. Agamemnon, who has quite unmistakably been compared to the leafage of the vine, is likewise not needed any longer. The foliage is not required, but the fruit of the vine is now gathered to make wine. As to ἀπ' ὄμφακος πικρᾶς, it must be remembered that no one makes wine from unripe grapes. Either, therefore, the meaning is that Zeus makes wine from grapes which had once been immature and sour (ἀπό referring to time as well as source, and meaning approximately 'when (the stage of unripeness) is over' or the word ὄμφαξ is used simply to mean any grape, without reference to its degree of maturity. In this latter case, πικρᾶς is a comment on the general flavour of grapes as the viniculture of the day produced them, and the wine, sweet by comparison, perhaps because spiced, is contrasted with the fruit from which it is made. The importance of the time of year is particularly emphasized: ὅταν δὲ..., τότ'ἤδη..., and the season is clearly distinguished from that in which the leafage and the heat go together—'But when...' Only Blaydes seems to have seen this point, appropriately quoting Hesiod, *Works and Days*, 609 f., and 672 (674) ff.:

μηδὲ μένειν οἶνόν τε νέον καὶ ὀπωρινὸν ὄμβρον
καὶ χειμῶν' ἐπιόντα, Νότοιό τε δεινὰς ἀήτας, κτλ.

Of ἀνδρὸς τελείου Fraenkel writes, "... Verrall irrelevantly introduces one of his double meanings (a secondary reference to 'the perfect victim, fit for the sacrifice')". With great respect to Professor Fraenkel, it seems to me that Verrall here is right. It is not impossible that the image of the vine, as it is used here, had religious overtones even for Aeschylus' time. We know too little of the doctrine of Dionysus as wine god but should not forget the apparent connection between the ceremony at Aigeus' death and the festival of the Oschophoria (see p. 44).

prayed for and expected. Agamemnon's blood corresponds to the wine, and is now awaited. The final image in the sequence of images to which Clytaemnestra likened Agamemnon on his arrival at the palace was that of 'a springing stream to the thirsty wayfarer' (901). After the slaying, she says (1389 ff.): 'And when the sharp edge struck him, he blew forth blood; the dark drops of bloody dew struck me, and I rejoiced as does the sown land in the god-given moisture at the birth-pangs of the buds'[90]. Clytaemnestra's strange manner in welcoming Agamemnon is, I think, due to her incipient ecstasy.

A possible stumbling-block to our interpretation is the description of Clytaemnestra's and Aegisthus' deed as one of guile or treachery, as in 1129: δολοφόνου λέβητος τύχαν σοι λέγω. It is usually taken that this means that an unexpected stroke, delivered by a cunning artifice, laid Agamemnon low. To see in this an objection is, however, to confine the essence of the ritual to the intention of the victim. Illumination is supplied by 1523 ff. Here it is said that Agamemnon laid a δολίαν ἄτην, a treacherous work of evil, on the house when he sacrificed Iphigeneia. It is still a treacherous deed although there is no doubt that it was a sacrifice. The δόλος, the guile, is what is necessary to overcome the anticipated unwillingness of the victim: it does not mean that the sacrifice is not a sacrifice because the victim was a free agent and would have resisted had he or she known what was intended. In the case of Agamemnon the treachery lay in Clytaemnestra's pretence that she was welcoming him as a loving wife in her plot with Aegisthus, by which Agamemnon had in the end to submit, helpless, to their will. There are willing and unwilling victims of sacrifice.

Every one knows that generations interpret und re-interpret history. This tendency is at its most radical at times of cultural change, and there is, in my view, no doubt that the story of Agamemnon, Clytaemnestra, Aegisthus and Orestes owes its fame to the fact that it became for the Greeks a symbol of a great crisis in their history. We have, if this is so, the strongest of reasons to think that the hostile picture of Clytaemnestra and the laudatory one of Orestes have at least in part been painted by the victorious cause. That Agamemnon met a violent end seems established. At least a part of the Late Mycenaean age appears to have been a time of violence and disorder. Kingdoms were snatched by force from their rulers. Obviously this was not a

---

[90] Cf. Apollon. Rhod. IV, 473 f., where the blood of Apsyrtos dyes the veil and robe worn by Medea.

favourable time for a matrilineal religious culture, and the princesses of this culture may well, as it began to weaken and collapse, have received much of the blame for the very evils which its destroyers brought with them. Thus a religious ceremony presided over by such a princess to secure immortality for her displaced and slaughtered husband might seem to condone that slaughter, performed, as it would have been, in the shadow, if not the presence, of his successor.

The story of Odysseus and Penelope may provide a parallel. Apollodorus says that after Telegonus had killed Odysseus he brought Penelope, Telemachus and the body of Odysseus to Circe, who made them immortal[91]. Acoording to Proclus[92], Telegonus married Penelope, Telemachus Circe. If Telemachus is simply a 'double' of Telegonus, renamed for the new version of the story which we find in our present Odyssey (as will later appear probable), then Penelope and Circe are also the same person. We may find some measure of support in Eustathius[93] for the equivalence of Penelope and Circe, in that he asserts Calypso to have been Telemachus' mother, while Hesiod[94] and Apollodorus[95] say that Telegonus was the son of Odysseus and Circe. It would seem, in short, that magical powers were ascribed to Penelope by traditions which the Odyssey excludes; in the Odyssey they are attributed to separate persons. The demonstration, however, that Calypso and Circe are indeed the bearers of powers and functions originally proper to Penelope (and it can, I think, be shown with some cogency) must await another occasion. The essence of Apollodorus' story would then be that Telegonus-Telemachus brought the body of Odysseus to Penelope and that she made him (Odysseus) immortal. In this light we may understand also the tradition of Clytaemnestra as a woman of power. For Aeschylus, Clytaemnestra murderously sacrificed Agamemnon in a state of ecstasy (and guided his soul to another world); an earlier story possibly related that Agamemnon was slain by Aegisthus and made immortal by Clytaemnestra. The version which we know, with the Apolline behest to Orestes that he should slay Clytaemnestra, is a product of the Olympian revolution and its principle of patrilineality[96].

---

[91] Apollod. *Epit.* 7.36; Schol. *Od.* 11.134.
[92] In Kinkel, *Epic. Graec. Frag.*, p. 55.
[93] Kinkel, p. 58.
[94] *Theog.* 1014, but some hold the line to be interpolated.
[95] *Epit.* 7.16.
[96] See the beginning of this chapter.

CHAPTER III

Penelope's Weaving and the Wedding of Nausicaa

I. Penelope's Weaving

If, as we suggested at the end of the last chapter, Penelope in some earlier form of the myth had had the power of conferring immortality on dead rulers, together with the mysterious and apparently magical qualities which in the Odyssey as we now have it are possessed by Calypso and Circe, the method of Homer in composing our Odyssey has not been unsubtle. For in refusing all that Calypso had to offer, evading the enchantments of Circe, and eschewing the allurements of the Lotus-eaters, Odysseus is moved always by his desire to return home to Ithaca and to a Penelope who was wholly of this world and possessed no powers beyond those that work-a-day mortals have. His goal was a home in which he was the master.

Penelope was, however, no ordinary mortal: even in Pausanias' time her tomb was shown in Arcadia[1] and Apollodorus and Cicero knew of a tradition that made her the mother of Pan by Hermes[2]. If our hypothesis is sound (and we claim no more for it here than that it is a hypothesis for which there is some *prima facie* evidence)—if the hypothesis is sound, then Homer has radically changed the quality of Penelope and consequently of Odysseus' home. Indeed, he has greatly magnified the wanderings of Odysseus, who in this case never crossed the seas to the islands of Calypso and Circe, for these two praeternatural figures were both united in his own house in the person of Penelope. Upon the broad waters of Olympian fable, the islands of Circe and Calypso, the countries of Cyclops and Lotus-eaters, float like will-o'-the-wisps to lead the traveller further and further away from the central reality of an earlier age.

We shall not attempt to examine this theory, which indeed has a far wider scope than is here suggested. Instead, we shall take notice of other radical revisions, in a not wholly dissimilar sense, of an earlier epic tradition, revis-

---

[1] Paus. 8.12.3.

[2] Apollod. *Epit.* 7.38; Cic. *de nat. deor.*, 3.22.56.

ions which reveal themselves readily to a critical reading of the existing poem. For this we shall, however, ask the reader to accept the view put forward in Chapter I, that matrilineality, though not universal in the earlier Greek and Aegean world, was very widely spread. At the moment, all that the reader—if he will accept the implications of Chapter I—is asked to bear in mind is its corollary, namely, that most of the patrilineal accounts of royal lineage in Greek myth are false: for the relationship of father and son we should substitute mere succession of the unrelated[3]. Perhaps we should also remind ourselves that the struggle between matrilineal and patrilineal in early Greece generated intense and often ferocious feeling, for with it two profoundly different worlds were at war.

There are references in late Greek writers to a poem called the *Telegony*, which narrated the deeds of Telegonus, the son, according to one tradition, of Odysseus and Circe, according to another, of Odysseus and Calypso. We learn of Telegonus that he set out from his mother's island home to seek his father. Landing on Ithaca, he ravages it (or carries off the cattle)[4]. Odysseus, coming up to beat off the robbers, is killed by his son, who does not know who he is. According to Apollodorus[5] Odysseus is killed by an exceedingly primitive weapon, a spear tipped by the spine of a sting-ray. Telegonus, when he sees what he has done, brings Penelope and Telemachus and the body of Odysseus to his mother, Circe[6], who makes them immortal. In another version, Telegonus marries Penelope, Telemachus Circe[7]. According to Apollodorus, Penelope and Telegonus are sent by Circe to the Isles of the Blest.

This story follows a familiar matrilineal pattern: the stranger from a distance (we notice the name Telegonus), of plainly aggressive intention (if he had really been seeking his father, he would hardly have laid waste what might have turned out to be his father's kingdom upon entering it), and the slaying of his 'father' 'in ignorance of who he was'. He then marries his 'father's' wife (or daughter). The tale begins and ends with the dominant

---

[3] It will be remembered that in certain cases the supposed father-son relationship was shown to be, almost certainly, that of grandfather and grandson.

[4] Apollodorus, *Epit.* 7.36.

[5] *loc. cit.*; also Schol. *Od.* 11.134.

[6] According to Eustathius, Calypso was Telemachus' mother (Kinkel, *Epic. Graec. Frag.*, p. 58).

[7] Proclus in Kinkel, *op. cit.*, pp. 55 f.

figure of a woman, who here, as in the stories of Medea, possesses magical
powers of renewing youth or conferring immortality.

In 1905 A. Gercke published an article on the relationship of the *Telegony*
to the Odyssey as we know it[8]. We may summarise that part of the argument
of this article which concerns us (omitting its disconcerting, if then fashion-
able, conclusion, which has no relevance to our theme) as follows:

In *Od.* 11.121 ff. Odysseus is told by Teiresias in the underworld that,
after he has slain the suitors in Ithaca, he is to travel to a land where the
people do not know the sea, carrying an oar on his shoulder. There he is to
plant the oar in the earth and sacrifice to Poseidon. Then he is to go home,
and a *gentle*[9] death (in contrast to that related in the *Telegony*[9]) will come
to him from the sea at the threshold of old age. This land will, Gercke holds,
have been Thesprotia, and his arrival there will have marked the end of his
wanderings. But the Odyssey as a whole makes the return to Ithaca the end
of Odysseus' journey. The suggestion that Odysseus' home was in Thesprotia
is not the only difficulty which this passage raises. That a man who had been
pursued by the anger of Helios and Poseidon, and has, by the skin of his
teeth, reached home *in spite* of their anger, should then show contrition and
gratitude towards one of them by a penitential journey, sacrifices and,
apparently, the institution of a cult, is self-contradictory. Moreover, the
propitiation of the deity comes too late: he had escaped the dangers of the
journey, and was at home. Nor is the sequence of events given in Proclus
and Apollodorus in any way convincing: this (it is in Gercke's view, plainly
a compilation) makes Odysseus return to Ithaca and massacre the suitors,
travel to Elis and return again, set out once more and travel to Thesprotia,
and return for the third time to Ithaca. In *Od.* 23.266 ff., Odysseus tells
Penelope that he must leave Ithaca once more and seek the inland people
who do not know the sea, and when he reaches them, he must sacrifice to

---

[8] *Telegonie und Odyssee*, Neue Jahrbücher für das klassische Altertum, Geschichte und
deutsche Literatur, herausgegeben von Johannes Ilberg (Leipzig) (New series of the
Jahrbücher für Philologie und Pädagogik, edited by Jahn), Vol. VIII (1905), pp. 315 ff.
It would seem that, if Eugammon's *floruit* was c. 566 B. C., he cannot have been the
author of the *Telegony*, unless indeed we are concerned here with an earlier poem
on the same subject. The *Telegony* is also ascribed to Kinaithon of Sparta, whose
date is given as the fourth Olympiad, c. 760 B. C., which Professor H. J. Rose regards
as 'suspiciously early' (*A Handbook of Greek Literature*, p. 68). This does, however,
suggest a tradition that the story of the *Telegony* was current in very early times.
There is no need for us to suppose that either Eugammon or Kinaithon invented it.

[9] Italics and comment in parenthesis are mine.—E. A. S. B.

Poseidon. But, Gercke asks, having reached home, was he to leave the island again and expose himself to the anger of the sea-god in order to appease him in Epirus? It is a compromise by the 'editor' of the Odyssey.

That there was a poem which associated Odysseus with Thesprotia and was called the *Thesprotis* we know from Pausanias[10]. This poem was held by Wilamowitz-Möllendorff to have formed the central part of the *Telegony*: Gercke holds it to have been the first part, the second part dealing with events in Ithaca. He observes also that there are two different accounts in the Odyssey of the oracle which gave Odysseus advice about his return home. One, that in the eleventh book, puts it into the mouth of Teiresias in the underworld. The other makes Odysseus enquire of the oracle of Zeus in the great oak at Dodona, not far from the borders of Thesprotia *(Od.* 19.206 ff.) Gercke points out that this latter tradition was that used by Sophocles in the *Niptra (fr.* 417–8, 422–3), and that Welcker and Wilamowitz have shown that Sophocles derived the substance of the *Niptra* from epic.

Gercke pays much attention to the nineteenth book of the Odyssey. He comments on the scene in which Eurycleia, the old nurse, while washing Odysseus' feet in Penelope's presence, recognises by the scar on his leg that he is indeed Odysseus. Eurycleia, dropping his foot with a clang into the basin, proclaims her discovery aloud and turns to Penelope—but Penelope notices nothing, 'for Athena had turned her mind away'. The nurse's failure to draw Penelope's attention is so improbable that Gercke, following Wilamowitz, holds that in an earlier form of the poem her recognition of Odysseus did in fact follow that of Eurycleia, but that it was excised in order to allow of the Shooting Contest. In this earlier version there was no massacre of the suitors. Indeed, Gercke holds the sole passage (130—60) in which they are mentioned to be an interpolation. He observes that Anticleia, Odysseus' mother, when in the eleventh book she speaks with her son in the underworld, also knows nothing of any suitors. Nor, in this earlier version which Gercke believes to have existed, was Odysseus a bald old man, or a badly-clothed beggar. It is indeed true that in the nineteenth book only Melantho[11], whom

---

[10] 8.12.3.

[11] Why this hostility of Melantho to Odysseus? Notice (a) that one of the suitors, Eurymachus, was her lover (18.325) (b) Odysseus in his transfiguration before Telemachus becomes dark-skinned and dark-bearded (see footnote 19) (c) 'Melantho' is formed from the Greek word for 'black', but its stem ends in the non-Greek *-nth.* It is apparently intended (even if used only as a diminutive) to show that Melantho is of non-Greek race. Her lover is apparently pure Greek. But this dark-skinned

Penelope sharply sends about her business, accuses Odysseus of begging.
Penelope treats him as a social equal: he sits and talks with her, not with
the servants, and she speaks of him as an honoured guest. (*Cf.* 308–334,
and especially 316.)

There is a good deal more that Gercke has to say, but it need not concern
us. There has been much further analysis of the Odyssey since Gercke wrote.
One may agree with him that the epic about Telegonus (as well as others,
including the *Thesprotis*) has left traces in Homer's poem. A part of the
subject of the *Telegony* was the slaying of Odysseus by Telegonus, who was
evidently a violent young chieftain in search of a kingdom, and not the son
of Odysseus at all. This would have been characteristic of succession to a
domain in the matrilineal Greece of very early times. On the other hand,
the Odyssey, on the surface at least, bears a patrilineal stamp. Descent is
traced from father to son. It opens with Zeus, the *father* of gods and men,
reflecting on the slaying of Aegisthus by Orestes, son of Agamemnon. The
event in which it culminates, the massacre of the suitors, may be regarded
as the husband's assertion of his right to the kingdom against those, including
Penelope's parents, who urged her to marry again[12]. Indeed, the contest with

Odysseus? Was he not, like herself, one of the race which was in process of being
submerged? Did she not prefer the new lords, and despise the men of her own people?
In 20.173 ff. it is a Melanthios who upbraids Odysseus. Is the name Odysseus Greek at
all? Why are the suitors spoken of as 'Achaeans' and as such sometimes apparently
distinguished from Penelope (*e. g.* 16.76, 17.513, 19.151) and, at times, from Odysseus
(17.413, 415) and from Eumaeus and Telemachus (16.133 f., 17.596 f.)? Notice especially
2.265, and also 3.100, 330, where Telemachus speaks of 'you Achaeans'. It is true
that the Achaeans often speak of themselves as 'Achaeans' (*e. g.* 2.106, 3.220, 16.376)
and that Odysseus includes himself among them in 8.259, 13.315 and elsewhere, and
that he is addressed as an Achaean in 12.184; nevertheless, the instances quoted above
(to cite no others) seem to imply a consciousness of different race, as of course does
the Achaean habit of referring to themselves as such. The meaning of 15.274 is worth
some consideration, particularly in respect of the use of the genitive, not the dative,
after κρατεῖν. About Odysseus there were evidently divergent traditions (see footnote 19). If 15.274 means that the kinsmen of Theoclymenus were stronger in Argos
than the Achaeans, how could Theoclymenus have sought refuge with Odysseus, after
making this statement, if Odysseus himself had been an Achaeans? The herdsman Melanthios is, like Melantho, a servant. He seems to see in Odysseus a competitor for the
benefits of his master's household (*i.e.* Laertes and his supporters were presumably
Achaeans: see footnote 36 below), for he tells him in effect to be gone and hang
about some other Achaean table. That is to say, he seems to take Odysseus as being,
like himelf, no Achaean.

[12] 19.147.

the bow takes place under emphatically and expressly masculine auspices, for it is held on Apollo's feast day, and this fact is repeated no less than five times[13].

To describe the way in which, as it seems to the author, our Odyssey may have originated may help the reader to appreciate the theme of this chapter. No one denies that a number of epic lays must have been in circulation when the Odyssey was composed. The subjects of these lays will have been episodes in the lives of typical, if also ideal, figures of the past[14]. But like the *Telegony*, they were, or at least some of them were, of a different character to the Odyssey as we know it. For one thing, they were grimmer. They not only told of the death of the old king but they told of it as occurring, not in heroic battle, but in something that, by Homer's time, appeared at best as a squalid killing, or as a repellent ritual of which they did not even wish to remember the significance. In particular, men no longer wished to recognise the part played by the princesses of the older world at the deaths of the rulers, or a kingship sustained by the spirits of royal predecessors, powerful in their immortality. They did not want to remember shamanism. The world in which these things had seemed natural, necessary, or reassuring had passed away. The poems which told of them, however, were still current, the stories, in their various versions, were familiar. What Homer did in the Odyssey was to retell one[15] of these stories in a way that appealed to the generation in which he lived. When he had finished with it, it was no longer the serious, savage tale that the parents and grandparents of his hearers had known. It is optimistic, there is (for the hero) a 'happy ending'. Indeed, one of its principal episodes, the meeting of Laertes and Odysseus, is given a humorous turn, or what has passed for such. Let us, then, look more closely at some crucial passages of the Odyssey.

The theme of the *Telegony* is, we have said, characteristic of the ancient matrilineal tradition. But it directly involves the succession to the domains of Odysseus. Was the action of Telegonus in killing Odysseus an exception, in that normally the descent was patrilineal in the estates over which he ruled,

---

[13] 20.276 ff.; 21.258 f., 267, 338, 364.

[14] That is to say, there will have been no single original from which the figures of Odysseus and Telemachus-Telegonus were derived. The main outlines, and much detail, will have been partly characteristic of the time in which the story was set, partly of the time in which it was composed.

[15] Or, rather, several. See below. R. Merkelbach, *Untersuchungen zur Odyssee* (Munich, 1951), holds that there were a number of epic poems about Odysseus.

or does it really imply that which it appears to imply? There is quite strong
evidence in the Odyssey that the original tradition was a matrilineal one,
which has been concealed by the construction of the Odyssey we know so that
it should conform with the patterns of patrilineal tradition. Thus, just as
Telegonus was made, in the accounts of him which have survived, to have
landed in Ithaca, quite implausibly, in search of his father, so in the Odyssey
Telemachus, whom Gercke calls a 'double' of Telegonus, goes out from Ithaca,
also in search of a father. But if, as we shall see reason to believe, the house
of Odysseus was really the house of Penelope, then Telemachus' name would
indicate the purpose of his journey, which would have been the same as that
of Telegonus, namely, to win a foreign kingdom.

Now Telemachus makes a most significant answer to a question which
Odysseus puts to him. The disguised Odysseus (who has not yet revealed
himself to him), having said that if he were in Telemachus' situation he would
fight the suitors and put an end to their unmannerly behaviour, asks whether
Telemachus is out of favour with the people or whether his κασίγνητοι are
to blame for not defending him as he could have expected[16]. Telemachus
replies that he is not out of favour with the people, nor are his κασίγνητοι to
blame, for he has not got any, Zeus having made his family go by ones:
Laertes was the only son of Arkeisios, Odysseus the only son of Laertes,
Telemachus the only son of Odysseus. Now this is an odd family: it is
especially odd for a ruling family, as a father is anxious to have sons to
support and defend his kingdom, however much they may quarrel among
themselves after his death. The word κασίγνητοι is properly used of maternal
relations[17]. That they should have been expected to defend Telemachus is
thus an indication that the house and land descended in the female line, since
they are implied to be its natural protectors. Even if we assume that the word
is here used loosely for kinsmen of any kind, the three generations of only
sons after Arkeisios is too remarkable to be passed over. The inference that
the 'sons' were not in fact related to their predecessors at all is strongly
indicated. The son of the ruler of a matrilineal kingdom cannot succeed his
father. That is obvious, as is its consequence, that this is the explanation of
the many examples in Greek legend of unrecognised 'sons' returning from
abroad to their reputed fathers' kingdoms and succeeding them, sometimes after killing them 'by accident' or in ignorance of the alleged relat-

---

[16] 16.113 ff.
[17] Cf. Iliad, 3.236 f., and Miller, 'Greek Kinship Terminology', *JHS*, LXXIII (1953).

ionship. These are the devices of the later patrilineal tradition to disguise or interpret a stage of history which was distasteful or unfamiliar to it. All this we have already seen in Chapter I.

There is indeed, in the nineteenth book[18] of the Odyssey, a distinct indication that Odysseus' own descent was matrilineal: he makes a journey to the house of his maternal grandfather, Autolycus, to receive 'presents'. In our Odyssey, Autolycus is still alive (though the emphasis falls noticeably on his sons), but the event reminds us of the journey of the children of Atreus' daughters, including Agamemnon, to Crete to receive their shares of his property after the king's death. (See pp. 12 ff.)

Now it is extremely striking that no one (except his dog Argos) recognises Odysseus when he returns to Ithaca. Even his wife does not recognise him when he sits and talks to her. Why? Surely the reason is that he was in fact a stranger, not that Athena had made him unrecognisably old. Indeed the implication of Athena's action in disguising him as an elderly beggar is that he was in fact and in appearance quite a young man, which he could hardly have looked if he had acceded to the kingdom and left a young son behind him when he had sailed away twenty years before to a life of battle and great hardship. And indeed when Athena disguises him in 13.429 ff. he is plainly in the vigorous prime of life, and when she restores him to his true condition in 16.172 ff., she gives him youth (ἥβην) and a dark beard[19].

But this, it may be said, is the licence of the poet and the teller of tales. Let us take some further evidence. When the suitors pressed Penelope to make up her mind and choose one of them as her husband, she put off the necessity of making a decision by saying that she must first finish weaving a piece of cloth (φᾶρος) which was to be a shroud for the hero Laertes[20]. The suitors accepted this statement of Penelope about her intention, and waited for three years. In the fourth year one of her maid-servants revealed to them that Penelope was unweaving at night all that she had woven during the day, and she was then unable to avoid marriage any longer, in spite of her reluctance.

The excuse which Penelope makes for not deciding immediately whom she would marry is at first sight a strange one. It is still stranger

---

[18] 399 ff.

[19] It is to be noticed that in 13.431 Odysseus' hair is ξανθός, while in 16.175 ff. he is dark-skinned and his beard is κυάνεος.

[20] 2.97 ff.; 19.142 ff.; 24.132 ff.

that the suitors accept it, and wait with remarkable patience. Penelope gives as her reason that she does not wish to waste the thread she has spun, nor to give cause to the women of the district to reproach her for letting Laertes, the lord of many possessions, lie in death without a winding-sheet.

We notice that the general rule that in Homer, at any rate in the Iliad, men are burnt, not buried, when they die, apparently does not apply in this case. We are dealing with another tradition. Having noted this important fact, we are bound to ask why the suitors so patiently wait for Penelope to finish her task. The only answer to this question that seems to be convincing is that they considered Penelope to have given a sound reason for putting off her decision. If this is the correct answer to our question (and it must be), we may next ask why Penelope could not have given the task of weaving the shroud to one of her attendant women, if marriage should prove an obstacle to her continuing it herself. To this there is only one reply which seems adequate to the situation of Penelope: her marriage involved Laertes' death[21]. She therefore could not marry until the shroud was finished. It is plain that the shroud, which is obviously a cloth of some elaboration, must have some special place in ritual, and that this ritual is one which could not rightly be denied to Laertes.

If we are right in our belief that Arkeisios, Laertes, Odysseus, and Telegonus-Telemachus are all unrelated, at any rate as fathers and sons, because they acquired their position only by marrying the successive heiresses of Ithaca (or some Thesprotian or Arcadian kingdom), Laertes is the father, not of Odysseus, but of Penelope. Her relationship to Laertes, the fact that her marriage involves his death, the ritual significance of the winding-cloth, all work together to make it a duty for her to finish the cloth before marrying. This duty is a generally recognised one, and the suitors accept her statement of it without question. The first two of these factors no doubt explain her reluctance to choose a husband.

If Laertes (and not Ikarios) was the father of Penelope, we may ask who her mother was. It is remarkable that the name of Penelope's mother is nowhere expressly stated in the Odyssey. We are told that the name of Odysseus' mother was Anticleia (11.85); in 19.339–406 it is certainly implied that she

---

[21] Greek myth contains more than one record of such a situation. It will be remembered that Oinomaos was said to be fated to die if his daughter Hippodameia should marry. W. J. Gruffydd, *loc. cit.,* thought the oracle about his death caused Akrisios to send Danaë out of Greece. *Cf.* also the story of Nisos and his daughter, Scylla. In general see Chapter I, § VII.

was Eurycleia[22]. But Eurycleia is also the supposed old nurse in Book XIX who washes Odysseus' feet und recognises him from the scar. Eurycleia, the 'nurse' then, is Odysseus' mother, and Gercke speaks of Pacuvius (frs. 1 and 2) as describing her preparation of the bath for her son. This makes the attempt in the Odyssey to represent Odysseus as returning to his old home even less credible. Neither his mother nor his wife recognise him. But was Eurycleia really Odysseus' mother? She is certainly not a nurse, although she is called that. Penelope addresses her as περίφρων Εὐρύκλεια[23], and περίφρων is an epithet commonly used of Penelope herself. In 20.147 she is called δῖα γυναικῶν. A servant would not be so addressed or described[24]. In 1.428 ff. it is said that Laertes bought her for twenty oxen when she was a young girl, and that he treated her in the hall as though she were his wife, but did not lie with her as he wished to avoid his wife's anger. But if Laertes treated her in public as his wife, one may wonder whether the anger of the supposed real wife (who never appears at all) would have been much less. (We except the solitary appearance of 'Anticleia' in the *Nekyia*).

Why is this curious effort made to prevent our knowing who Eurycleia really was? There is an attempt in Book XIX, and in other books, to represent her as a nurse, but it is not carried through consistently, and she is also implied in Book XIX to be Odysseus' mother. But in Book I, as we see, although Laertes treats her in public as he would treat his wife, yet she is not his wife or his concubine, and so cannot be Odysseus' mother. The poet evidently found himself in a difficulty over Eurycleia. What was the difficulty? A very simple one: she was Penelope's mother, but the poet was seriously concerned to disguise all traces of the matrilineal world in the poems which he used in composing the Odyssey. If he had admitted that Eurycleia was Penelope's mother, he could not have represented Odysseus

---

[22] That this is the implication of, in particular, 11.405—6 is, to my mind, incontrovertible: 'And Autolycus answered her (Eurycleia) and said: My son-in-law and daughter, . . .' In addition to this, there is the fact, most uncharacteristic of Homer, that she, the mother about whom the story is told, is not otherwise named at all. Furthermore, what woman would place a child on its maternal grandfather's knee and ask him to name it, if not its mother?

[23] 19.357. The same epithet is used in 491; 20.134; 21.381.

[24] δῖος ὑφορβός is used of Eumaeus, but the incongruous juxtaposition has been held to be humorous. Another possibility is that it is a courteous reference to his royal descent. I cannot help suspecting, however, that in a much earlier epic the prototype of Eumaeus was an important figure, the keeper of a 'temple herd', such as was known in ancient Mesopotamia.

as returning to Laertes', his father's, home. Thus he has reversed the truth: she *was* Laertes' wife, but she was not the mother of Odysseus. (Anticleia, who is only mentioned once, in the *Nekyia,* and is there said to be Odysseus' mother, is clearly a substitute name for Eurycleia.)

We can now begin to understand Odysseus' reluctance to have his feet washed by any of the women of the household, and his insistence that they should only be touched by an old woman of serious mind, who has endured as much in her heart as he has. That is to say, it must be done by a responsible person. The foot-washing is a symbolic rite. It was not recognition, in the sense of a discovery that the stranger was really no stranger, that accompanied it: it was acceptance of a man and recognition of his claim to the position of spouse and ruler. It could only be performed by the mother of the bride, and it was Eurycleia, Penelope's mother, who performed the foot-washing for Odysseus. Indeed, she says she is going to wash both his feet and Penelope's, and on his account, for her heart is moved by troubles[25]. Thus *before* the discovery of the scar, Eurycleia has already symbolically joined Penelope with Odysseus, and recognised their status as the heads of the household. The incident of the finding of the scar, is, then, another device of the composer of the Odyssey to disguise the true nature of the scene. We may therefore differ from Gercke when he supposes that 'recognition' by Penelope originally followed recognition by Eurycleia: Penelope gave no sign of recognition because no 'recognition' was required or possible.

Penelope had been compelled to finish the φᾶρος which she had been weaving for Laertes. She had been engaged on exactly the same task as Clytaemnestra when she wove the 'robe' for Agamemnon. Laertes, the old king, had now to die.

The Odyssey as we have it now has a 'happy ending'. Laertes, at the end, watches with joy his son and grandson competing in valour as they attack the avenging kinsmen of the slaughtered suitors. Then Zeus and Athena stay the victorious onslaught of Odysseus and Telemachus and their men, and Athena makes a lasting peace between the two parties. Yet there are traces in the Odyssey of a different theme, grave, or rather savage, in character, which culminates in the death of Laertes. To be precise, there are two other themes: one of these culminates in the death of Laertes, the other in that of Odysseus.

---

[25] 19.376 ff. What was it that troubled Eurycleia's heart? Surely it must have been the impending fate of her husband, Laertes (see below).

The theme which ends with the death of Odysseus has, it is true, been almost entirely obliterated, yet some traces of it are visible to those who know what to look for. They are, very probably, the remains of those parts of the *Telegony* which have been taken up into the Odyssey. Before we start to examine the text we must first decide what sort of signs we should seek in the cases both of Laertes and of Odysseus. We shall certainly expect them each to be slain by a stranger, a man who has come from over the sea. The slaying, being the prelude to marriage with the lady of the house and land, is not done without her knowledge. If the slaying takes place in a fight, it will have no ritual character, yet after it there will certainly be a religious ceremony. This may in part take the form of relaxation in funeral games (of which there is no trace in connection with the deaths of Laertes and Odysseus), but in any case, before such celebrations, there will be a solemn ritual of wholly religious intent. We may find a clue to the nature and intention of such a ritual in the scenes on the Hagia Triada sarcophagus, which we have touched on in the last chapter, and in the allusions in literature to the deaths of rulers, of which we have already taken notice in Chapter I, § VII, and Chapter II. When the old ruler is a consenting participant in the ceremony that reaches its climax in his death, the rites, as we have seen, appear to begin with a meal which the principal participants take together. The victim is then bathed and dressed in a special robe. When the execution takes place, it would seem that the old ruler only dies to the corporeal eye: he is translated to the Isles of the Blest or the Elysian fields, that is, he becomes an immortal. As an immortal, age cannot touch him, and he is to be conceived of as in the prime of his vigour. Thus the ritual death of the old ruler must have been thought of as bringing about his transfiguration, that is, a change in his appearance. The translation of the dead to the Isles of the Blest, or the rendering of them immortal, is, as we saw in the cases of Penelope, Telegonus and Odysseus at the beginning of this chapter, achieved by the agency of the Medea-like princess, whether wife or wife's mother, with whom they were associated in life[26]. She conducts the sacrifices and

---

[26] Whether the story correctly associates Penelope with those made immortal by Circe may be doubted. She surely became immortal by right at her death. The transference of the power to Circe alone is perhaps intended to enhance the fame of Telegonus. Another possibility is that Κίρκη is the feminine of κίρκος, which is some kind of hawk. In Mycenaean religion the relation of a bird and a human figure denotes that the figure is in some sense divine (even if also human). Athena, *Od.* 3.372, takes on

ritual. Her power derives from that of the palace-goddess and guardian of
the dynasty, living and dead. The presence of Athena with Odysseus or
Telemachus or Penelope in the Odyssey is thus a sign that the affairs of the
dynasty itself are concerned. We may, however, be sure that Penelope's
dynasty, being matrilineal, had nothing to do with Athena, who is, in this
context at least, an insertion by the author of our Odyssey.

Let us now turn to see what evidence there is of the death of Odysseus.
Odysseus, it will be remembered, was, according to the legend, slain by Telegonus. Now Telemachus in the Odyssey is undoubtedly at times a substitute
for, or the equivalent of, Telegonus. The scansion of the names is the same,
their resemblance quite close. Each man travels over the sea 'seeking his
father' in the patrilineally-modified version of the story, although they start
from different islands. When Telegonus arrives in Ithaca he does so of course
as a stranger. Telemachus, on his return to Ithaca, is a stranger to all except
Eumaeus. His only supporters (apart from Eumaeus) are the companions who
arrived with him in the ship. Telemachus' isolation is so striking that it moves
Odysseus (before he had revealed himself to him) to ask whether he is out
of favour with the people, or whether his kinsmen are to blame[27]. Telemachus-Telegonus has thus arrived in Ithaca. We know that when Telegonus
did so, he killed Odysseus. Is there any sign of this in the Odyssey?

There are, I think, two features that point in this direction. The first is
that when Telemachus returns, Odysseus is an elderly man. We know that
this appearance of age is due, according to Homer's account, to Athena, who
by a stroke of her wand disguises him. Nevertheless, it would seem that
Athena's action in disguising him with advancing age is very likely due to
the necessity of combining two widely separated events in his life. These
events are the arrival of Odysseus himself as a youngish man in Ithaca, and
his meeting with his slayer in later life. In the Odyssey, however, Odysseus
and Telemachus return to Ithaca at about the same time. For the successful
vindication of his claim to Penelope's hand, Odysseus has to be in the prime
of life: he alone can string the bow, and he slays the suitors. Gercke rightly
points out that in his interview with Penelope in Book XIX Odysseus does

the form of a kind of vulture. 'Circe' may therefore simply mean 'the power of the
goddess'.

[27] 16.95 ff. We should also notice the suggestion that Telemachus' descent from Odysseus
and Penelope is not quite certain, 1.215 f. and 2.274 f. Why is the subject raised?
Perhaps in order to obtain a suspension of disbelief among those who knew another
tale.

not appear to be old. He is only travel-stained. Yet his son Telemachus was
at least twenty years old. When Telegonus arrived on the island Odysseus
was long past his youth. The appearance of age had therefore, in our Odyssey, to be a mere disguise for his dealing with the suitors, while it correspond-
ed to the reality when he met Telemachus.

The second feature is to be found after Telemachus has sent off the swineherd to tell Penelope of his safe return from Pylos. Odysseus is left alone
with Telemachus. Athena appears to Odysseus as a tall woman. Telemachus
does not see her, 'for the gods do not appear to all for them to see'. She tells
Odysseus that it is time for him to reveal himself to his son, and for the two
of them to plot the destruction of the suitors. She will not be far from
Odysseus and his son in the fight. Athena then touches Odysseus with her
wand and clothes him with a cloak and a tunic. She makes his body young,
fills out his cheeks, makes his beard dark.

Telemachus is astonished, and takes him for a god. Odysseus assures him
that he is no god but his father, now at home after many sufferings and
wanderings. In the twentieth year he returned to his native land. This (*i.e.*
the change in his appearance) was the work of Athena Ageleia, who had been
wont to make of him what she would, for she had the power. At one time he
was like a beggar, at another like a young and well-dressed man. It was easy
for the gods who dwell in the broad heaven to exalt a man and to destroy
him.

Odysseus reminds us then that he has been abroad, enduring good and
evil fortune, for twenty years. It is clear that in the condition of youth and
strength in which Telemachus now sees him he is younger in appearance than
his putative age and adventures would seem to allow. There is moreover a
certain splendour about him which compels Telemachus to think he is god.

Odysseus seems to undergo a somewhat similar transformation on one
other occasion. He orders a mock wedding, to conceal the fact that the
suitors have been slain[28]. It begins with music and dancing. Odysseus is
bathed by Eurynome, looking more like a god than a man. He goes and sits
opposite Penelope. Penelope is still not convinced that he is really her husband Odysseus. She only loses her doubts when he describes how he had
made the bridal chamber when they were married many years before. That
is to say, it is only because he knows of a particular event in the distant
past that she is persuaded that he is her husband, although he is now looking

---

[28] 23.130 ff.

handsome and strong, and is no longer wearing rags. There is nothing in his personal appearance which assures her that he is her husband. This is quite incredible. The beautiful scene is clearly not, as it claims to be, the reunion of husband and wife at a pretended wedding cermony. Odysseus is a stranger to Penelope and she is silent and reserved because she does not know him. He has won her by force of arms. The celebrations end with Odysseus and Penelope entering the bridal chamber. It is their real wedding[29].

The transformation in Odysseus' appearance after the bath is also said to take place by the grace of Athena. It is however not parallel to that which happens when he reveals himself to Telemachus. Before the wedding, Athena simply removes the disguise of age which the combination of the stories of Odysseus and Laertes and of Telegonus-Telemachus and Odysseus within the single frame of the Odyssey had made necessary. He appears handsome and strong, with a thick head of hair, because he is really young.

It is quite otherwise in the transformation before Telemachus. Here there is no possibility of his being a young man. He is transformed to look other than his age and condition make him. In the speech that he makes to Telemachus there are two phrases that draw our attention. The first occurs in line 206: ἤλυθον εἰκοστῷ ἔτεϊ ἐς πατρίδα γαῖαν. It is difficult to be entirely positive on such a matter, but both the use of the aorist and the phrase as a whole seem to remove Odysseus' return into a fairly distant past. It would hardly seem a natural way for him to express himself to his son two or three days after that return[30].

The second phrase occurs in the next line: 'This (i.e. his transformation) is the doing Ἀθηναίης ἀγελείης'. Why of Athena *Ageleia?* Athena Ageleia is 'Athena who drives off the spoil'. The epithet particularly refers to spoil in the form of cattle. We remember that Telegonus is said to have driven off cattle when he landed on Ithaca, or, more generally, to have ravaged the

---

[29] The device of a suddenly-arranged mock wedding ceremony would of course in any case be totally impossible in the small communities of Ithaca, where impending marriages could not fail to be known long before. And what wedding could take place in the royal home on the morrow of the massacre of the suitors if not that of Penelope?

[30] In spite of the ἐς πατρίδα γαῖαν and the suggestion of long wanderings, the phrase really means, I believe, 'I came here in my twentieth year'. It is a relic of the older tradition, not fully assimilated into the new context. The ἐς π. γ. then replaces a phrase which would have given too much away. The interpretation which our Homer wishes to put on it, as well as a prophecy of Odysseus' unrecognised return, is put into the mouth of the aged Halitherses in 2.175. Notice the genitive in -ου in 2.177.

island. Apparently Odysseus is saying that his state of transformation is due
to Athena when she brought him into contact with cattle-stealing or free-
booting. He is then made to imply that what he means is that his changes of
clothes, now rags, now of fine quality, as also those in physical appearance,
are due to vacillations of fortune. But as the change takes place while he is
in Telemachus' presence, there has been no possibility of a change of fortune.
The suggestion of vacillations between misery and prosperity is particularly
misleading, and was no doubt intended to be so, for if the two lines
(209–10) which suggest this meaning are disregarded, the general trend
of the speech seems to suggest that the change that had just occurred was
unique. Moreover the feeling that this change which appears to bring an
almost god-like splendour with it is somehow a melancholy condition is
unmistakeable: the goddess can exalt a man or destroy him.

Odysseus, according to the legend about Telegonus, was killed by the
latter while he was trying to drive off the cattle-raiders. Himself a freebooter, he met a freebooter's end. This is the most obvious, as it is certainly
a reasonable, explanation of the ascription of his condition to Athena Ageleia. In other words, Odysseus is dead, and the scene is his transfiguration
as an immortal being as seen in the imagination of Telemachus-Telegonus[31].
No considerations of an ordinary, common-sense kind can account for the
transformation. It certainly did not help Telemachus to recognise his 'father'.
Afterwards, of course, the scene is merged into the general scheme of the
Odyssey.

If, then, we can agree that the apparent transformation of Odysseus into
a man in the prime of life which occurs in Book XXIII is not transformation
at all, but the removal of a disguise, Odysseus only undergoes one transformation or, rather, transfiguration. On this ground at any rate the suggestion
that Odysseus had met his death when this transfiguration takes place
remains unshaken[32].

We may now turn to the transfiguration of Laertes. With the twenty-

---

[31] This may be compared with Nilsson's interpretation of the Hagia Triada sarcophagus.

[32] Attention is drawn once more to the *Argumentum* to Euripides' *Medea*: 'Pherecydes
and Simonides say that Medea boiled Jason and made him young. About his father
Aison the author of the *Nostoi* says,

αὐτίκα δ' Αἴσονα θῆκε φίλον κόρον ἡβώωντα,
γῆρας ἀποξύσασ' εἰδυίῃσι πραπίδεσσι,
φάρμακα πόλλ' ἕψουσ' ἐπὶ χρυσείοισι λέβησιν.'

fourth book of the Odyssey the story reaches its culmination: Odysseus and
Laertes at last meet and the former is accepted by the people as the rightful
ruler of Ithaca. As a prelude to these events a scene has been introduced
which portrays the meeting in the underworld, first of the souls of Achilles
and Agamemnon, and then of Amphimedon and the other suitors who had
just been slain by Odysseus. The conversation which takes place between
Achilles and Agamemnon is designed to point out the contrast between the
dignified and glorious death of Achilles and his comrades in battle, and the
renown that stills adorns their memory, with the miserable end of Agamemnon at the hands of Aegisthus and his baleful wife. It may be compared with
the eulogy of war in the *Eumenides*. The shade of Amphimedon tells of the
deception which Penelope practised on the suitors and of the cunning and
strength by which Odysseus got the better of them. Agamemnon concludes
with lines in praise of Penelope and in condemnation of Clytaemnestra, and
of all women after her:

'How excellent a heart and mind had the blameless Penelopeia, daughter
of Ikarios! How well she remembered Odysseus who married her as a young
man! The praise of her virtue shall never perish, and the immortals will
make for dwellers upon earth a lovely song about the constant Penelopeia.
She did not devise evil and slay her husband like the daughter of Tyndareos,
of whom a hateful song will be sung; but the daughter of Tyndareos has
brought an evil repute upon all women, even upon those who do good.'

Surely the shade of Agamemnon protests too much. It has already been
remarked that Penelope signally *failed* to remember Odysseus. Why should
the deceptions of Penelope and Odysseus earn praise in spite of the great
slaughter they brought about, whereas the death of Agamemnon at the hands
of Clytaemnestra and Aegisthus brings infamy not only on Clytaemnestra
but upon all women after her? Because Penelope was faithful to her husband?
No doubt, if she was faithful, she deserved praise, but why should she not
ennoble all women as much as Clytaemnestra brings them all to shame? Yet
she does not: her conduct is spoken of as though it were rare, even unique.
Surely, only one explanation is possible: the conduct of Clytaemnestra is
regarded as typical of the earlier time, not that of Penelope. It is clear that
the poet of this scene in the underworld is very anxious that the right doctrine
should be drawn from the story. There was, then, another point of view
which might have been taken.

The scene in Hades ends, and we find Odysseus on his way to the house of
Laertes in the country. The first thing that Odysseus does on arriving there,

before even seeking his father, is to order a meal to be prepared, although it is not even his house. This is a point which deserves the closest attention.

Odysseus finds Laertes alone and in great sorrow. He debates in his mind whether to embrace him as his father or first to ask him questions and taunt him. He decides first to taunt him. We are not told why Odysseus decided on this way of greeting his aged and grieving father after an absence of twenty years, only that he thought it 'more profitable'. He taunts him with his poor clothing, with working so hard for a master, with the contrast between his condition and his royal appearance, and ends his mockery with the words: 'You look like one who, after he has bathed and eaten, would sleep softly, for this is what is due (δίκη) to old men'[33]. The sinister brutality of the last sentence is in keeping with the heartless grossness of the lines that lead up to it. It has of course been misunderstood as an indication of kindnesses to come at the hands of the filial Odysseus. Odysseus is really referring to the ritual bath and meal that precede the execution of the old king.

All this speech (244–254) was, I believe, for Homer's first hearers, strongly reminiscent of an older poem, a poem which told a different story about the meeting of Odysseus and Laertes from that which Homer intends to relate. Indeed, the whole scene, up to the recognition, has an intended ambiguity: what is Odysseus' mood? What is he going to do? On the one hand, the course of events seems to suggest the ending which the audience already knew; on the other hand, there are curious new turns given to the conversation. Thus Odysseus, who is of course unrecognised, now pretends that Laertes' son, from whom he distinguishes himself, had visited him years before and received hospitality at his hands, and he asks if he has really reached the country from which his guest came. We, the audience, know that this is not true, and we are therefore uncertain of Odysseus' intention: if his intention is not an ill one, why this deception?

Laertes replies that it is indeed the country of the stranger's former guest, and asks how long ago that guest, who was his own son, left him. He thinks he must have perished in the sea. He then asks Odysseus who he is, whence he came, and how he reached Ithaca. Odysseus answers by giving himself a fictious name ('Insulter') and descent, says he has sailed from Sicania, and adds that Odysseus left him four years before, with good omens, and they had both wished to meet again in friendship.

At this a dark cloud of grief descends on Laertes. He takes up dust in both

[33]   254 f.

his hands and pours it on his head, moaning loudly. But Odysseus' spirit was roused (ὠρίνετο θυμός) and as he looked at Laertes the keen power (or anger) (δριμὺ μένος) struck up his nostrils, and he sprang (ἐπιάλμενος) upon him—and kissed him[34].

Nobody, I think, can contest the total inappropriateness of the climax of this last passage to the phrases that lead up to it. They all point in one direction: Odysseus leaped upon Laertes and killed him. A phrase such as ὠρίνετο θυμός is ambiguous: is his spirit moved, or roused to action? What has δριμὺ μένος to do with affection[35]? And ἐπιάλμενος strongly suggests the spring of the aggressor: it cannot fitly be used of throwing oneself upon another in affection or embrace. If this be conceded, it enables us to answer a question: why did Laertes moan and pour dust on his head? Because he thought his son was finally lost, or because he knew that his time had come and that his successor confronted him? The answer is, surely, that in the older poem, the latter was the reason; in Homer's Odyssey it turned out to be the former (although Laertes admits that he had already given Odysseus up for lost). The uncertainty is maintained up to the very end: 'What is Odysseus feeling? What is he going to do?' must have been the question in the minds of the first listeners who heard the words

τοῦ δ' ὠρίνετο θυμός, ἀνὰ ῥῖνας δέ οἱ ἤδη

δριμὺ μένος προΰτυψε ...

They must have found something astonishing in the rest of the sentence:

φίλον πατέρ' εἰσορόωντι.

Homer stays very close to the pattern of the old poem which, it is suggested, his hearers knew. In this older poem, however, the slaying, and the line and a half just examined, were part of the ritual scene. The bathing of Laertes (365 f.) and the meal now follow. We notice that *it is not Odysseus, the returned traveller, who is bathed, but Laertes, in his own house.* Dolios enters, and after his surprise at seeing Odysseus is over, his first care (for he was Penelope's steward) is to ask him if Penelope has been told of his return. Just so had Telemachus sent off the swineherd to tell Penelope when he arrived. But before finally leaving the place where Odysseus and Laertes confronted each other, we must remark once more that Odysseus is a stranger to Laertes,

---

[34] 315 ff.

[35] *Cf.*, for example, *Iliad* 1.282, where Nestor, urging Agamemnon and Achilles to restrain their anger with each other, says to Agamemnon, Ἀτρεΐδη, σὺ δὲ παῦε τεὸν μένος.

who never recognises him personally but requires evidence that he is, as he asserts, his son. This evidence is supplied once more by the scar on his leg, by mention of the visit of Autolycus to the house, and by Odysseus being able to quote the numbers of pear and apple trees and vines which Laertes had planted for him. It is all circumstantial evidence; like Odysseus's supposed mother, Eurycleia, and his wife, Penelope, his supposed father is unable to recognise him personally. We return to the sacrificial meal and the bath:

'Meanwhile the Sicilian serving-woman bathed the great-souled Laertes in his own house, and anointed him with oil, and put a beautiful cloak about him. Then came Athena and stood near and filled out the limbs of the shepherd of the people, and made him look taller and stronger than before. He stepped from the bath, and his son wondered at him when he saw that he looked like an immortal god. He said to him with truth, 'My father, surely one of the everlasting gods has made you greater in stature and finer to look upon'.'

This transformation of Laertes is precisely parallel to that of Odysseus, which we have already discussed. It takes the same form, the restoration of the old man to the prime of life; it is the work of Athena, the guardian goddess of the dynasty; it is a vision which appears to the younger man when he is apparently alone, or at any rate no one else sees it; and in each case the older man takes on the likeness of an immortal god. It is a remnant of the old ritual scene.

If the view of the original form of the story advanced here is correct, Laertes plainly would not have lived apart, as the Odyssey represents him as doing, in the main house. Homer takes great pains to show that Penelope was not present at the transfiguration of Laertes or that of Telemachus. The transfigurations take place in Eumaeus' hut and Laertes' separate dwelling, and it is stressed that Penelope has to be informed of Telemachus' and Odysseus' presence. In reality, however, she would have been intimately concerned, and have taken a leading part in the immortalisation ritual. The obvious use of devices to draw attention to the fact that Penelope is not present lend weight to the hypothesis we advanced that Circe's power of conferring immortality was really Penelope's.

Meanwhile the people are making lamentation and uproar in front of the house of Odysseus, that is, the house of the dynasty, Penelope and her mother and kinsmen (413 ff.). It is said to be because of the slaughter of the suitors, and it may have been so, but one is reminded of Plutarch's description of the scene at Aigeus' death in the Life of Theseus. The resemblance becomes the more striking when Medon, the herald (like the herald who, after the sacrifice performed by Theseus, announces the death of Aigeus), arrives and announces that Odysseus is king:

'Listen to me, men of Ithaca! Odysseus has only done these things by the will of the immortal gods. For I myself saw a deathless god who stood beside Odysseus in the likeness of Mentor, an immortal god, who appeared, now in front of Odysseus, encouraging him, now rushing down the hall and affrighting the suitors, and they fell in heaps[36].'

The deathless god was of course Athena, who was wont to take on the appearance of Mentor. If Athena, the palace-goddess and dynastic guardian, appeared as Odysseus' champion and protector, he was indeed King. Laertes had been King; there could not be two kings: Laertes was no more. The end of the last book of the Odyssey is devoted to trying to show that what had happened had not happened, and to portraying the prospect of an ordered world under the governance of Zeus and Athena. It is a gentle death from the sea that now awaits Odysseus, not that ungentle one that came upon him, also from the sea, in an earlier poem. An ancient and in some ways more wonderful world, of which Penelope and her like had been the centre, had become intolerable because it could not control the increasing disorder of the times. The religious world had to retreat before the political and military.

---

[36] 443 ff. R. Merkelbach, *op. cit.*, pp. 6 ff., and D. L. Page, *The Homeric Odyssey* (Oxford, 1955), pp. 124 f., hold that the poet of 18.158—204 and 206 ff., in which Penelope is inspired by Athena to present herself formally to the Suitors in consent, had in mind an earlier epic, in which Odysseus and Penelope had by this stage already met and recognised each other and had plotted together her apparent surrender to the suitors. This suggestion, in spite of all that is to be said for it, assumes that the suitors were 'suitors' in the earlier epic. There are, however, difficulties about such an assumption, for some of which see footnote 67. Not the least of the improbabilities is their patience. Troublesome no doubt they were, but so were King Lear's henchmen in the houses of his daughters and sons-in-law: they need not be suitors on that account. Their apparent readiness to live (and die) together as a body in relative amity, when but one of them could win the bride and that only after waiting several years, strains credulity too far. If the 'suitors' were originally Laertes' adherents, then Penelope's formal appearance to them must have signified that she intended to marry *Odysseus*. There was no one else for her to marry. Notice the reference to the stranger in 222 f.

II. The Wedding of Nausicaa

Before we pass to Odysseus among the Phaeacians, there is a passage in the third book which we should not overlook, namely, the sacrifice to Athena before the departure of Telemachus from the palace of Nestor. The account has been fitted into the context of the story of our Odyssey (Nestor gives[37] as his reason for holding the sacrifice the appearance of Athena at the sacrifice to Poseidon on the previous day, and he is made to refer to the ship in which Telemachus arrived) but there are signs that the account of the ceremony and some parts of the passage as we have it are derived from another setting.

From what epic story the account of the sacrifice might have been taken, one cannot say. Whether or not the names of Nestor and Telemachus are original to the scene, the passage opens with a reference to the house and to Nestor's predecessor which has a certain sombre solemnity of tone. Nestor, awaking at dawn, comes out of the house and sits upon the polished white stones, shining with oil of anointment (ἄλειφαρ), in front of the high doors of the palace. Neleus, the equal of the gods in counsel, had sat there, but he had now been subjected to death (κηρί) and had gone to the house of Hades. Now Nestor sat there in his turn, and held the sceptre. There is a certain gravity about this opening, which suggests that we are being invited to bear in mind that what follows may concern the succession to the seat where Nestor now sits. This impression is partly confirmed by the explicit state-ment[38] that Athena came to the sacrifice. Athena, as we have remarked, does indeed, in the Odyssey, play the part of, in Nilsson's phrase, the 'palace-goddess'; in particular she is present when the succession to the kingship is involved. The exceptional importance of the sacrifice is emphasized by the instruction that the horns of the victim should be tipped with gold and by the presence of the queen and Nestor's daughters, sons and daughters-in-law. Nestor, however, is not the centre of the ritual. That place is reserved for Telemachus. He is led out by the six sons of Nestor[39], himself making a seventh prince, and placed beside Peisistratos, in whose charge, as it would seem, he has spent the night[40].

The sacrificial beast is slaughtered, the queen, her daughters and her daughters-in-law wailing (or exulting) at its fall. Telemachus is bathed by

---

[37] 3.420.   [38] 435.   [39] 415 f.   [40] 400.

Polycaste, one of Nestor's daughters, anointed with oil, and robed in a
pharos and *chiton*. There is no doubt whatever that this bathing and robing
is a part of the ceremony. We have already noticed that the word φᾶρος is
used of the shroud woven by Penelope for Laertes. It is not a normal garment
of epic heroes, but the word is also used of the robe or wrapping worn by
Agamemnon at his death[41]. Eustathius, commenting on 8.85, supposes that the
pharos was drawn over Telemachus' head and face[42]. Telemachus steps from
the bath looking like one of the immortals[43], and goes and sits by Nestor.
There follows a banquet. The statement that on stepping from the bath, the
hero 'looked like the immortals' surely implies that he has undergone a
change that gives him a divine quality. We have seen this simile used in order
to describe an act of the imagination, of the inward eye beholding the spirit
of the dead man, glorious in immortality. In its place in the third book of
the Odyssey, Telemachus is said to look like the immortals, but to what end

---

[41] See p. 84.

[42] κἀκ κεφαλῆς, κτλ. ὃ δήπου καὶ ὁ τούτου υἱὸς Τηλέμαχος ἐν τῇ Πύλῳ ἐποίει ἀλλ'
ἐκεῖ μὲν ἡ αἰτία οὐκ ἐτέθη. A little oddly, Eustathius makes no mention of this in his
commentary on Book III, but we may perhaps assume that, since it is not described in
the text of Book III, he was only reminded of the account on which he based his
note on 8.85 by the actual description of the event in the latter passage. Nevertheless,
the last seven words of Eustathius' comment seem to suggest that the event *was* to be
found in his text.

[43] Line 468 attracts attention: ἐκ ῥ' ἀσαμίνθου βῆ δέμας ἀθανάτοισιν ὁμοῖος. If the
scene described is really supposed to take place at Pylos, the word ἀσάμινθος calls
for comment. The bathing of Telemachus is certainly part of the ceremony, which
takes place in front of 'the high doors' of the palace, and obviously needs space for its
accomplishment. The bath in the palace at Pylos, however, was in a small room in the
south-west corner; the main gate-way was only indirectly accessible from it. (See plan
of palace attached to C. Blegen's article, *Illustrated London News,* April 7th., 1956,
p. 257). The bath, with its permanent stepping-stone, was apparently always in this
place. It might, of course, be argued from the τόφρα of 464 that Telemachus was bathed
and robed out of sight of the place of ceremony and led to it only after this had been
done. This is possible, although, as the bathing is clearly a part of the ritual, it seems
improbable. The ceremony is a single one and is not, at least at first sight, likely
to have been carried out in two different places at the same time. If, as we provisionally suggest, the ritual here is, in its externals, similar to that in which Agamemnon
died, the bathing and robing of the victim seem to have been important features of it.
An ἀσάμινθος might also take a portable form, as 4.128 implies; but if the ritual
were *essentially* the same as that surrounding Agamemnon's death we must remember
that Telemachus would never have stepped from the bath in a material sense.

he was bathed and robed with this result we are not told: he merely goes and sits beside Nestor. In other words, he has simply had a bath as part of a ceremony. There is something missing, an explanation of the change that has come over Telemachus. The change was one which in some way related him closely to Nestor, for after the bath he goes and sits beside him, whereas before it he was escorted by Nestor's sons. The banquet then follows, and is made the link between the ceremony and the start of Telemachus' and Peisistratos' journey to the home of Menelaus. In the other cases which we have examined, the banquet seems to have preceded the bathing and robing, but disguise and the need to connect the ceremony with the story have, as it would appear, caused the sequence to be inverted.

Homer gives no adequate explanation of the sacrifice, solemnly introduced, attended by Athena and the whole royal household and distinguished by the ununsual features of the tipping of the cow's horns with gold, Peisistratos' guardianship of Telemachus, the indication that Telemachus attended as the seventh of the princes[44] and the change which he undergoes.

The most extraordinary element in the scene is the rôle played by Telemachus. The whole ceremony centres round him. It is certainly no parting courtesy: why bathe and robe him in a φᾶρος before sending him off on a journey by chariot? Unlike the sacrifice to Poseidon on the previous day, it takes place, not on the sea-shore, but in front of the palace. It is addressed to Athena and Athena attends it[45]: there is no doubt that it concerns the dynasty intimately. In general, the pattern seems to be clear. It is strongly reminiscent of that of other instances we have considered; it looks in its procedure like that which accompanies the slaying and immortalisation of a royal person.

Nevertheless, we should be cautious here. Telemachus is a young man. Moreover, there is perhaps, after all, a connection between the sacrifice to Poseidon on the seashore and that to Athena. In the next chapter we shall notice both the intimate relationship between these two deities in a shamanist context and also the very close resemblance between the ritual accompanying a king's death and that of an initiation ceremony, particularly that of a

---

[44] There is, as far as I know, no other example in Greek literature of this last peculiarity, but there is certainly evidence (to be set out on another occasion) that the number seven was significant in Mycenaean times.

[45] It is worth noticing, in connection with Athena, that one of Nestor's sons is called Perseus.

shaman. Several of the heroic rulers of Greek myth were evidently shamans, as we shall see, even if sometimes only in a formal and traditional sense. It is tempting to see in this curious passage a description of the initiation ritual by which the young Telemachus is solemnly inducted as a shaman by Nestor as 'shaman father', with Nestor's sons as the 'shaman sons'[46]. During the period of solitude and unconsciousness which precedes the initiation of a shaman, at least among some Siberian peoples, the shaman-to-be may only be served by pure youths and maidens. Telemachus sleeps at the palace of Nestor attended, as is expressly remarked, by the unmarried Peisistratos. After the Siberian ceremony the meat and soup from the sacrifices are eaten by the participants, after some has been thrown into the air or into the fire. The likeness to the Homeric sacrificial ritual is worth noticing. Moreover, the drawing of the *pharos* over the head (if we may follow Eustathius) is strongly suggestive of shamanist practice[47]. In spite of its other similar features and quasi-identity of conception, the ceremony at Pylos may not have, probably did not have, the same purpose as that in which, as we believe, Agamemnon, Laertes and other rulers died.

We have, however, not yet done with the traces of other, apparently pre-Olympian, epic which disclose another world than the 'Homeric' behind the narrative of our present Odyssey. They have so far centred round, as we suggest, the slaying and immortalisation of the king, his successor's battle for the hand of the queen (or her daughter) and his marriage. Perhaps, too, there is the initiation of a young prince as a shaman. There seems to be little doubt that in the story of Odysseus among the Phaeacians appear parts of the same sequence of events. The tale in the Odyssey does not hold together.

First of all, Athena announces quite plainly[48] that Nausicaa's wedding-day is near: it is so near that it is time for her to wash her clothes for it. The bridegroom therefore must be known, for the day of the wedding is evidently known. The lines that follow Athena's announcement contradict it: the firm declaration is changed into the vague general assurance that, with so many

[46] See next chapter. If fitness for the kingship and the status of a shaman went together, and if in this context the support of Athena implies both, it would be possible to read 3.218–238 as bearing directly on the ceremony in which Telemachus plays a central *rôle* next day. Not even 232–235 necessarily suggest that Odysseus might return; the rest, including Telemachus' words 225–8, seems to refer to Telemachus' expulsion of the suitors.

[47] See p. 89 ff.

[48] *Od.* 6.27.

suitors, she is bound to marry soon. This would be no reason for Nausicaa to wash her clothes for an imminent wedding.

There is another vague generality: an argument for getting the wedding apparel ready is that a well-dressed bride and her attendants give pleasure to her father and mother, for such things give her a good name. Yet when Nausicaa goes to ask her father for a waggon to carry the clothes down to the washing-place, she is reluctant to speak of her marriage to him and pretends she is going to wash his and her brothers' clothes. Why, if it would give her father pleasure? The interpretation of αἴδετο[49] as 'she felt bashful' (which some, apparently moved thereto by θαλερόν, have adopted) is surely one that would not only be unique in Homer but quite remote from any attitude of mind which we encounter in the *Iliad* or the *Odyssey*. Homer is not prudish. Indeed, 6.286 ff. show that this is not Nausicaa's way. Further, if her marriage is so near, it must have already been spoken of with her parents. No, 'bashfulness' will not do. She surely hesitates to mention marriage, which is normally thought of as a joyful event, because for her father her marriage would be no occasion for joy.

Yet no bridegroom's name is ever mentioned. Instead we have Alkinoos' extraordinary remark[50] that he would gladly have Odysseus as his son-in-law, Odysseus, the melancholy, destitute, ship-wrecked stranger, whose very name he does not know[51]. And this just before his daughter's marriage! Alkinoos is here represented as being not merely friendly to Odysseus, but quite unthinkingly and irresponsibly so. Why?

Odysseus himself did not expect a friendly welcome. In 7.32 he is told by Athena that the people are not friendly to strangers; in 50 ff. he is urged not to shrink at breaking in upon the feasting company in the palace. It was not the people whom he feared: as he says in 304 ff., he was afraid that Alkinoos himself would not look kindly on him. Possibly it may have been wise for lone wanderers to be wary of unknown peoples in general (even if beggars and strangers are under the protection of Zeus), but the unnatural cordiality and lack of common prudence attributed to Alkinoos and the specific fear of Odysseus should give us pause. Is the poet of our Odyssey perhaps over-reaching himself in an attempt to disguise the fact that Odysseus had good cause to expect a hostile Alkinoos? Did Odysseus originally arrive without ship and companions? We notice at any rate both that we are told in Book V

[49] 6.66.   [50] 7.311 ff.   [51] 8.28.

how it came about that Odysseus arrived alone and destitute in the country
of the Phaeacians, and that he repeats the story himself in the next book,
taking 56 lines to do so: we are not intended to be in any doubt about it. We
notice further that, when Odysseus, clasping Arete by the knees, has made
his request to her, there is total silence in the hall[52], and, when the silence is
broken, it is neither Arete nor Alkinoos who speaks, but the old noble
Echeneos. He reproves Alkinoos for leaving Odysseus sitting by the hearth,
on the ground, and tells him to take him by the hand and seat him on a
silver-studded throne. Neither Alkinoos nor Arete seems at this stage to welcome Odysseus. Alkinoos moreover seems to have lost his authority. I
suggest that Alkinoos' sudden declaration that he would fain have Odysseus
as his son-in-law is designed to hide the fact that Odysseus was indeed the
bridegroom and that he was in the highest degree unwelcome as such. It
therefore fell to the eldest of the nobility to declare his acceptance, perhaps
with Nausicaa's consent.

When Nausicaa, on the seashore, sees Odysseus transformed, after washing
himself, into a splendid figure of a man, shining with the beauty and grace
which Athena has poured upon him, she says that the gods who dwell on
Olympus have had a hand in this. She would like to have such a man for her
husband: would that it might please him to stay there. There is no suggestion
that there is any other bridegroom, in spite of her approaching wedding, and
Athena is noticeably present when the succession to the kingship is involved.
Having so declared herself, Nausicaa says that she does not wish Odysseus
to accompany her to the palace, for people who see them together will assume
that he is to be her husband. A shipwrecked mariner, just rescued from the
strand? Alkinoos and Nausicaa both want Odysseus as son-in-law and
husband respectively, the people will assume that he is the bridegroom, the
wedding day is imminent and no other bridegroom is mentioned. Athena has
poured her grace upon him. Is not the conclusion certain?

Nausicaa had gone to wash her own clothes. She is nonetheless able there
to clothe Odysseus, not in women's garments, but in a *chiton* and a *pharos*[53].
These were precisely the garments worn by Telemachus in the ceremony of
which we have spoken above. It is clear that they are ceremonial robes: when
Arete eventually breaks silence she asks him who gave them to him. She
recognises them as garments she and her women have made: who then

[52] 7.154.   [53] 7.234 with 296.

should have given them to him but Arete herself? It is impossible to believe that Nausicaa simply happened to have them among her washing.

There is not the slightest doubt that the Phaeacian royal house is matrilineal. The immense prestige of Arete, who is regarded as a goddess by the people, and who settles even the quarrels of the men, and Alkinoos' own attitude to her[54], make that clear. Moreover, when Odysseus enters the hall, he is to go straight to Arete, not to Alkinoos, and this he does. We have already seen in Chapter I how the succession to the kingship of a matrilineal dynasty was regulated: Alkinoos cannot have welcomed Odysseus, and we understand both Odysseus' fears and the silence of king and queen when he had made his demand. This will certainly not have been that he should be returned to his 'fatherland'. Nor should we overlook the reappearance of Arete, Alkinoos and Echeneos in Book XI. The passage is curious in more than one respect, but our attention is particularly seized by Alkinoos' remark in 348 f.: 'These words will be observed, if I at any rate am to rule, a living man, among the Phaeacians' (αἴ κεν ἐγώ γε ζωὸς ... ἀνάσσω). What is the sense of this if Odysseus is to leave the next day or soon after? (See the lines immediately following). Does not the king imply a doubt of his own survival?

The games in Book VIII give rise to questions. Why should an unknown castaway take so prominent a part in them? Why do the games follow on Odysseus' arrival? Are they not a strange way of entertaining a weary traveller? Why should he be 'put to many tests'? Why did Athena again pour grace upon his head and shoulders, and make him taller and stronger to look upon, so that the Phaeacians should be in awe of him[55]? If he is just on the point of departure, it seems quite pointless. If, however, he is now the king, it is quite a different matter. But if he is the new king, who is showing himself for the first time to the people, what are the games if not funeral games for Alkinoos? This conclusion may at first sight seem too bold a contradiction of Alkinoos' apparent presence at the games, but reflection may bring persuasion that it makes better sense of the events recounted than the manifold self-contradictions and improbabilities of our Odyssey.

If we accept the view that the present story in the Odyssey disguises a quite different narrative, culminating in funeral games for Alkinoos, with Odysseus as the new king, wedded to Nausicaa, we should look very much

[54] 7.67 ff.   [55] 8.18 ff.

more carefully at the song which Demodokos sings of the love of Ares and Aphrodite, their capture in the net and their merciful release through Poseidon. Is it just a slightly bawdy tale, told for no particular reason other than idle entertainment? On examination it seem to be nothing of the kind but to be highly relevant to all that has gone before.

In order to understand the tale we must recall certain of the conclusions that we came to earlier in this book. Firstly, we must remember that a matri-lineally-descended grandson of a ruler almost certainly had a claim to his grandfather's throne[56]. Thus for example, a Pelopid ruler, who represented Poseidon and Hermes in cult, might be succeeded by an Ares-worshipper, but the Ares-worshipper might be followed by a Pelopid, and so by a celebrant of Poseidon and Hermes, especially if there were already a Pelopid or Poseidonian faction in the kingdom. Secondly, we should remember that, as we saw, there is a hint that Agamemnon at his death may have been fastened in a net beneath his robe. Thirdly, not only the old king but the *Potnia Meter* herself was sometimes slain, particularly by representatives of the cult of Ares. Fourthly, we must not overlook the fact that the Olympian revolution, in its exaltation of certain deities and attempted suppression of others, tried to substitute Athena for Ares, as one can very clearly see in the Iliad[57]. Lastly, although Odysseus compared Nausicaa to Artemis, Artemis is not to be distinguished from a certain Aphrodite, as may be seen in Appendix I.

Now Demodokos' story in its essentials is that Hephaistos, warned by Helios, caught his wife Aphrodite sleeping with Ares and trapped them both under a net. After telling them that soon neither of them would want to sleep at all, he summoned the other gods. Those that come are Poseidon, Hermes and Apollo. They stand and roar with laughter at the pair caught under the net. Poseidon persuades a reluctant Hephaistos to release them.

The song of Demodokos, beneath its surface of bawdy cheerfulness, has a serious theme. In the original story Odysseus and Nausicaa, as we believe, were to become the new king and queen. Whether Odysseus had in the older tale been an Ares-worshipper or not, their situation would be essentially that of Ares and Aphrodite under the net. The song may be a coarse prothalamion for Odysseus and Nausicaa, but it is something more. One day Odysseus at

---

[56] See pp. 50 f.

[57] The demontration must be made on another occasion, but a principal context is the Diomedeia in the Iliad.

least will be 'under the net'. He has, we think, just slain his predecessor in order to obtain the kingship and be the spouse of the representative of Artemis-Aphrodite. He cannot fail to have at the back of his mind the thought that his turn will come too.

The gods comment. Apollo (who, as an Olympian, helped to bring this older world to an end) asks Hermes (that most ancient god) whether he would like to sleep with golden Aphrodite under the weight of the net[58]. Hermes answers that beneath three times the weight of net, and beneath the eyes of the other gods (i. e., knowing that another would supplant him), he would still wish to sleep with golden Aphrodite. In that early world it was worth it, because she was 'golden Aphrodite'. The other gods laughed, except for Poseidon. Poseidon did not laugh, but begged Hephaistos to let Ares go. Hephaistos asked how, if he let Ares go, he could bind the other gods with his net, including Poseidon himself. Poseidon replied that, if Ares escaped without paying what he owed (i.e., to the injured husband), he, Poseidon, would pay Ares' debt[59]. This offer Hephaistos cannot refuse: very unwillingly, he releases Ares and Aphrodite, who flee to Thrace and to Cyprus respectively. Homer does not say that Odysseus laughed at this story, any more than Poseidon did, but that he rejoiced, and the seafaring Phaeacians with him. The recital seems to have been taken seriously.

Why did Odysseus and the Phaeacians rejoice? The answer is, I think, that the story gave Odysseus hope of escaping the fate which seemed to await him. There must have been something in the situation of Ares which Poseidon saw as affecting himself. If one work out the generations from Poseidon who married Periboia, and whose 'son' was Nausithoos, king of the Phaeacians, who in turn had a 'son' Alkinoos who married his brother's daughter Arete, we find that, on the principle enunciated above, Alkinoos will have cultivated Poseidon (as the prefix Alk- suggests[60]), and Odysseus' successor would probably be of the same cult. Odysseus, it seeems to be implied, cult-

---

[58] 8.334 ff.

[59] What is the debt which Ares owes? Line 332 implies that it is the fine for adultery payable to the cuckolded husband. It is impossible to believe that any such quittance was recognised among the sacred dynasties of the matrilineal world. Why moreover should Poseidon offer to pay the fine? The original tale has obviously been tampered with. Poseidon may have been less merciful and the debt may have been the ultimate service of immortalisation. This answer however can only be tentative.

[60] See Appendix II.

ivated Ares[61]. But Poseidon is a merciful deity, as it appears, unlike Odysseus, who in another epic had jeered at the aged Laertes whom he was about to kill. Poseidon will be satisfied with deposition and banishment and this assurance brings joy to Odysseus.

Some of the Phaeacians celebrated Poseidon[62], *i.e.*, as we have seen, a dynasty cultivating Poseidon was not unknown in Phaeacia. The gold and silver dogs, immortal and ageless, on either side of the doorway of Alkinoos' house, were made by Hephaistos and set there to guard it. It looks therefore, if we take Demodokos' story together with these statements, as though Hephaistos and Aphrodite (Artemis), had been the first tutelary deities, then Poseidon and Aphrodite (Artemis) alternating with Ares and Aphrodite (Artemis). Perhaps, however, Helios, who is recorded as the spouse of Aphrodite[63], and who warned Hephaistos, was the original male deity of the house. Hephaistos may indeed in some sense represent Helios, or be regarded as the latter's agent. It is to be observed that the genitive in -ου only occurs in lines that refer to Ares' deception and Hephaistos' feigned journey to Lemnos (8.287 f., 301). These events may therefore be late devices. Hermes belongs to an older world than Poseidon, but may have become associated with him as he seems to have been in the Pelopid dynasty. The real reason for the absence of the goddesses is thus apparent: only the male deities represented by the successive kings, consorts of Aphrodite, are concerned, and the rising power of Apollo, who represents the new, patrilineal, order.

If, however, Demodokos' second song, that about Ares and Aphrodite, reflects the implicit situation of Odysseus and Nausicaa, is not his first song[64] likely to reflect an earlier stage in the sequence of events? He sings, we are told (though, unlike the second song, we never hear it), the famous lay of the quarrel of Odysseus and Achilles, when they strove with each other with terrible words θεῶν ἐν δαιτὶ θαλείῃ. Agamemnon, it is added, rejoiced that the noblest of the Achaeans were quarrelling, because Phoebus Apollo had spoken thereof when he went to consult the oracle, just before, by the design of Zeus, the Trojan War broke upon the world.

---

[61] In 8.518 Odysseus is compared to Ares. Comparison is a common Homeric device for indicating a special relationship between a human being and a divinity. See Appendix I, on Helen as Artemis. *Cf. Il.* 19.282, *Od.* 4.121 f., and remarks on ἀθανά-τοισιν ὁμοῖος at the end of this chapter. See also *Il.* 7.200 with Chap. I, n. 180.

[62] There is a temple of Poseidon near the harbour of the Phaeacians (6.266). See also 13.130.

[63] See Appendix I.   [64] 8.73 ff.

We do not know the story of the quarrel between Odysseus and Achilles, although guesses may be, and have been, made about the occasion of it. Homer attempts in the present passage to connect their quarrel, by means of the statement about Agamemnon, with the expedition to Troy, and by the mention of Phoebus Apollo and Zeus, with the Olympian world. The attempt, however, only attracts attention by its awkwardness[65]. It seems certain that something is here being camouflaged. The quarrel took place and the terrible words were uttered, we are told, 'at a feast of the gods', that is to say, at a sacrifice or a ritual meal. So far as this information goes, it would be consistent with the examples quoted in Chapter I, § VII, of the challenging of a ruler by his successor at a sacrifice. This was at least at times accompanied, as we have seen, by the cursing of the new king by the old, and, if we may judge by Odysseus' greeting of Laertes, by the new king's jeering at his doomed predecessor.

We are in fact on the right track. Demodokos sang this first song after a banquet at which Odysseus and Alkinoos are present. We have already noticed that the death of the king is several times related as following upon a meal. No sooner has Demodokos finished the song than, almost unbelievably, but quite unmistakably, there comes a description of the drawing of the cloth over the king's head, just as it was done at the death of Agamemnon and as it is depicted in the relief shown in Plate II. Here are the lines:

πορφύρεον μέγα φᾶρος ἑλὼν χερσὶ στιβαρῇσι

κὰκ κεφαλῆς εἴρυσσε, κάλυψε δὲ καλὰ πρόσωπα (84 f.).

Homer has again been astonishingly clumsy. Odysseus, sitting at dinner with a great purple cloth over his head and face, apparently attracts no one's attention. So too, we have seen, in the passage which has been converted into Eurycleia's recognition of Odysseus, when Eurycleia drops the hero's foot with a clang into the basin, and tries to draw Penelope's attention, Penelope notices nothing. Only Alkinoos, sitting near Odysseus, realises he is weeping because he hears him 'groaning heavily'. This cannot possibly be accepted: the whole picture is simply absurd. Scholars have sometimes been no better than Homer: some have actually supposed the *pharos* in this case to be Odysseus' dress[66]. The μέγα shows clearly that it is nothing of the kind.

[65] Lines 81 and 82 are in any case dubious. The accounts offered in the scholia on 75 and 77 reveal no trace of old tradition. I suspect, but cannot prove, that at least the name 'Achilles' is a substitute.

[66] Eustathius began it by citing *Od.* 4.154, χλαῖναν ... ἄντ' ὀφθαλμοῖϊν ἀνάσχων. But this is no parallel, for it does not explain κὰκ κεφαλῆς, as Plate II does.

And if it were a dress, how could it be drawn κὰκ κεφαλῆς, '*down* over the head', and so cover the face? It is absolutely impossible.

The lines quoted do not tell us who was beneath the great cloth, nor does line 95, by itself, tell us who sat near whom and heard him groaning. Lines 84–85 and 95 are surely taken from the older epic. The whole trend of the story, as we have followed it, points to the clear conclusion that it was Alkinoos who sat beneath the cloth and that it was Alkinoos who groaned so heavily.

The sequence of events is not changed. The funeral games, as we hold them to be, now follow, and after them Demodokos sings the 'prothalamion' in which the theme is the plight of Ares and Aphrodite. We noticed in the first part of this chapter that, after the slaughter of the 'suitors', there is dancing and singing[67]. Then Odysseus is bathed[68], and the wedding with Penelope follows. Originally, the slaughter of the 'suitors' will have immediately preceded the death of Laertes. The killing of Laertes in the disguised form given to it in our present Odyssey follows the 'reunion' of Odysseus and Penelope, but this latter event, being, as we have seen, in fact their wedding, must have taken place *after* the death of the old king. In Phaeacia the original sequence seems to be retained. After the funeral games, as we hold them to have been, there is song and dancing[69], and Odysseus is given costly presents by twelve βασιλῆες, Alkinoos, it is said, making a thirteenth (but originally Odysseus himself, the new king, will have made the thirteenth, if, as we believe, Alkinoos was already dead[70]). It is clear that these presents are

---

[67] 23.133 f. and 143 ff. We call them 'suitors', as Homer does, but they do not seem to be rivals: they are hostile only to Odysseus and Telemachus. They live at the cost of the palace, apparently year after year. One may suspect that they are the supporters of Laertes: they are slain at a banquet in the hall, just as were the supporters of Agamemnon. The occasion seems to be a religious feast (21.258). It should be noticed that there are twelve axes. Considerations which I hope to discuss in another work suggest that the feat performed by Odysseus in the 'Shooting Contest' was really of a shamanist character and may be compared to sailing between Scylla and Charybdis or Clashing Rocks. There was originally no 'shooting contest' in the accepted sense. See footnotes 36 and 70.

[68] 23.154 ff.

[69] 8.261 ff., 370 ff. The song is made by Demodokos.

[70] This is the earliest example of the significant group of a leader and twelve known to me. It is essentially religious, appearing later not only in the New Testament but in the persecuted secret covens which persisted in Western Europe at least until the seventeenth century. The 52 (4×13) young men (8.48) may also be significant, although it is difficult to be certain about this without more evidence. They appear to dine

wedding presents: they are not (except for the sword) handed to Odysseus, but are taken by heralds to the palace, where they are received by the children of Alkinoos, who hand them to their mother[71], in other words, to the mother of the bride.

Odysseus is then bathed[72]. After the bath[73] in the main story he is 'recognised' by Penelope and goes to the marriage-bed with her, while after the bath in the Phaeacian narrative Nausicaa, who has not been seen since she left Odysseus on the sea-shore, is standing waiting for him[74]. They enter no bridal chamber, for Odysseus is supposed to be on his way to his Ithacan home, but Odysseus addresses her as Alkinoos might have addressed Arete: after invoking divine aid on his journey, he adds

τῷ κέν τοι καὶ κεῖθι θεῷ ὣς εὐχετοῴμην
αἰεὶ ἤματα πάντα · σὺ γάρ μ' ἐβιώσαο, κούρη.[75]

It seems reasonable to think that in the original poem Odysseus here wedded Nausicaa. Indeed, Odysseus is plainly the master at the feast which follows: it is he who cuts the portion of meat for Demodokos, and he who bids Demodokos sing.

In the passage which follows upon Demodokos' song of the Wooden Horse lines 532–4 are a repetition of 93–5. Of 95 we have spoken in its place; it told, as we believe, of Odysseus listening to Alkinoos groaning heavily beneath the *pharos*, although the poet of our Odyssey has inverted the relationship of the two heroes in his use of the line. Here, in the sequel to the song of the Wooden Horse, we find certain other lines which likewise belong properly to the earlier passage. They occur in a simile (523–530), in which Odysseus, sitting at the feast, is compared, unaccountably and inappropriately, to a woman who falls weeping upon her dying husband, slain in front of his city and before the peoples while defending his citadel and his children, and who then is 'driven in' to a life of labour and sorrow[76]. The simile is

---

separately from the sceptre-bearing princes (βασιλῆες). Odysseus chooses twelve men from his ship to accompany him to the Cyclops' cave.

[71] 8.420.   [72] 8.426 ff., 449–457.   [73] 23.153 ff.   [74] 8.457 ff.
[75] 8.467 f., Cf. 7.66 ff.
[76] For the reader's convenience the passage is given below:

ὡς δὲ γυνὴ κλαίησι φίλον πόσιν ἀμφιπεσοῦσα,
ὅς τε ἑῆς πρόσθεν πόλιος λαῶν τε πέσησιν,
ἄστεϊ καὶ τεκέεσσιν ἀμύνων νηλεὲς ἦμαρ,
ἡ μὲν τὸν θνῇσκοντα καὶ ἀσπαίροντα ἰδοῦσα

525

grotesquely inapplicable both to someone sitting at a banquet and to the attitude of a victorious Greek leader towards vanquished Troy. It is equally inapt to Odysseus' ostensible situation, secure as he now is of his return. Further, Odysseus is not merely weeping, but like a woman 'wailing shrilly'. Indeed, the simile does not even stand on its own feet: the scene is presumably meant to be taken as one of battle before the walls of a city, but where else do we hear of women flinging themselves in lamentation upon the dying on a battlefield? Such nevertheless is the apparent implication of 526–7, *if taken as part of the simile*. If, however, the simile originally ended at 525, we are not compelled to make any such supposition: it is then naturally implied that the *dead* body, as is customary in Homer, had been brought back from the field. There can be no doubt that we have before us a clumsy attempt to use lines composed for another context. In particular, 526–7 certainly belong to the description of the death of Alkinoos, which took place at some point in the lines that follow line 84. The scene is not a battlefield: the husband has received his death-blow in his wife's presence. It can only be Arete of whom it is said that 'she, seeing him dying and gasping, embraced him, shrilly wailing' (reading λίγ' ἐκώκυε for λίγα κωκύει).

The original simile was short, as the older Homeric similes are, and was contained in the three lines 523–5; the ἡ μέν of 526 resumed the narrative. Whether 528–30 are substantially unchanged is much less certain: they hardly seem apposite to the original situation and may be an addition. They have at least been modified by the poet who turned the whole sequence 523–530 into a simile. Line 529 in particular, with the verb in the present tense, seems to have been composed as part of a simile. Indeed, the εἰσανά-γουσι, 'drive back into', stems from the 'battlefield' picture. Even so, the poet understood the original sense of the passage, for the word εἰσανάγουσι, 'drive

> ἀμφ' αὐτῷ χυμένη λίγ' ἐκώκυε (*codd.* λίγα κωκύει).
>   οἱ δέ τ' ὄπισθε
> κόπτοντες δούρεσσι μετάφρενον ἠδὲ καὶ ὤμους
> εἴρερον εἰσανάγουσι, πόνον τ'ἐχέμεν καὶ ὀϊζύν·
> τῆς δ' ἐλεεινοτάτῳ ἄχεϊ φθινύθουσι παρειαί·   530
> ὣς 'Οδυσεὺς ἐλεεινὸν ὑπ' ὀφρύσι δάκρυον εἶβεν.
> ἔνθ' ἄλλους μὲν πάντας ἐλάνθανε δάκρυα λείβων,
> 'Αλκίνοος δέ μιν οἶος ἐπεφράσατ' ἠδ' ἐνόησεν,
> ἥμενος ἄγχ' αὐτοῦ, βαρὺ δὲ στενάχοντος ἄκουσεν.

The punctuation of line 525 has been somewhat changed from that which is generally received, in that a comma is substituted for a colon.

back into (the palace)', used instead of some word meaning 'carry off', suggests that the queen's future life of toil and tears was to be lived in the building in which she had reigned. So it seems to have been with Eurycleia, the mother of Penelope. Of 523–27 we may surely say that they are part of the description of Alkinoos' death which followed somewhere after[84]: their meaning, and the fact that 532–4 repeat 93–95, clearly show us their true context. The incompatibility of λίγα κωκύει with βαϱὺ... στενάχοντος is obvious. It is a final ludicrous but significant absurdity that Odysseus' lamentations escape the notice of all present except Alkinoos (532 f.). The poet seems to have been inhibited by a certain fidelity to the epic which he was revising: we may perhaps conclude that in the earlier poem the dreadful scene was conducted in a silence broken only by the groans and gasps of the dying king and the wailing of his wife.

Like line 95 (see p. 130), line 534 does not, by itself, tell us who sat near whom and heard his groaning. If 533, with its mention of Alkinoos, be excised, lines 531–2 and 534 would fit very well into the theme of the older epic: Odysseus, the successor, weeps unobserved for the king to whom he has given the death-blow. An Odysseus who (for no good reason) wails shrilly like a woman yet is at the same time said to be groaning heavily, while he is in any case heard by only one man of all those present, is a piece of nonsense which can only have arisen from a botcher's attempt to change the whole sense of the passage.

Like all Demodokos' songs (which are intended to serve as parables of the true story to those who can understand them), the song of the Wooden Horse is relevant to Odysseus' situation in the original epic. Odysseus is an intruder in the citadel, as was the Wooden Horse in Troy, and at first stood in great danger. We have already noticed his fear of entering the palace. As 506 ff. tells us, the question was whether the Horse, that is, Odysseus, should be cloven with pitiless bronze, cast down the rocks (two customary forms of execution) or allowed to remain. He was allowed to remain, that is, was accepted as the new king, and as such brought death with him into the heart of the citadel.

Almost the whole scheme of this pre-Olympian epic lies now before our eyes. To identify the pre-Olympian poems which have been drawn upon in the composition of the Odyssey is a task we shall not attempt[77]. It looks as

---

[77] It is not my purpose to enter into detailed structural analysis. The approach made here to some problems of the Odyssey sets out from the findings of the two preceding

though Odysseus was the hero of at least two, used in the composition of the Odyssey, in one of which he is associated with Penelope, in the other with Nausicaa.

The present Odyssey is of course at pains to show that Odysseus represented no deity; Odysseus emphatically denies to Alkinoos that he 'resembles' any god, and says flatly that he has no likeness to (*i.e.* does not represent) the immortals who dwell in the broad heaven, οὐ δέμας οὐδὲ φύην, but is like only to mortal men[78]. Yet Alkinoos thought that Odysseus might well be an 'immortal'; the Phaeacians were, like the Cyclopes and the Gigantes, related to the gods, and sometimes encountered them. The common use of the phrase ἱερὸν μένος 'Αλκινόοιο hints at something in Alkinoos which may be akin to the divinity which he suspected in Odysseus. In spite of the denial put into Odysseus' mouth, at the opening of the next book the herald expressly describes the stranger who has just arrived, that is, Odysseus, as δέμας ἀθανάτοισιν ὁμοῖος[79]. If, as appears to be certain, Odysseus was originally the successor of Alkinoos, it is unlikely that he would have been accepted as king had he not been able to claim, like his predecessor, to be in some way divine. We remember that Menelaus was able, as the spouse of Helen, to claim to be the son-in-law of Zeus. Before marriage, however, a claimant to the kingship would have had to be able to say that he was at least, in the herald's words, ἀθανάτοισιν ὁμοῖος: an ordinary mortal without ἱερὸν μένος would not have been princely and therefore not eligible. So much at least we are probably right to assume. It was this power perhaps whose presence was formally confirmed by the ceremony undergone by Telemachus, a ceremony which we have already examined. We may now begin to consider certain aspects of this quality which rendered some men like to the immortals, like to the gods.

chapters and thus differs too widely from that of scholars in the succession from Kirchhoff and Wilamowitz to P. von der Mühll, R. Merkelbach, D. L. Page and C. S. Kirk for such discussions to be useful at this early stage. One advantage, however, of the view here advanced of the story behind our Odyssey's account of events in Phaeacia is that it supports and explains their sequence as we now have it.

[78] 7.208 ff.
[79] 8.14.

CHAPTER IV

Shamanism

I

This chapter is an enquiry into the earliest evidence for shamanism in the world of Greek myth. We shall not interest ourselves in the shamanism of archaic Greece, but in that of the pre-Olympian world alone.

Professor Dodds holds[1] that the Greeks came for the first time into contact with a culture based on shamanism when the Black Sea was opened to them in the seventh century. K. Meuli[2] had seen hints of shamanism in Greek epic, but Dodds, while fully appreciating the importance of the main substance of Meuli's article, considers his suggestions in this context to be 'hazardous speculations'[3]. It is worth observing in the first place that, if we may take myth for evidence, there had been some contact in Mycenaean times between Greece and the lands lying round the Black Sea[4]. Greek myth, as we shall see, quite unmistakably shows that shamans were known to the ancestors of Mycenaean rulers. Indeed, it seems that in shamanism is to be found the origin of at least three of the most important clan-cults contending for existence in mainland Greece during the fourteenth and thirteenth centuries.

Tantalus' treatment of his son Pelops has long been recognized as having the character of a rite of regeneration[5]. Tantalus is said to have cut Pelops

---

[1] *The Greeks and the Irrational* (California and London, 1956), p. 142.

[2] 'Scythica', *Hermes*, 70, 1935.

[3] *Op. cit.*, p. 164, note 47.

[4] One may recall, for instance, the legends of Phrixus and of Jason.

[5] See, for instance, F. M. Cornford in J. E. Harrison, *Themis*, pp. 243 ff., referred to with approval by A. B. Cook, *Zeus* I, p. 679. Cornford is, however, wrong in connecting the story with Zeus, Dionysus, Zagreus or the Kouretes, which he does through the slender links provided by the statements of Bacchylides that Rhea drew Pelops alive from the cauldron, and of Strabo that Rhea was worshipped (in the first century B. C.) on Mt. Sipylos. The deity with whom Pelops is indissolubly connected is Poseidon (see below), whom Cornford barely mentions, while the myth says nothing of Dionysus,

up in pieces, boiled him in a 'purifying'[6] cauldron, and served him up to the gods to eat. He was then restored to life by divine action, blooming as never before[7], all the parts of the body, except the shoulder, for which an ivory substitute was found, being replaced. Various deities are credited with the act of restoring him to life[8]. To see in the story an account of a ritual of regeneration is, however, not enough, if we are to understand the story, we must ask what sort of rebirth is here described.

As a rite of rebirth, the ceremony is in some sense one of initiation. Fundamentally, all rites of initiation are the same, in that they enact the death, or putting behind one, of an earlier existence, and entry thereupon into a new life. 'It is often difficult to distinguish between the rites of tribal initiation and those of a secret society, or between the rites of admission to a secret society and those of shamanist initiation'[9]. Nevertheless, there are real differences, and in this case we can come to a certain conclusion. In the first place we must observe that in Siberia and Central Asia, a region which provides highly important analogies for our study, there are no initiatory rites on the passing of youths from one age-group to another[10]. This is not a final argument against a view that the myth describes tribal initiation, for not all the forces at work in Mycenaean Greece originated in Asia, nor does the fact that no such rites are observed to-day preclude their having been practised in the distant past. Nevertheless, it is perhaps a consideration of a certain weight, for most of the shamanism traceable in earlier Greek myth seems to have had an Asiatic origin.

Secondly, the story apparently describes a selective ritual: not every 'Pelops' went through it to the same end, for we learn of one 'Pelops' who was thrust out of the company of the gods[11]. We notice too that this Pelops

---

Zagreus, the Cretan Zeus or the Kouretes. Pindar mentions Zeus (*Ol.* 1.42 [66]), but there is no suggestion that this is the Cretan Zeus.

[6] Pindar, *Ol.* 1.26 (40).

[7] ὡραιότερος, Apollod., *Epit.* 2.3.

[8] See Schol. Pind. *Ol.* 1.24 (37).

[9] M. Eliade, *Le Chamanisme et les techniques archaïques de l'extase* (Paris, 1951), p. 74.

[10] *Ibid.* The Spartan and Cretan *agelai* seem, in all probability, to have been a Dorian institution, although R. F. Willetts, *Cretan Cults and Festivals* (London, 1962), p. 66, thinks that the possibility that they were of 'Minoan' origin cannot be excluded. On the *agelai* see also Willetts, *op. cit.,* pp. 41 (with 39 f.), 45 f., 112, 116 f., 175, 190 f., 201, 204 ff.

[11] Schol. Pind. *Ol.* 1.38 (61).

is not said to have been thrust out of the company of his fellow-clansmen but out of that of the gods. Thirdly, and most significantly, Poseidon is said to have given winged horses to the Pelops who was the son of Tantalus and to have wished to bear him off with the golden steeds to the dwelling of Zeus[12]. What this means we shall shortly see, but we may here anticipate our general conclusion: the story describes Pelops' initiation as a shaman.

Tantalus is said to have stolen the nectar and ambrosia of the gods and given it to his companions and fellow-drinkers. Because of this the gods made him immortal. At the consecration of a new shaman among the Buryats the flesh of the sacrificed animals is boiled and placed in special vessels. After a little of this meat and soup has first been offered to the 'lord of the fire', the 'shaman father', the 'shaman sons' (i.e. attendant youths) and the other shamans stand in a row and, each holding a vessel of meat and soup in his hand, pray to the gods to accept the sacrifice of the new shaman. After this, the flesh and the soup are thrown either into the air or into the fire. Then the 'shaman father' and the others begin to eat[13]. This is consistent with a relationship of Tantalus as 'shaman father' to Pelops and with the story of his sharing the food of the gods with his companions. It does not, of course, by itself prove that Tantalus was a shaman, and we must show that close parallels to his further actions, and what we are told of Pelops, are to be found in accounts of the initiation of shamans.

The traditional pattern of a ceremony of initiation is suffering, death, and resurrection. Among the sufferings of the canditate is the dismemberment of the body and removal of the internal organs. H. Findeisen finds[14] that the essence of the 'mystical' dismemberment of a man (or woman, for there are female shamans) who is in process of becoming a shaman is the fact 'that the shaman can only heal such illnesses as are caused by spirits which, in the terrible process of dismemberment, have received their share of his body.' The accounts of the dismemberment are various[15], and various ghostly

---

[12] Pind. Ol. 1.41 f. (65 f.).

[13] U. N. O. (Holmberg) Harva, Die religiösen Vorstellungen der altaischen Völker (Helsinki, 1938), p. 494.

[14] Schamanentum (Stuttgart, 1957), p. 51. See M. Eliade, Le chamanisme etc., p. 48.

[15] For the dismemberment of the shaman in the psychical and psychosomatic experience attendant on his preparation for the vocation Findeisen refers to G. V. Ksenofontov, Legendy o šamanach, published by the Yakut Section of the East Siberian Department of the Russian Geographical Society, Irkutsk, 1929. Eliade gives the title of the second edition (Moscow, 1930) as Legendy i rasskazy o shamanach u jakutov, burjat i tungusov.

powers are said to carry it out, from the 'animal mothers' to the spirits of
ancestors who were shamans, or even the souls of ordinary people who have
died. Among the tribes in the Tungus region of Siberia the spirits of shamanizing ancestors carry out the *sparagmos*. They eat the flesh of the 'slain'
man raw, and only after this process can he become a shaman. Among the
Buryats, ancestral spirits cook the rent flesh, and further torture the candidate while demanding that he become a shaman. Generally, the head is
severed first: it is placed in some position from which it can observe all that
follows. Iron hooks are driven between the joints to tear them apart; the
flesh is scraped off the bones. Sometimes it is hung upon stakes[16]. During this
experience the shaman-to-be lies by himself or herself, separated from all
contact with ordinary and sinful mankind. Only pure youths or maidens may
serve him.

After the spirits have torn the shaman asunder, they revive him. The disjoined bones are brought together in their proper positions, the head is restored to its place, new flesh is laid upon the bones. The spirits take the new
flesh from other human beings and from domestic animals, and it is believed
that those from whom it is taken are, as a result, bound to die. In general,
it is apparently only relations of the shaman who are thus affected, though
relationship may be extended to all the members of a clan, and, in the case of
the initiation of a great shaman, all may be doomed to perish. It is reported
that, among the Tungus peoples, the spirits conclude their operations by
drinking reindeer blood and offering it to the shaman himself.

During this experience the shaman may lie insensible for days, sometimes
with froth trickling from the mouth, and bleeding at the nose, or with dark
purple and blue marks upon his body, caused by congested blood beneath the
skin. Or the shaman may lie as if asleep, but his clothing (it is alleged) becomes covered with blood[17]. A woman in the Altai, who practised all the
traditional religious rites but was not a shaman, explained why the spirits
did not accept her as a shaman. She fell ill, and everything became dark all
round her. Then, in a vision, some people appeared who cut up her body,
joint by joint, and boiled the pieces in a cauldron. 'Then two further people
appeared, who cut up her flesh anew, drew out her intestines, and boiled the
whole. Then they took the flesh from the cauldron, laid it upon an iron plate

[16] Further details will be found in Eliade, *op. cit.*, pp. 47 ff., and Findeisen, *op. cit.*,
pp. 53 f.
[17] Findeisen, *op. cit.*, pp. 54 ff. See also M. A. Czaplicka, *Aboriginal Siberia* (Oxford,
1914), pp. 171 ff.

with claws, and long and carefully examined all the portions of her body, to see whether all the bones and muscles were suited for the calling of a shaman. It was, however, found that there was one small bone too many, and for this reason she could not become a shaman'[18]. In the case of a Teleyut from the *ulus* Čolchoi, a bone fell out of his neck before he became a shaman. Eliade quotes accounts of the (imagined) dissection of a Yakut shaman-candidate while in a state of trance[19], and of a Samoyed candidate, the pieces of whose body were placed in a cauldron[20]. The dismemberment and boiling of Pelops in the purifying cauldron fits exactly into the pattern of this part of a shaman's initiation, as exemplified in these stories. The story in itself is so strange, as well as being characteristic of shamanist initation, that no other explanation can reasonably be given of it[21].

Findeisen, like Eliade, sees in the mystical dismemberment and its issue in the initiated shaman an experience of death and resurrection. It has also an ethical element, 'a becoming conscious of the strange forces of the soul which are at the disposal of man himself'. 'These people are armed against the trivialities of existence, for they have not only recognized destiny in the crushing power of death, but have experienced all the demands of the human soul, which they have shaped and undergone in personified images ... For these people there can be no more fear, after they have subjected themselves to such terrors. This they did at first unwillingly, but later under the overpowering compulsion of the power that dwells in the creative function of the soul[22].'

According to a Buryat shaman, before the flesh of the candidate is cooked, 'to teach him the art of shamanizing', the spirits of ancestors carry the soul of the canditate before the 'Assembly of the Saaitans' in the heavens and there he is instructed[23]. The flight of shamans through the upper air and over land

---

[18] Findeisen, *op. cit.*, p. 58.

[19] *op. cit.*, pp. 47 ff.

[20] *Ibid.*, p. 52.

[21] Tales of dismemberment and resuscitation are of course to be found in the folklore of many countries: see Stith Thompson, *Motif Index of Folk-literature, s. v.* Dismemberment, Rejuvenation by dismemberment and boiling, Resuscitation with missing members, etc., for references.

[22] *Op. cit.*, p. 59. See also the important study of the 'dismemberment' of shamans and of the concept that lies behind it in *Schamanengeschichten aus Sibirien,* translated from the Russian by A. Friedrich and C. Buddruss, (Otto Wilhelm Barth-Verlag, München-Planegg, 1955), Introduction, pp. 31–43.

[23] Eliade, *op. cit.*, p. 54.

and sea in a state of ecstasy or trance is a well-known and distinctive characteristic of shamanism, and indications of it in descriptions of initiation tell us
that the initiation is that of a shaman. The shaman is often borne aloft on
a bird, but Buryat shamans ride on a horse, which is represented by a stick
with a horse's head and is called the shaman's horse[24]. The ecstasy of the
shaman is strongly promoted by his drum, and among the shamans of the
Altai this drum is called a 'horse'. Eliade draws attention to the tradition that
a 'horse' may be the vehicle of the ecstatic flight in commenting on the words
of 'the long-haired ecstatic' in *Rigveda* X, 136: 'In the intoxication of ecstasy
we are mounted upon the chariot of the winds. You, mortals, see only our
bodies ... The ecstatic is the horse of the wind, the friend of the god of the
tempest, winged by the gods ...[25]' The nature of the winged horses given by
Poseidon to Pelops, with which the god wished to carry him to the house of
Zeus, is, if we take the evidence for shamanist initiation as a whole, clear
beyond reasonable doubt.

We turn to the story of Pelops' ivory shoulder. No religion is pure and
unmixed with elements of other religions. A marked feature of Central Asian
and Siberian shamanism is the belief in animal ancestors or protectors. The
shaman, may, in a state of possession, himself embody this animal ancestor[26],
and this identification would seem to be an important source of the story of
Pelops' ivory shoulder. Among the Yakuts there used to be a ceremony of
consecration of a new shaman, in the course of which the candidate ascended
with his teacher to the Spirit of the upper world. This Spirit possesses a herd
of stallions 'with wings on their shoulders'. This last expression is used, in the
case of horses of the terrestrial world, of white patches on the neck near the
shoulders or withers, which Yakuts hold to be symbolic of the horse's wings.
Horses so marked are dedicated to this spirit of the upper world[27]. In the
legend of the offering of his dismembered body to the gods, 'Pelops' is plainly
regarded as the original ancestor of the Pelopidae. It is thus likely that, as
such, he would have also been identified by tradition with the *animal* ancestor of the Pelopidae, which seems to have been the horse. Medusa, who mated

---

[24] Eliade, *Ibid.* See also M. A. Czaplicka, *Aboriginal Siberia*, p. 224.

[25] pp. 365 f.

[26] Findeisen, *op. cit.*, pp. 28 ff. See also M. A. Czaplicka, *Aboriginal Siberia*, p. 183, citing
Troshchanski, *The Evolution of the Black Faith:* the 'animal-protector' of the shamans
'seems to be of a totemic and personal nature, to a certain extent "of one blood and
flesh" with his *protégé* ...'

[27] Findeisen, *op. cit.*, p. 69.

with Poseidon, and from whose body, after her decapitation by Perseus, sprang the winged horse Pegasus, is, as we shall notice later, actually represented on a seventh-century Boeotian *pithos* by a centaur-like figure, with a woman's head and upper parts, and the body and legs of a horse. It is therefore not unlikely that 'Pelops', as clan ancestor, was identified with the animal ancestor of the Pelopidae, the horse. This probable identification should be considered in connection with the story of the shoulder eaten at the meal served to the gods by Tantalus and replaced by the gods with an ivory shoulder. The ancient authorities[28] held that the story explained a white mark on the shoulder of the Pelopidae. I would suggest that this explanation is almost correct, but that the mark it explains is a white patch on the shoulders of horses sacred to Poseidon, himself very closely associated with the Pelopidae. Pelops, whom Poseidon 'especially loved'[29], has been identified with the animal ancestor. Horses so marked, as we have seen, are called 'winged' by the Yakuts. These horses were, it seems, the terrestrial images of the divine steeds of the spirit. The implication is that Pelops, the human ancestor of the Pelopidae, rode a divine steed with which he was at times virtually identified. That Pegasus was the winged horse of Pelopid, or at least of Poseidonian, shamanism is a conclusion which we shall argue further below.

There is, however, a possible second source for the story of the ivory shoulder. In itself, the suggestion which we have just made seems to provide a sufficient explanation. Nevertheless, another explanation has been advanced, of which we must take account. There are many legends of resuscitation with a portion of the body missing after dismemberment and collection of the disjoined pieces[30]. The explanation of the missing member is surely that it represents that which one gives up in order to be reborn spiritually. So, for instance, may one interpret the missing generative organ of Osiris[31]. 'And if thine eye offend thee, pluck it out: it is better for thee to enter into the Kingdom of God with one eye, than having two eyes to be cast into hell fire[32].' (This, be it remembered, was spoken to the disciples.) There are also stories of the replacement of the missing part which are to be understood differently. Eliade quotes an Armenian story of a hunter who was present at a marriage

---

[28] Schol. Pind. *Ol.* 1.24 (37).

[29] Pind. *Ol.* 1.25 (39); 41 (65).

[30] See J. A. MacCulloch, *The Childhood of Fiction* (London, 1905), pp. 90, 97 ff.; also above, footnote 21.

[31] MacCulloch, *op. cit.*, p. 99.

[32] *Mark*, 9.47.

of the spirits of the wood[33]. Invited to the banquet, he abstained from eating, but retained the rib of an ox which was offered to him. The bones of the animal were then re-assembled so that it might be resuscitated, but for the rib the spirits were obliged to substitute a branch of a nut tree. This is clearly to be understood in the context of the tree-cult: a sacred element is introduced into the body at re-birth. Eliade[34] gives many examples from the aboriginal tribes of Australia of the imagined opening of the body of a medicine-man at his initiation and the insertion therein of magical substances, from which the new medicine-man is to derive his power. In one of these stories, a tibia and shoulder-blade are taken out, stuffed with magical substances, and re-placed. The same kind of (imagined) practice is to be found in the initiation ceremonies of the medicine-men of South America[35].

In the case of Pelops' ivory shoulder both the explanations we have given might be applicable: horses with a white patch on the shoulder may have been deemed to be so marked as a symbol both of the wings of the divine steed and of the magical ivory shoulder-blade of the Pelopid shamans[36]. Either explanation (but especially the former) confirms the conclusion that the myth of Tantalus and Pelops describes a shaman's initiation.

That their shamanism was not unopposed appears from tradition. Tanta-lus, indeed, has something of the quality of a religious innovator. As we have seen, he seems to have reduced the high gods from their estate, and to have asserted that there was a capacity in human beings for communion with the gods. An Aeschylean fragment[37] makes him receive the heavenly warning; 'Learn thou not to revere things human beyond their desert.' We may recall Findeisen's view of the spiritual *sparagmos* undergone by the candidate for the office of shaman as having an ethical element, 'a becoming conscious of

---

[33] Also referred to by J. Bolte and G. Polivka, *Anmerkungen zu den Kinder- und Haus-märchen der Brüder Grimm* (Leipzig, 1913–30), I, pp. 422 f.

[34] *Op. cit.*, pp. 55 ff.

[35] *Ibid.*, p. 62.

[36] The shamans of certain northern Asiatic tribes bear on their robes models made in iron of the principal bones and other parts of the human body as well as of parts of animals' bodies. Thus among the Yakuts, in addition to representations of human bones, there are, near the junction of sleeve and shoulder, iron plates which are held to represent the bone in a bird's wing which corresponds to that of the upper part of the human arm. Other shamans speak of these bones as shoulder bones. (Find-eisen, p. 88).

[37] 159 (Nauck).

the strange forces of the soul *which are at the disposal of man himself*[38]. The traditions of modern Siberian shamanism show astonishing parallels to the offence, or sin, of Tantalus, explaining the decadence of contemporary shamanism by the pride of the 'first shaman', who entered into rivalry with God. The Buryat story is that, Khara-Gyrgän, the first shaman, having announced his limitless power, God put him to the test by shutting up the soul of a girl in a bottle, which he stopped with his finger. The shaman, mounted on his drum, flew to heaven, where, in order to liberate the girl's soul, he changed himself into a spider, and stung *(sic)* God in the face. God withdrew his finger from the bottle and the girl's soul escaped. In his wrath, God limited the power of the first shaman and the capacities of succeeding shamans have consequently been diminished. The Yakuts also have a tradition of the pride of the first shaman and of God's enmity towards him[39]. Eliade thinks that these stories may only be marks of 'black' shamanism, that is, of a shamanism with infernal, or chthonic, associations. A celestial shamanism apparently shows no signs of enmity towards the supreme and heavenly being.

The nature of Tantalus' innovation, and of his offence, may also be seen from another angle. It has commonly been accepted[40] that two kinds of sacrifice were practised among the Greeks, one in which the whole offering was given to the gods, and one in which the offering was shared with the gods by those who performed the sacrifice. That is to say, in the former kind of sacrifice, the whole victim (if it was an animal sacrifice) was burnt or otherwise destroyed; in any case, no man partook of it, whether it was an animal sacrifice or not. The verb properly used for this kind of sacrifice was ἐναγίζειν, and the offering was made to the spirits of the dead who inhabited the underworld. The motive behind the sacrifice was fear: it was a ceremony of ἀποτροπή, riddance. 'The formula of the religion was not *do ut des* "I give that you may give", but *do ut abeas* "I give that you may go, and keep away".' There was no communion between the sacrificer and the spirit or spirits to whom he sacrificed: on the contrary, he wanted to have nothing to do with such dangerous and malevolent beings.

There was however, another kind of sacrifice, that for which the correct

---

[38] My italics. See, however, Horst Kirchner, 'Ein archäologischer Beitrag zur Urgeschichte des Schamanismus', *Anthropos*, vol. 47 (1952), p. 256.

[39] Eliade, *op. cit.*, pp. 76 f.

[40] Among English writers by, *e. g.*, Miss Jane Harrison, *Prolegomena to the Study of Greek Religion*, Chapter I and pp. 55–65.

verb was ϑύειν. In this ritual the sacrificer took part of the offering and
ate it himself: the victim, or the food and drink, was shared between men and
gods. Between gods and man there was communion, not fear alone. This
sacrifice has been distinguished as Olympian. Karl Meuli has, however,
shown[41] that the meal taken in common by men and spirits is characteristic
of the 'Speisungsopfer' or 'feeding-sacrifice' made to the dead, to heroes, to
gods at *theoxenia*. The Olympian sacrifice was originally of a different
nature, but acquired some of the characteristics of the sacrifice once offered
in the family or a select company to presences other than Olympian gods.

Now it was precisely the offence of Tantalus that he and his companions
ate and drank with the gods. It is implied that others did not do so, and the
inference that their offerings were apotropaic is possible, though not inevitable. It is, however, clear that the sharing of a meal with the gods is a form
of communion with them: Tantalus and his companions were evidently
different from other men of their time in that they alone claimed to communicate with the gods. This, however, is precisely what a shaman does. The
shaman originally seems to have operated in, and on behalf of, a circle of
kindred. Shamans alone, in a somewhat more developed setting, are able to
encounter spirits face to face and converse with them. Tantalus, the scholiast
tells us, wished to live like the gods; that is, he wished to live on an equal
plane with them. Nothing inconsistent with our view that Tantalus was a
shaman appears if we apply this analysis of the two kinds of sacrifice to this
legend. Eliade[42] indeed makes the point explicitly: 'In the archaic cultures,
the communication between Heaven and Earth was used for sending offerings to the celestial deities, and not for undertaking a concrete and personal
ascension (to them); this remained the prerogative of the shamans. They
alone know how to perform the ascent through the 'central opening'; they
alone transform 'a cosmo-theological conception into a *concrete mystical
experience* ... the privileged *régime* of the shaman is due to his faculty of
mystical experience.'

A constant feature of shamanist cosmology in Asia is the Tree of Life (as
the World Tree). The Tree of Life varies in its form and in its attributes: in
Siberia, for instance, it is commonly thought of as a birch or a conifer, but
elsewhere it may have great fruits hanging from its branches. The Water of

---

[41] 'Griechische Opferbräuche' in *Phyllobolia für Peter von der Mühll* (Basel, 1946), esp.
pp. 191–200.

[42] *Le Chamanisme* etc., pp. 240 f.

Life often springs from beneath its roots, or flows past it as a stream, or lies as a lake at its foot. Tantalus, in myth, was punished for his impiety by being compelled to stand in water up to his waist, only to find that as, thirsting, he sought to put his lips to it, the water receded. Above his head were the branches of a tree from which hung an abundance of fruit, but for all his hunger they evaded his grasp as he reached for them. The image is clear beyond mistake: Tantalus is standing under the Tree of Life[43]. Once more he is involved in the world of shamanism. It is a chthonic shamanism, for Tantalus is below the earth. It is true that the Tree of Life also appears in contexts which we should not call shamanist in the ordinary sense, but there we enter into the difficult and little-explored borderland between shamanism and the yogic practices. The evidence we have already cited shows clearly that it is a shamanist background that relates Tantalus to the Tree and the Water of Life.

It appears from the myth of Tantalus and Pelops that Poseidon, who 'especially loved' Pelops, was intimately connected with shamanism[44]. We shall see other evidence that this was so, and a probable piece of such evidence we may bring forward now.

A characteristic feature of shamanism in parts of northern Asia is mutation of sex[45]. The change may take place in either direction: a man may take on secondary female characteristics, or a woman, especially after the age of

[43] The description is taken from Hyginus. Apollodorus, *Epit.* 2.1., speaks of trees growing on either side of Tantalus, the branches hanging over either shoulder until the winds carried them up to the clouds out of his reach. This is another form of the same conception: the tree or its substitutes may be double. Homer, *Od.* 11.582 ff., speaks of fruit-bearing trees of many kinds. In some narratives about the Tree of Life the tree becomes a grove or forest.

[44] As two members of the staffs of university classical departments (neither of them named in the preface) who claimed to have read this text were under the impression that I had said that Poseidon, and other deities to be mentioned later, were shamans, it seems necessary to explain that a god cannot be a shaman, who is a human being. Poseidon and other deities were spirit powers with whom the shaman was in relation. In early Greece, however, a man might represent a god and be known by the god's name. If 'Poseidon' was the chief power with whom shamans had to do at a certain time and in certain regions, and if a number of these shamans were known by the name Poseidon, it was natural that the god Poseidon should acquire the trident as an attribute (see below). Similarly, Athena gained her aegis in this way. Before studying the shamanism of ancient Greece, those who wish to go more deeply into the subject will find it necessary to make some study of Asiatic shamanism.

[45] Findeisen, *op. cit.*, chapter XIII.

childbearing is over, may become man-like, and follow the calling of a sha-man. Greek myth records[46] a change of sex in a woman, who, after inter-course with Poseidon, asked to become an invulnerable man[47]. This desire was granted. As a man this person went by the name of Kaineus. Kaineus, who was accounted most noble, lived in Thessaly. Though invulnerable, he was buried by centaurs beneath pine trees. Striking the earth with his foot, he vanished beneath it in a chasm which opened below him. Afterwards, according to Ovid, a bird with yellow wings rose from the pile of logs, and was declared by Mopsus to be Kaineus transformed. Kaineus was distinguished by a singular impiety in that he worshipped no deity but his 'spear' or staff (δόρυ) alone, which he set up in the market-place and commanded people to worship. He contended with Apollo, but was defeated. The evidence that Kaineus was a shaman is largely circumstantial: the irrefutable signs of trance, suffering, death and rebirth, of descent into the underworld, and ascension or flight into the heavens, are mostly missing. One may perhaps see a part of this in his burial under pine trees by the Centaurs, for the burial replaces death (in that he was invulnerable), but one cannot say that this is its unambiguous sense[48]. His subsequent descent into a chasm, however, would certainly seem to mean that he visited the underworld: the chasm would only have opened for him if he had had the power of entry there. His invulnerability is distinctly suggestive of shamanism, and the change of sex is, on the analogy of Siberian and North American shamanism, very strong circumstantial evidence. Ovid's story of his transformation into a bird reproduces a common feature of shamanism in many parts of the world[49], but the phenomenon is not restricted to shamans.

In such a context the fact that Kaineus as a woman had intercourse with Poseidon is striking, and we may justifiably hold that the connection of Poseidon with Pelops in an unmistakably shamanist setting strongly suggests

[46] Apollod. *Epit.* 1.22; Schol. *Il.* 1.264; Apollon. Rhod. 1.57—64, with Schol. on 57; Ovid, *Metamorph.* 12.459–532. See Frazer's note on the passage of Apollodorus for other references.

[47] On the claim to invulnerability of Ostyak Shamans, see Adolph Erman, *Travels in Siberia,* Vol. II, p. 45 (English translation, London, 1848). It is a common belief of shamans in many parts of the world that they are invulnerable.

[48] It may mean exactly what it says: shamans are sometimes buried under a pile of logs in the Siberian forests. See Czaplicka, *op. cit.,* p. 184.

[49] '... la faculté de se métamorphoser en oiseau appartient à toutes les espèces de cha-manisme, aussi bien turco-mongol, qu'arctique, américain ou indien et océanien' (Eliade, *op. cit.,* p. 362).

that here too we have the remains of a myth about a famous shaman. Conversely, the circumstantial evidence of shamanism in the case of Kaineus reinforces the view that Poseidon is to be regarded as a power intimately concerned with chthonic shamanism.

That his staff may well have been the sacred shaman's staff is plain[50]. We should observe the apparent analogy with an aspect of the caduceus of Hermes, noticed by Professor P. Raingeard in his *Hermès Psychagogue*[51]. The caduceus often appears on vases by itself (that is, without the god); winged, it has a self-sufficient quality which prompts Professor Raingeard to raise the question whether there was a deity 'Caduceus', a question which he answers negatively. Instead, he points out that the Christian Cross appears by itself, and is a centre of worship, without being confused with Him whom it symbolizes. Perhaps we may go so far as to maintain that the legend of Kaineus is perfectly correct, and that the staff of Kaineus differs from the caduceus only in the fact that there was no god which it directly symbolized: it stood for the power of the shaman alone, whose spirit helpers were personal to himself.

The soothsayer Teiresias also possessed a staff. It was presented to him by Athena as a recompense for his having been blinded; such was its quality that Teiresias by means of it was able to walk like those who see. Of Teiresias it is also recorded that he twice underwent a change of sex, the change resulting apparently from his having on each occasion struck a pair of snakes which he saw copulating on Kyllene. It is worth remembering that, according to those who have seen them, snakes in copulation adopt exactly the interlaced attitude of those which appear with the caduceus[52]. Snakes entwined in this pattern appear of course in ancient religious contexts outside Greece. Kyllene was the birthplace of Hermes.

Teiresias also bade Odysseus sacrifice to Poseidon[53]. Since his mother was so close a friend of Athena that she sometimes travelled in the goddess's chariot, Teiresias is connected both with Poseidon (and, it would seem, Hermes) and with Athena. We shall later notice the association of Poseidon and Athena in an unmistakably shamanist setting. The journeys of Teiresias' mother in Athena's chariot are strongly suggestive of shamanist flight. These

[50] See Findeisen, *op. cit.*, pp. 115 f.
[51] Paris, 1935, p. 415. On the various forms of the caduceus see F. J. M. de Waele, *The Magic Staff or Rod in Graeco-Italian Antiquity* (Ghent, 1927), plate facing p. 213.
[52] A. Butterworth, *The Southlands of Siva* (London, 1923), p. 111.
[53] Homer, *Od.* 11.130.

facts, taken together with Teiresias' prophetic powers, staff and, especially, change of sex, seem to point clearly to his having been a shaman.

We may observe in connection with Teiresias that the cult of chthonic deity may have been characterised by some association with sexual intercourse, and that the celestial powers were by contrast, as we suggested in speaking of the *partheneia* of the Danaids and Tyndarids, ascetic. Hera and Zeus referred to Teiresias for decision a dispute on the question whether in sexual congress men or women experienced the greater pleasure. Teiresias replied that if the pleasure of love be reckoned at ten, men enjoyed one and women nine parts. Hera thereupon blinded the sage: the answer seems to have been unacceptable to the goddess[54]. Teiresias' observation of snakes copulating on Kyllene, whatever else it may imply, may perhaps imply also some connection with sexual intercourse as an element of cult. Hermes, the Kyllenean, who is undoubtedly intimately connected with a chthonic shamanism (although the demonstration of this must be made elsewhere), is of course at times represented as phallic. This however, has nothing to do with shamanism as such, and it is with the manifestations of pre-Olympian Greek shamanism that we are here concerned.

II

This is a suitable point for some discussion of a question which our argument has raised: what has the shamanism of twentieth-century Siberia to do with Mycenaean or pre-Mycenaean myth? Are there any signs of historical connection? The subject is a very large one, and we shall not do more than brush the surface of it in observing that there are some indications of a connection. We may begin with asking whether Poseidon or, to anticipate, Hermes can provide a connecting link.

A story related by a Yakut to Findeisen[55] describes the way in which a man who died, yet retained consciousness without the power of movement, was buried and his soul carried off by spirits in human and animal forms, first to the worlds below and then to the region above the present world. He was then brought back to this world to inhabit a new body and to follow

---

[54] This story may of course have been invented after, and as a consequence of, the tradition of Teiresias' double change of sex.

[55] *op. cit.*, pp. 38 ff.

the calling of a shaman. Certain features of the story draw our attention. In the spring of the year in which the man died, a roan foal was born which showed every sign of growing into a good horse. When he returned to earth, the foal had become a horse of great fame. The manner in which the man was borne from his grave to the underworld was as follows. While in his grave he heard sounds of digging above him. The lid of his coffin was opened, and four black men stood above him. They set him, in a seated position, on the coffin, facing his house. There was a light in the windows of the house and smoke arose from the chimney. Suddenly, from somewhere deep down in the earth came the bellowing of a bull. The bellowing drew nearer and nearer. The earth then began to tremble, to the terror of the dead man. From the bottom of the grave rose a great black bull with horns that curved closely towards each other. The bull took the seated man upon its horns and returned into the hole from which it had risen. Later, after the dead man had visited the underworld and had been weighed in the palm of the Ancient there, the bull brought him back to this world, whence he was carried into the upper world by a raven.

The rest of the story does not directly concern us, but three features of the portion we have related are to be noticed, namely, the horse, associated with the time of the man's death and his re-birth as a shaman, the bellowing bull which rises from below, and the fact that this bull makes the earth tremble. Earthquakes and the bull are, as one knows, associated with Dionysus, but it is only Poseidon who is associated with all three manifestations. Whether this is coincidence or real connection is a question which cannot on this evidence be answered, but the three features are, we observe, here associated with shamanism.

Perhaps we may come closer to the answer if we consider a single attribute of Poseidon, namely, the trident. Not only Poseidon carries a trident-headed staff. On an Attic black-figured vase from Vulci which is in the British Museum[56], Hermes carries a *kerykeion* with an unusual three-pointed head. This is evidently the staff called τριπέτηλος in the Homeric Hymn to Hermes[57]. Another black-figured vase, possibly of Chalcidean manufacture[58], shows a variant of the normal caduceus, but below the head is a cross-bar, a highly significant feature which may some-

---

[56] Brit. Mus. cat. B. 248. Illustrated on Plate III.

[57] 530. Raingeard, overlooking this vase, finds the τριπέτηλος 'très obscur' (p. 405).

[58] Brit. Mus. cat. B. 16. Illustr. Pl. IV.

times be traced on the trident of Poseidon[59]. A caduceus with two crossbars is shown on an Attic black-figured vase in the Louvre[60].

The shamans of the Kets, or so-called Ostyaks of the Yenisei, a tribe which may by now have disappeared as a distinguishable people, used to carry a staff which often had a trident head[61]. After the death of a shaman, the top of his staff was sometimes set at the masthead of one of the boats that ply on the Yenisei[62]. The cross-bar associated with the trident is a distinctive feature of some of these Yenisei shamans' staffs, as will be seen from Plate VII (a), (b), and (c). It appears in other shamans' staffs also, for instance, those of the Dolgans[63]. There are several theories of the origin of the trident, and into the question of its origin we shall not enter, save to mention its possible connection with the sacred World Tree, which is a very important part of the spiritual cosmology of Siberian shamans[64]. The cross-bars are held by some to be stylized branches, and to have a significance, for the souls of shamans-to-be are reared in nests placed upon the branches of the World Tree. Whatever the origin of the cross-bars upon ancient Greek and later Asiatic tridents, the fact that this feature is common to both is very striking.

There is at least a presumption to be drawn from these different considerations that a relation exists between the form of the Yenisei shaman's staff and the trident of Poseidon and the 'three-leafed' caduceus of Hermes.

Whence did the Yenisei shaman derive this shape of staff? It seems that the Kets, or Yenisei Ostyaks, formerly lived, for the most part, much further south, in a region (the Sayan Mountains) where they must have come into contact with lamaism[65]. It is possible, therefore, that the trident-headed staff was modelled on a lamaistic original. Certainly, the trident head is

---

[59] See plates V and VI.

[60] CVA Louvre III He, Pl. 51,4. The cross-bar on the caduceus appears also on a black-figured Attic vase shown in E. Langlotz, *Griechische Vasen Würzburg*, pl. 53,188. Langlotz quotes *Bonner Studien 251;* Hackl, *Merkantile Inschriften,* 27.

[61] Pl. VII (a) and (b).

[62] Pl. VIII. See Findeisen, *op. cit.,* p. 115, and G. Nioradze, *Der Schamanismus bei den sibirischen Völkern,* p. 78.

[63] U. N. O. Holmberg (Uno Harva), *Mythology of all Races: Finno-Ugric Siberian,* p. 511.

[64] See Holmberg (Harva), *loc. cit.,* and Findeisen, *op. cit.,* p. 114.

[65] I owe this information to Dr. Ulla Johansen, of the Museum für Völkerkunde und Vorgeschichte, Hamburg, who also made the suggestion that the trident form may be derived from a lamaistic model.

found on ritual staffs from Mongolia[66] to Tibet[67], and, as we shall immediately notice, much further south. We find trident-headed shaman's staffs
again in Korea[68]. In India, the trident is a very frequent concomitant of
Siva. Illustrations of Siva bearing elaborate forms of the trident will be
found at Plates XII and XIII, where the cross-bars below the trident are
also visible. At Plate XIV a plain form of the trident reappears. The trident
may also be carried by Siva's consort, Kali (who is also known by other
names) as will be seen from Plate XV, which shows the figure of a masked
dancer from the festival of Kali. (To this figure we shall return.)

The origin of the trident associated with Siva is no clearer than the
aspect of the god with which it is associated. There are in Saiva, the worship
of Rudra-Siva, two distinct streams of tradition, the one Aryan and Vedic,
the other, the Agamic, which is non-Aryan, springing from a variety of
local sources. It is difficult to associate the trident with one or the other
stream exclusively. Plate XI (a) shows a trident from a pariah altar at
Vellore, S. India. On the other hand, the trident is associated with Siva in
Vedic tradition, and it is possible that its appearance in settings outside the
Vedic tradition is due to borrowing. The itinerant holy man of India is said
sometimes to carry a trident. The association of the trident with ecstasy or
possession appears from Plate X, which shows a Tibetan medium entering
into a trance (at Kalimpong, Sikkim) with a trident placed at his side[69].
This trident appears to be virtually identical with a form of that associated
with Siva.

The figure of the masked dancer from the festival of Kali (Pl. XV) is of
singular interest. A question which one may legitimately ask about Medusa,
whom we shall later consider in more detail, is why, if she, unlike the other
two Gorgons, was a mortal, her face was so terrible that no other mortal
could look upon her. There can surely be little doubt that the answer is that,
on ceremonial occasions, she wore a terrifying mask[70]. If this was so, the
description of her as having a boar's tusks and snaky hair becomes immed-

[66] See the photograph of a Mongolian Cham dancer on Pl. IX.
[67] See Plate X.
[68] Pl. XI (b).
[69] There is an interesting account of the *séance* in R. de Nebesky-Wojkowitz, *Oracles and Demons of Tibet,* (Oxford/The Hague, 1956), pp. 432 ff.
[70] Miss Harrison, *Prolegomena,* p. 187 ff., is right in seeing the Gorgoneion as a mask, but, in my view, wrong in thinking that a body became attached to it only later. Obviously, a mask is worn by somebody.

iately comprehensible, for these would then have been a part of the mask. The Gorgoneion in art has also a pendent tongue. The masked figure in Plate XV has boar's tusks, a pendent tongue and a somewhat stylized cobra in her hair. The snake in the hair is also a feature of Siva and may be seen in Plate XIII. The dancer holds a trident and so does Kali, Siva's consort, depicted on the raised screen-like headdress, in two of her fourteen hands. When we remember that Medusa mated with Poseidon, it can hardly be dismissed as coincidence that these four very distinctive features, the boar's tusks, the pendent tongue, the snake in the hair, and, by implication, the trident, are common both to Medusa and to the dancer for Kali, Siva's terrible spouse. (Kali only carries the trident, which is Siva's emblem, as Siva's consort.)

The trident occurs also in Africa. Professor K. G. Lindblom, who examines the subject in an essay, 'Spears with two or more heads, particularly in Africa'[71], thinks (though expressing himself cautiously) that the zone of distribution in Africa shows signs that the use of the trident spread from certain centres, probably through being used as symbols of authority in kingdoms set up by the Hamites (but not in ancient Egypt). He adds that 'one cannot altogether disregard the possibility of influence from Asia, and perhaps also, here and there, from Poseidon-Neptune'. If one may comment on this last remark, it should be observed that one cannot 'influence' a trident into existence: surely either the ultimate source of the African trident lay outside Africa or it did not[72]. The greater part of the 57 African bidents and tridents considered by Professor Lindblom are symbols of rank for 'rulers, chiefs, high priests or other prominent personages'. Others possess a religious or at least a magical, significance. One or two are purely cult objects, while about the use of ten nothing is known. The temporal use of some of these African bidents and tridents is a striking fact. Professor Lindblom does not comment further on the fact that some are used in a

---

[71] *Essays presented to C. G. Seligman*, ed. by E. E. Evans-Pritchard, R. Firth, B. Malinowski, I. Schapera (London, 1934), pp. 178 ff.

[72] It is just possible that Professor Lindblom means that the source from which bidents came is uncertain, while that of the trident perhaps lies outside Africa, although it could be simply a development from the bident. It may be relevant to point out that at least one example of a bident Yenisei shaman's staff is known: it is shown on Plate VII (c). It should be remembered that the Hamites are held to have migrated from Asia to Africa.

religious context and some in a secular, simply saying that they are symbols of rank for temporal or spiritual authority. In the absence of further information, one may suppose that the use of the symbol in a secular context is a mark of degeneration from the religious to the political plane, which occurred either because many of the chiefs largely lost a religious character which they once possessed, or because, from whatever causes (possibly because its origin lay outside Africa), the symbol itself lost its religious significance in the course of its distribution.

In Europe and Asia there is no doubt that the trident is always associated with supernatural power. We have perhaps said enough to show that the trident of Poseidon and the 'three-leafed' caduceus of Hermes can scarcely be considered in isolation from other appearances of the trident. So far as they, that is to say, the deities that bear them, are connected with shamanism (which has yet to be shown in the case of Hermes), we have assumed the existence of a shamanist context common to both Mycenaean Greece and to twentieth-century Siberia. This is a considerable assumption. I would, however, refer the reader both to K. Meuli's essay in *Hermes*, 70, 1935, and to an essay by H. Kirchner published in 1952. Professor Kirchner[73] after referring to A. Alföldi's work, and particularly to his lecture to the Berliner Archäologische Gesellschaft in 1931, writes: 'Since then further research in the same direction has shown ever more clearly how great an influence religious conceptions of a kind which are still familiar to us to-day in the form of shamanism, principally from Central and Northern Asia (without being limited to this part of the world), exercised upon the spiritual life of Europe and the Mediterranean region in prehistoric times'[74]. He quotes J. Wiesner as holding the view that a wave of shamanist horsemen ('diese reiterlich-shamanistische Welle'), impelled by the pressure of peoples in the steppes further east, reached the Mediterranean principally by sea from the region of the Euxine and Asia Minor (though some may have passed by land north of the Black Sea and through the Danube countries). This wave will have reached central Europe and left its marks at Hallstadt and Villanova about the turn of the second millennium B. C.[75]. There is, however, evidence of shamanist practice in late Neolithic times, that is, a thousand years earlier[76]. In Professor Kirchner's opinion there was cultural inter-

---

[73] Horst Kirchner, 'Ein archäologischer Beitrag zur Urgeschichte des Schamanismus', *Anthropos,* vol. 47 (1952). See also Meuli, *op. cit.*, pp. 137–141.

[74] pp. 245.   [75] p. 248.   [76] p. 249.

communion within a great region stretching from Western Europe to Central
Asia. He sees the development of this area of cultural contact as involved
with the spread of the late Palaeolithic culture, which, in his view, had the
plains of south-western Siberia for its place of origin rather than Western
Europe[77]. The influence of this culture spread northwards as well as west.
The possibility exists, it would seem, of a common origin for shamanism in
early Greece and in modern Central Asia and Siberia, however much the
detail may be open to dispute.

III

Let us return to the Pelopidae. As a Pelopid, Agamemnon would celebrate
Poseidon. Nevertheless, as Raingeard shows[78], his characteristic emblem is
the caduceus of Hermes. The prime function of the caduceus is to be the
instrument of Hermes as conductor of souls[79]. In Homer it puts men to sleep,
a property which makes Raingeard ask whether behind this tradition of
its qualities lies an association with hypnotism or cataleptic trance[80]. If,
however, as we shall see to be the case, Hermes is a shamanist power, there
can be little doubt that the soporific quality of the staff was a symbol of
the shaman's trance, and its capacity to restore a man to a state of youth
and beauty[81] is to be associated with the same shamanist context: the issue
of successful initiation is, as in the case of Pelops, revival in a new youth
and in a greater beauty; in a word, rebirth.

A small detail may be significant. When Achilles, in the first book of the
Iliad, is hurling abuse at Pelopid Agamemnon, one of the epithets which he
selects is οἰνοβαρές[82], 'heavy with wine'. Now there is no suggestion that
Agamemnon is drunk at the time of the quarrel: the adjective plainly
describes a general condition of the king. Speaking of a great shaman of the

[77] pp. 282 ff.

[78] op. cit. pp. 407 ff.

[79] Ibid. p. 403 f.

[80] If we remember that Hermes was 'the Kyllenian' and that the former name of Kyllene
was Mēkōnē ('Poppy Town'), we may infer that the sleep sent by Hermes' wand was
sometimes induced by opium. Its true nature, however, is of another kind.

[81] Raingeard, p. 404.

[82] 1.225.

Goldi of the Amur river, Findeisen[83] says that he had the onerous and
responsible task of conducting the souls of dead members of the clan into
the other world. Sometimes people waited for years for him to arrive in
their district, with the result that on occasion he had twenty souls to conduct, an extremely strenuous duty. He could not have carried this task out
without the help of his principal deity, who was female. She never deserted
him, but he had to supply her continually with nourishment, as a result of
which he was himself in a state of chronic alcoholic intoxication. Astonishingly, he never lost his clarity of mind, nor was the strength of his will
impaired (a circumstance which may perhaps be ascribed to the fact that his
drunkeness was due not to psychical disturbance or weakness but, as he
believed, to the necessity of his calling). The pious intoxication of the
Koryaks in celebration of a shamanist deity is recorded by a French traveller
of the eighteenth century[84]. This in itself proves nothing except that
shamanism and habitual intoxication may go together. When however we
hear Agamemnon called 'heavy with wine' we should remember that the
name of the ruler whom Pelops slew was Oinomaos, 'Wine-mad'. We may
recall also Aetolian Oineus. These two names[85] suggest a practice of religious
drunkenness, and such may have been the condition of Agamemnon himself.
There is some evidence that connects Oinomaos with an ecstatic discipline,
but in themselves these hints are not enough to enable us to assert that
Agamemnon practised shamanism.

The sceptre which Agamemnon received from his predecessor had, as
Homer tells us[86], been handed to Pelops by Hermes, the conductor of souls.
It is possible, though our evidence does not justify us in definitely concluding
so, that it was a function of Pelopid kings to conduct the souls of the dead.
We have however seen that Clytaemnestra speaks of herself as conveying

---

[83] *op. cit.*, pp. 121 f.

[84] *Journal Historique du voyage de M. de Lesseps du Kamschatka en France* (Paris, 1790),
Seconde Partie, pp. 93 f: de L., describing the attitude of the Koryaks to their malevolent deity (co-equal with their good deity), says, 'par-tout ce dieu fantastique peut
être honoré; il écoute le Koriaque qui le prie seul dans le désert, comme la famille
réunie qui croit se le rendre favourable en s'enivrant pieusement dans sa yourte: car
l'habitude de l'ivrognerie est devenue chez ce peuple une pratique de religion et le
fondement de toutes les solennités. Ce démon . . . est sans doute le même que le Koutka
dont les chamans Kamschadales se disent les ministres et les organes . . .'

[85] 'Oineus', who, as the story of Meleager suggests, was an enemy of Artemis, and whom
myth connects with Dionysus as wine-god, has the appearance of a cult-leader.

[86] *Il.* 2.104 f.

the soul of Agamemnon[87]. The identification of the deity from whom Pelops received the sceptre with Hermes may, on the other hand, be the work of a later generation which knew simply that this had been a Pelopid function. Similarly, in spite of the close association between Poseidon and shamanist features of Greek myth, it may be that Poseidon too is a name and unifying concept besowed by later Greeks upon a complex of spirits and functions[88]. That this may have been so is suggested by a contradiction in the myth of Kaineus: as a woman, she is said to have lain with Poseidon; as an invulnerable man he worshipped no deities, but only his staff. If, as we hold, Kaineus was a shaman, he will certainly have believed in the power of the spirits of dead shamans and most probably in a deity, male or female, who was primarily his personal guardian and helper, and therefore of no direct concern to ordinary people. This patron may or may not have been Poseidon. What is, however, clear is that Poseidon and, as we shall see, Hermes, at one time were gods whose nature fitted them to be the personal deities or spirits of shamanist 'kings' and 'noblemen'.

Were the Pelopid kings shamans? Certainly, as we have seen, there was shamanism in their clan traditions. A scholiast on Pindar's first Olympian ode[89], however, says that a 'Pelops' was thrust out from the company of the gods. The only meaning which can be attached to this would seem to be that a 'Pelops' of whom there was some individual tradition was not accepted as a shaman. What other evidence is there?

At first sight the 'banquet of Thyestes' might seem to offer a parallel to the dismemberment of Pelops, but the curse uttered by Thyestes and the facts that the children were not restored to life, and that their flesh was not offered to 'gods' but to Thyestes, show that this meal was of another kind: there was here a real killing.

The presentation of Agamemnon in the Iliad is neither uniform nor consistent. In particular, the description of him by Achilles in Book I as having 'the heart of a deer', and the remarkable picture of the King in Books II and IX are quite inconsistent with his (as it may be felt) perfunctory *aristeia* in Book XI[90]. In the light of all that has just been said, the words addressed by

---

[87] See p. 94.

[88] See also J. E. Harrison. *Prolegomena*, pp. 333 ff., on the 'nameless' gods of the Pelasgians, and my remarks on Chrysaor, pp. 24 f.

[89] 38 (61). *Cf.* 65 (105).

[90] 91 ff.

Diomedes to Agamemnon at *Il.* 9.37 ff. are in particular worth reflecting upon:

σοὶ δὲ διάνδιχα δῶκε Κρόνου πάϊς ἀγκυλομήτεω ·
σκήπτρῳ μέν τοι δῶκε τετιμῆσθαι περὶ πάντων,
ἀλκὴν δ' οὔ τοι δῶκεν, ὅ τε κράτος ἐστι μέγιστον.

'The son of Kronos, him of crooked counsel, gave thee contrary gifts: he granted it to thee to be honoured above all men for thy sceptre, but gave thee no *alke,* which is the greatest power of all'.

It seems unlikely that, if by 'sceptre' Homer meant simply the sovereign authority of the royal office, he would have used the phrase σοὶ δὲ διάνδιχα δῶκε, which implies that the two gifts, though different, are personal powers of the same order, even if one be a negative quality. This sceptre, which Hermes had given to Agamemnon's ancestor, is a power that may be compared with *alke,* that is to say, it is a personal ability conferred by the son of Kronos. But if Agamemnon lacked *alke,* he can hardly have been a great warrior. An indication of the sense in which Diomedes may have intended the word σκῆπτρον it to be found in *Il.* 13.59. Here Poseidon fills the two Ajaxes with *menos* by the touch of his σκηπάνιον. This suggests that the σκῆπτρον was a channel of superhuman power, but in this passage it is in the hands of a god. Nevertheless, the god was one who especially loved Pelops, and to Agamemnon's σκῆπτρον may have been attributed power as the channel of a *menos* which resided in the king. The implications of the carpet scene in the *Agamemnon* have already been demonstrated, and they support such an interpretation. In the earlier part of Book II of the Iliad Agamemnon is presented wholly as a religious figure with an incapacity for generalship[91]. The hints are few but they are not without significance. Pausanias[92] says that the people of Chaeronea revered Agamemnon's sceptre as the chief of their gods. It had no temple but was kept by each priest in turn for a year in his house. We are reminded of the staff which Kaineus bade the people worship and which likewise was housed in no shrine[93].

[91] *Cf.* the implied reproach in Nestor's words 2.362–8 and contrast them with the part played by Agamemnon up to that point from the time when Zeus sent him the deceitful dream.

[92] 9.40.6. The word I have translated 'priest' is ὁ ἱερώμενος. It appears that a man was consecrated for a year as keeper of the sceptre.

[93] In Homer the sceptre held by Agamemnon is handed first by Zeus to Hermes, and by Hermes to Pelops. Why, it may be asked, does Zeus first bestow the sceptre when Pelops was especially beloved of Poseidon? If we leave on one side the ambiguity of at

There is thus ground for suspecting that Agamemnon was, if only formally, a shaman, but the question remains open.

That very early god, Hermes, as we have seen reason to think, and as we shall discover in more detail, is also intimately connected both with the Pelopidae and with shamanism[94]. The connection with the Pelopidae gives rise to a question: how is it that the Pelopid king seems to be under the protection of *two* male deities, Poseidon and Hermes? The answer is, I suggest, quite simple: Hermes was not, strictly speaking, a Pelopid deity at all, but a god represented by the male line of a dynasty whom the Pelopids had supplanted, possibly in Asia Minor, but whose deity they added to their own Poseidon. In the Odyssey, Hermes is found on Circe's isle, and he is the messenger to Calypso. It was suggested at the beginning of Chapter III that Circe and Calypso are really detached aspects of Penelope, a figure of very ancient epic whom the Olympian revolution has completely transformed. The demonstration of this must await another occasion, but it seems most probable that Hermes belongs to the oldest matrilineal dynasties[95].

The Homeric *Hymn to Hermes,* being a product of the Olympian revolution, is careful to avoid touching on these connections. Nevertheless, it cannot disguise the opposition between Hermes and the chthonic world on the one side and that of Apollo and the sun-god on the other. In the *Hymn* the relations between the two gods are treated with a delightful humour which is designed to reduce the proportions of the antagonism between them.

least some deities of Asia Minor, who, as we saw in the case of Chrysaor, may partake of the nature of both Poseidon and Zeus, we may yet recall that Menelaos, by marrying Helen, had, as Proteus told him in the Odyssey, become the son-in-law of Zeus. The prestige of the cult represented by the *potnia meter* was very high, and the authority of the king's sceptre will have been regarded as *properly* derivative from Zeus, the divinity to whom the queen stood so close. Hermes, however, seems to be peculiarly associated with male rulers, even when they are under the patronage of a second deity. Pelops himself is related not only to Poseidon but to Hermes, Perseus to Athena and Hermes, and, apparently, Minos also to Hermes (Paus. 8.53.2). See below in main text. As to the sceptre itself, *cf.* de Waele, *op. cit.,* p. 119: 'the sceptre must have been originally an *independent staff,* a staff made by its bearer to a kind of protecting deity and bearer of a special magic power.'

[94] To expound in full Hermes' connection with the concepts associated with Asiatic shamanism would take us too far afield. I hope to supplement the observations made in this chapter by others in a later work.

[95] The Perseids were presumably once matrilineal; there are signs even of a connection of Athena with fertility.

Hermes himself is represented as anxious to enter into the Olympian world: βέλτερον he says,

> βέλτερον ἤματα πάντα μετ' ἀθανάτοις ὀαρίζειν
> πλούσιον ἀφνειὸν πολυλήϊον ἢ κατὰ δῶμα
> ἄντρῳ ἐν ἠερόεντι θαάσσεμεν ...[96]

'It is better to converse all one's days with the immortals, rich and wealthy with many cornfields, than to sit at home in a shadowy cave.'

But he *had* stolen the cattle of the sun god, and his home (like Calypso's) *was* a cave[97]. The *Hymn* does not allude to the decisive fact that Hermes was the conductor of souls. His enmity to Apollo is turned into the mischievousness of an incurable, but pleasing, trickster. This is at least in part the device of a poet who sought to reconcile to the Olympian world a deity whose nature was in its essence hostile to it. Whether Hermes' journey with the cattle over sandy seashores and rocky hills, before he returned to the cave and crept into his swaddling clothes again, is really derived from the flight of the shaman over wild landscapes and seas is a question we cannot enter into here, if indeed it admits of a definite answer. Yet in the *Hymn* Hermes shows himself to possess the shaman's gift of recitation (418 ff.) and the substance of his recital (427 ff.) is precisely that of the shaman's. Moreover, his capacity to change his size is one that is attributed to shamans[98] and in art his sandals are winged for flight.

It is certainly clear that Hermes and the sun once represented two spiritual worlds which were at issue with each other, the chthonic and the celestial. Tantalus is said to have declared himself against the divinity of the sun, by announcing it to be a mass of red-hot iron[99], but found it possible for certain men to have intercourse with gods. Apollo and the Olympians represent, in the later world of the Homeric *Hymn*, the conventional religion of men of ordinary ambitions: one can converse happily with the immortals if one is rich and owns many cornfields. In a world dominated by a celestial shamanism the great cleavage is between the two lower worlds (this world and the underworld) on the one hand and the upper world on the other[100]. Hermes,

---

[96] 170 ff.

[97] A fact which bears witness to his very great antiquity.

[98] *E. g.* by the shaman's becoming an insect in order to pass through a small aperture, as does Hermes in the *Hymn* (though without becoming an insect).

[99] Diels, *Frag. d. Vorsokr.* Anaxagoras, A. 20 a = Schol. Pindar, *Ol.* 1.97.

[100] See Ulla Johansen, *Die Ornamentik der Jakuten* (Museum für Völkerkunde und Vorgeschichte, Hamburg, 1954), pp. 11 f.

who wishes to live in the middle world but dwells in a cave, is clearly a power from the world of chthonic shamanism.

IV

The matrilineal clans were subjected to attack from two opposite quarters. The one attack arose from a development within the cult of Ares, himself a god of possession or of ecstasy, who probably belonged to an earlier stratum than Poseidon. The other attack came, less violently and by way as much of dynastic marriage as of direct force, from Athena. Athena was apparently, at any rate in Late Mycenaean times, no goddess of ecstasy[101]. She was also a patrilineal deity. Homer recognizes her as a protagonist of the individual reason in the face of collective emotion, but other evidence suggests that she had begun to show an aspect of rationality before the end of the Mycenaean age. In order to understand Athena's position as a goddess so different from all other Mycenaean goddesses, we must study her in connection with Perseus and with Bellerophon.

When Perseus arrives in the island of Seriphos, he is under the protection of two deities, Athena and Hermes. Now we have already seen reason to connect Hermes, as Psychagogos, with shamanism, because it is an especial function of shamans to conduct the souls of the dead to their next abode. Hermes, moreover, gave the sceptre to 'Pelops', whom we have seen to be deeply embedded in shamanist legend, though more obviously so through the power of Poseidon. Perseus, however, once he has left Seriphos and has established himself on the Greek mainland, does not appear as a religious or magical, but as a military and political figure. Yet the story of his visits to the Phorkides and the nymphs and of the help they gave him, his journeys that needed winged sandals and the cap of darkness, are very strongly suggestive of shamanism, of which invisible, that is, spiritual, journeys, in which the shaman encounters dangers which he overcomes with the aid of supernatural helpers, are eminently characteristic[102].

The 'cap of darkness' would seem without doubt to be the shaman's cap. Miss Czaplicka writes: 'Shashkoff enumerates the following items as indis-

---

[101] At one time however Athena too was a shamanist deity. See below in this chapter, § VI ad finem.

[102] See K. Meuli, 'Scythica', in Hermes, 70, 1935, especially pp. 169 ff.

pensable to the shaman's dress all over Siberia—the coat, the mask, the cap, and the copper or iron plate on the breast. The Samoyed *tadibey* (shamans) substitute for the mask a handkerchief tied over the eyes, so that they can penetrate into the spirit-world by their inner sight...'[103] Perseus' cap of darkness was given to him by spirit beings. Miss Czaplicka tells us: 'In his description of the Tungus shaman's garment, Gmelin relates how the shaman whom he saw had no cap because the old one was burnt and the spirits would not grant him a new one'[104]. Nioradze writes[105] that among the Yakuts a shaman must, at his consecration, see his guardian spirit in a dream, and receive from him the command to make himself a hat. Cap and mask seem occasionally to be combined among modern shamans[106], and the name given to Perseus' cap shows that, if it rendered its wearer invisible, it also covered the eyes. This duality of function in some of the accessories of a shaman, namely that they should both aid the spiritual sight of the shaman and also protect him, will come to our attention again.

The *kibisis* or wallet with which Perseus was also equipped for his journey is not regularly recorded as an accessory of modern shamans, although occasionally such bags are mentioned. An object very closely resembling it (as depicted in vase-paintings) appears on Akkadian seals with a shamanist subject[107]. Nioradze refers[108] to the iron replica of a purse or bag to be

---

[103] *Aboriginal Siberia*, p. 203. Miss Czaplicka adds, 'These four accessories... are worn by the Neo-Siberians only, since among the Palaeo-Siberians the dress is much less complicated.'

[104] *op. cit.*, p. 205.

[105] *op. cit.*, p. 59.

[106] Czaplicka, *Abor. Sib.*, p. 226.

[107] See, for instance, H. Frankfort, *Cylinder Seals* (London, 1939), Pl. XIX f., where it is carried by the man-headed lion, and Pl. XXIV h, where it appears immediately below the ascending bird on the right. As far as I know, the subjects of these seals, and the myth of Etana, have not yet been recognised as related to shamanism; I hope to deal with them in a second work. About the second of the two seals named I do not think an informed scholar would have any doubt: it is a classical yogic-shamanist scene (the lions taking the place of the serpent). This is not the place in which to enter at length into the nature of the bag, but I would draw attention to the 'life-water bag' which is in the possession of Ereshkigal, the Sumerian and Babylonian queen of the underworld (S. H. Hooke, *Middle Eastern Mythology*, Pelican, 1963, p. 40), and to a scene (Hooke, *Ibid.*, plate 10, from the Mansell Collection) in which two divinities, standing on either side of a stylised Tree of Life, are apparently squeezing drops of water over the Tree out of sponges which they have dipped in the bags which they are carrying. The Tree of Life is intimately connected with shamanism and the bags

found among the objects hung upon a shaman's belt. Whether the 'adamantine sickle' was originally part of the legend is doubtful. G. Loeschke[109] remarks that in archaic representations Perseus frequently carries no weapon at all, a statement which corresponds to my own observations of the British Museum's black-figured vases (except that I would substitute 'sometimes' for 'frequently'). He adds that when he carries a weapon in archaic art, it is a sword, and points out that this corresponds to Hesiodic tradition. Loeschke's statement that the *harpe* is found only in fourth century art is mistaken: K. Schauenburg[110] shows that it had already appeared in archaic times. The *harpe* usually has the shape of a sickle but later sometimes becomes a pointed staff with a hook at the side, resembling an elephant-goad. Something like a sickle-shaped *harpe* is carried by certain divine beings in scenes on Akkadian seals[111]. In this connection we may notice that Miss Czaplicka records[112] an observation made among the Tartars of Chern, that the shaman used two crutches, of which one was supposed to be a horse, while the other was a crook. The latter might have been described as a *harpe* in ancient Greek if its purpose had been to catch spirits as the modern shaman sometimes does with his drum. In this connection we should certainly not overlook the 'hooked rays' of the spirit beings of Tibetan lamaist cosmology[113]. It is at least far from certain that the *harpe* is simply a weapon for beheading Medusa.

Lastly, there is the brazen shield into which Perseus looked when he slew

---

are of the same characteristic shape. Surely only water of life would be poured ritually by deities over the Tree of Life.

[108] *op. cit.*, pp. 67 f. Hesiod, *Scut.*, 223 f., however, seems to suggest that the *kibisis* was the belt. Vase paintings, on the other hand, very frequently show Perseus carrying a bag or satchel slung over his shoulder on a strap.

[109] *Archäologische Zeitschrift*, 1881, 30.

[110] *Perseus in der Kunst des Altertums* (Bonn, 1960), pp. 121 f.

[111] e.g. The Akkadian 'saw of decision', Frankfort, *op. cit.*, Pl. XVIII k (and elsewhere), and the curved stick from which hangs the plant of life, carried by a divinity, *ibid.*, Pl. XXIII d. The 'saw of decision' seems to be toothed on its outside edge, and according to Schauenburg the *harpe* is occasionally toothed but apparently on its inside edge. In Hesiod, *Theog.* 175, 180, Gaia gave Kronos a ἅρπην καρχαρόδοντα. Schauenburg (*op. cit.*, p. 123) is uncertain about the origin of the *harpe*.

[112] *op. cit.*, p. 219.

[113] These 'hooked rays' are the saving grace or hook of salvation with which the compassionate powers catch hold of the soul of a dead man to save him from the dangers of the *Bardo*. See W. Y. Evans-Wentz, *The Tibetan Book of the Dead*, 3rd. Ed. (Oxford, 1957), pp. 109 (with note), 110, 112, 114, 117—8, 130.

the mortal Gorgon. I am most grateful to Dr. E. J. Lindgren for drawing my attention to a formerly unknown type of shaman dress which she discovered in north-western Manchuria and described in an article published in 1935[114]. Dr. Lindgren examined several dresses of shamans and shamanesses of the Dagur, Solon and Numinchen tribes. One of the striking features of these dresses is that they have numerous bronze Chinese mirrors, which overlap like scales, representing armour[115]. Dr. Lindgren refers to Nioradze[116], who says that the mirror on the breast of the Goldi shaman 'als Abwehrschild für die Feinde dient' and that the Yakuts refer to the whole shaman dress as a cuirass[117]. C. A. S. Williams (to whom Dr. Lindgren also refers) says[118] that the earliest mirrors in China were circular and made of polished bronze mixed with an alloy. On the back they were beautifully chased with decorated *motifs,* of which some were probably introduced from the Graeco-Bactrian kingdom in the second century B. C. Ancient mirrors, according to Williams, are held 'to have magic power to protect their owners from evil . . . They are believed to make hidden spirits visible, and to reveal the secrets of futurity'. Evil spirits approaching will be frightened away, for they will see themselves reflected in them. When Perseus looked with averted gaze into a bronze shield in which the image of the Gorgon was reflected, one cannot doubt that the 'bronze shield' was a mirror of the kind which hangs upon some shaman dresses to ward off its wearer's spiritual foes[119].

'None but a shaman', writes Miss Czaplicka, 'can fly or be represented by wings'[120]. Not only does Perseus wear winged sandals, and frequently a winged cap: on a black-figured Etruscan vase[121], heavy with symbolism, he

---

[114] 'The Shaman Dress of the Dagurs, Solons and Numinchens in N. W. Manchuria', *Geografiska Annaler,* 1935, published by Svenska Sällskapet för Antropologi och Geografi. One of the dresses, together with the other parts of the complete apparel, is now in the University Museum of Archaeology and Ethnology at Cambridge. I should add that Dr. Lindgren has no responsibility for the conclusions which I have suggested may be drawn from her work.

[115] *Ibid.,* p. 372.

[116] *Der Schamanismus* etc., p. 64.

[117] *Ibid.,* p. 85. Is the Minoan 'cuirass' something of this kind?

[118] *Outlines of Chinese Symbolism and Art Motives* (Shanghai, 1932), pp. 272—5.

[119] Pls. XVI and XVII.

[120] *Abor. Sib.,* p. 217. See also Nioradze, *op. cit.,* pp. 84, 90.

[121] Brit. Mus. cat., B. 63. Those interested in the evidence for shamanism among the Etruscans may consult W. Muster, 'Der Schamanismus bei den Etruskern', in *Frühgeschichte und Sprachwissenschaft,* ed. W. Brandenstein (Vienna, 1948). Muster is wrong

has a bird on each foot and great wings springing from his hips. We have
already drawn attention[122] to the similarity of shape in a form of the head
of Hermes' *kerykeion* to the head of the staff carried by shamans in parts
of the Yenisei basin.

If we turn to Medusa herself, whom we have held to be a shamaness, we
notice that, according to Apollodorus, the Gorgons had great tusks like
those of wild boars. Dr. Lindgren[123] mentions that on the dress of a Solon
shamaness a large boar's tusk was attached to each shoulder, and the costume
of a Dagur shamaness had 'a large tooth (probably the same kind) on each
side of the breast.' From the body of the dead Medusa sprang Pegasus. On
the former of these two dresses, says Dr. Lindgren, 'on each side of the...
skirt, hangs a brass animal (a horse?) *[sic]* facing towards the centre. An
iron stirrup about one inch high hangs from the...collar on each side.' That
a common image and conception lies behind these features of the dress of
these shamanesses and behind the description of the Gorgons seems to be very
probable: the parallel is so remarkable that it is scarcely acceptable as
coincidence. The reader will recall the connection which we have seen
between the masked dancer at the festival of Kali[124] and the description of
Medusa in Greek literature.

The cessation of magical, shamanistic, activities in Perseus as soon as he
arrives on the Greek mainland is striking. The reason for it is probably that
the shamanism once practised by the dynasty to which Perseus belonged was
already dying out when the proto-Perseids invaded Greece[125]: it had perhaps
become a matter of tradition rather than of current usage. The politico-
military outlook of Perseus, indicated by the legend of his development and
fortification of Mycenae while himself (as it appears) in occupation of
Tiryns, could hardly, as we have already remarked, consort with the mental
and psychical constitution of a true shaman. Athena rather than Hermes
was becoming the distinctive Perseid deity. There is, if one consider the
account in Apollodorus[126] of Perseus' actions after he had turned Polydektes

---

in stating that the 'Zerreissung' of the shaman (candidate) takes place when he is in
a state of 'Erregung'. It takes place when he is in a kind of coma.

[122] pp. 149 ff.

[123] *loc. cit.*, p. 373.

[124] Pl. XV. See pp. 151 f.

[125] It is not, I would suggest, necessary to hold that the Perseus who occupied Seriphos
was the same man as the Perseus who held Tiryns and 'founded' Mycenae. The shamanist legends attach to the period of residence in Seriphos.

[126] 2.4.3.

and his friends to stone with the Gorgon's head, a distinct indication of the abandonment of shamanism and of a decision to follow the way of Athena. Apollodorus' words are as follows: 'Having appointed Dictys king of Seriphos, he gave back the sandals and the wallet and the caps to Hermes, but the Gorgon's head he gave to Athena. Hermes restored the aforesaid things to the nymphs and Athena inserted the Gorgon's head in the middle of her shield. But it is alleged by some that Medusa was beheaded for Athena's sake; and they say that the Gorgon was fain to match herself with the goddess even in beauty[127].' The prize of the expedition is awarded, not to Hermes, but to Athena. Why? If Hermes had helped him to slay Medusa, surely the grateful *protégé* would have given him, the god, the recognition due. But although Hermes had given him 'an adamantine sickle', with which he flew over land and sea, it was Athena alone who guided his hand when he struck Medusa. The last sentence of the passage quoted tells us why: Medusa, who alone of the Gorgons was a mortal woman, was Athena's enemy and rival, because, though a mortal, she could also embody a divinity. No woman embodied Athena: she was, as the goddess of the male Perseid line, the patroness only of its secular ambitions.

The rest of the myth is an adventure on the spiritual, psychical, or imaginative plane. Medusa, in spite of being a mortal, is, in Apollodorus' account, found by Perseus with the two immortal Gorgons on the shore of Okeanos, that is to say, at the end of the world. After killing her he flies to Ethiopia. Why should a mortal woman be found in such a place and in such company? The tradition of the Argives that Medusa was buried in their city, and Perseus' activities on the mainland both point to a 'Medusa' having been the princess of Argos. Towards her, the embodiment of the divinity of another cult, Athena was, as we have said, deeply hostile. The flight to Okeanos, the Gorgons and Ethiopia with the aid of Hermes and the nymphs has, it would seem, nothing to do with Perseus on the Greek mainland but is a relic of the dynasty's pre-Grecian and, as I suggest, shamanist past[128]. Indeed, it seems to be implied in the passage we have quoted that Perseus,

---

[127] Frazer's translation.

[128] There is a parallel in the case of Pelops: there is the Pelops who was dismembered and offered at a banquet to the gods, and there is the Pelops who slew Oinomaos and took to himself the kingdom of Pisa. We have already noticed the tradition that a Pelops was cast out of the company of the gods. The Pelopidae, however, were immediately re-absorbed into the religious matrilineal tradition, which they found in Greece when they arrived there.

when he returned the winged sandals, cap and wallet to Hermes, had no further use for them: Athena was the goddess of his choice, for he was wrestling, not with the principalities and powers of the spirit, but with the flesh and blood of this world. There is therefore possibly a deeper reason why the mortal Medusa was found with the Gorgons on the shore of Okeanos. Where Medusa was, there surely her attendant Gorgons were to be found. A Medusa, however, was, we think, princess of Argos, and there, in Argos, should her two spiritual companions have been: they seem to form a 'triad'. It may be a mark of the unwillingness of the later Greeks to accept the existence of a mortal woman with supernatural powers or ghostly companions as the ruler of a known city of the Greek mainland that Medusa, the shamaness, is banished to the shore of Okeanos, and that after she is slain, Perseus appears in the Argolid in the worldly *rôle* of a military invader. As we suggested at the beginning of Chapter III, magic was apparently thrust outward to the untravelled edges of the world in order that at the centre, where men lived, they should lead ordered lives undisturbed by present knowledge of the matrilineal tradition or of human beings with divine powers and divine associates who had been ascendent where now the *polis* was beginning to arise.

The Perseids who followed Perseus at Tiryns and Mycenae will have had no interest in restoring in their own persons the true function of Hermes as conductor of souls. Gods of possession or ecstasy were incompatible with the *rôle* the Perseids chose to play (or so the myths now suggest), and Hermes sank to the status of a deity of the second rank. It is for this reason that Athena became the dominant Perseid deity.

At this point we may return to Medusa with a question which we have passed over, no doubt to the reader's dissatisfaction: why was Medusa, the mortal princess, confused with the Gorgon and associated with two other, immortal, Gorgons? We have already given the answer: Medusa was a shamaness, as Perseus was by dynastic tradition a shaman. He had to meet her on the plane of the spirit as well as on that of the body. The story that Pegasus sprang from her body when her head was struck off shows this: the winged steed of the spirit must be immortal, and when the shaman dies it presumably escapes from the shell of the body, bearing the shaman's spirit with it. The horse that appears in the names 'Hippodameia' and 'Nikippe' is, as will shortly appear from the parallel with Athena Hippia, this same winged horse of the spirit. The implication is then inevitable: some princesses were shamanesses, and they appear to have sometimes had two spiritual companions. Indeed, Nikippe, daughter of Pelops, had a daughter Medusa[129]. Why they were called 'the horse-tamer' or 'victorious over the horse' will appear from the part played by Athena in the story of Bellorophon, which is spoken of immediately below. It may be that the active shamanizing, as distinct from ritual observance, was carried out more by the women than by the men[130]. This would be consistent with the dynasty's matrilineality. Athena, however, was different: she, not Hermes, guided Perseus' hand when he struck, because the hero had turned his back on shamanism. He struck in the cause of descent from father to son; of politics, not religion; of rationality, not divination or possession. So, at least with the aftersight of history, must we understand Perseus.

V

Yet at one time, it is clear, Athena herself had been a patroness of shamans. Her 'many-tasselled' aegis is strongly reminiescent of the fringed shaman's coat[131]. In *Eumenides* 403 f. Athena flies, without wings, upon her aegis, a clear tradition of ecstatic flight. She would never have accompanied Perseus, with Hermes, on his flight to seek out the Gorgons had she not once had a place in the shaman's world. Most clearly, however, does this appear in Pindar's account of the story of Bellerophon[132]. There, Athena actually gives Bellerophon the bit with the golden headstall with which he is to control Pegasus. The story of Bellerophon's connection with Pegasus, like that of Perseus' flight with Athena and Hermes, has its setting outside the Greek mainland, if we may accept the testimony of Homer[133] and Apollodorus[134]. Nevertheless, the existence of Athena Chalinitis at Corinth[135] shows that she was known in Greece in her connection with the winged horse.

---

[129] Apollod. 2.4.5.

[130] Nioradze, *op. cit.*, pp. 51 ff., holds that the original shamans were women, and that as long as the practice of shamanism was confined mainly to the family, the women continued to be the principal shamans. Shamanism became a predominently male function when professional shamanism arose. The matrilineality of the Pelopids and Danaids is perhaps some confirmation of the correctness of Nioradze's view. Nioradze's thesis seems, however, not to apply to all tribes.

[131] See Nioradze, *op. cit.*, p. 60.

[132] *Ol.* XIII, 63 (89)–92 (131).   [133] *Il.* 6.168.   [134] 2.3.1–2.

[135] *Paus.* 2.4.1. See also Soph. O. C. 1070 for the conjunction of Athena Hippia and Poseidon. The evidence for the cult of Athena Chalinitis and A. Hippia, and for the con-

Pindar's account is of quite extraordinary interest, for it is nothing less than a description of the process by which Bellerophon became a shaman, and agrees very closely with the descriptions of the candidature of modern shamans which we have quoted in this chapter. Pindar speaks of the candidate's sufferings: in his desire to bridle Pegasus he suffered much (ἦ πολλ' ... Πάγασον ζεῦξαι ποθέων ἔπαθεν), until Pallas gave him the bit with the golden headstall. These sufferings are, like the shaman candidate's (pp. 137 ff.), experienced in a state of apparent insensibility (κνώσσοντι). He lies unconscious at the altar of the goddess, and she appears to him as a real vision with the words, 'Art thou sleeping, Aeolid king?' The bit, she says, is a charm for the horse. Her words wake him from the darkness of his slumbers: he springs to his feet. Pindar seems to know quite well that the world of these events is a spiritual one, for the bit becomes in line 78 (111) 'the spirit-taming gold' (δαμασίφρονα χρυσόν): indeed it is no piece of metal, but a philtre (68), a drug or gentle charm (85). A philtre or a *pharmakon* is something that works upon the inner constitution, whether physiological or psychic. To an external mechanical device the word is quite inappropriate. Bellerophon relates his vision to a seer, the son of Koiranos (Polyidos). The seer bids him obey the vision, and, when he has sacrificed a bull to the Earthshaker, raise an altar to Athena Hippia. Poseidon, it will be recalled, was the father of the winged horse, and according to the scholia on 69 (98 and 99) he was also the father of Bellerophon. Bellerophon bridles Pegasus, and mounts upon his back. When he does so, he is χαλκωθείς, 'covered with bronze'. What does this mean? I would suggest that it means that Bellerophon is now invested as a shaman with a shaman's coat, possibly laden with bronze mirrors. He has bridled the steed of the spirit and can ride it: he is a shaman, and puts on the 'cuirass'[136] which is the mark of his office. The seer, the son of Koiranos, is plainly the older shaman who, as we know from modern accounts[137], performs the induction of the new shaman. And what does Bellerophon do now? Surely the scholion which interprets ἐνόπλια ἔπαιζεν as 'he performed an armed dance' is essentially right: the climax of a shaman's performance is his dance[138], and so it was with Bellerophon.

---

junction of A. Hippia with Poseidon, has been collected and set out by N. Yalouris in 'Athena als Herrin der Pferde', *Mus. Helv.*, 7 (1950). This is a valuable article, although I cannot accept the author's view of the original nature of the cult.

[136] See pp. 162 f.

[137] See, for instance, Findeisen, *op. cit.*, Chapter VI, *Shamanistische Weihen*.

[138] ἐνόπλια is apposite: the shaman's coat, hung about with mirrors and other metal

On the back of his steed Bellerophon then mounts on high and slays his spiritual enemies[139]. The words of Eliade, commenting on *Rigveda* X. 136, are highly relevant: 'Rappelons-nous que le tambour des chamans altaïques est appelé "cheval" et que chez les Bouriates . . . le bâton à tête de cheval, qui d'ailleurs porte le nom "cheval", joue un rôle important. L'extase provoquée par les sons du tambour ou par la danse à califourchon sur un bâton à tête de cheval (sorte de hobby-horse), est assimilée à une chevauchée fantastique dans les cieux. Comme nous le verrons, chez certaines populations non-aryennes de l'Inde le magicien utilise encore aujourd'hui un cheval de bois ou un bâton à tête de cheval pour exécuter sa danse extatique'[140].

There is a curious ambiguity about the relations of Athena and Poseidon. On the Acropolis of Athens they share the Erechtheum, yet legend makes them rivals for the soil of Attica. Perseus, whose patroness was Athena, showed a marked hostility to the worshippers of Poseidon. Yet the association of the two deities in Pindar's account of the Bellerophon myth seems inconsistent with rivalry: the son of Poseidon accepts the aid of Athena in mastering Pegasus, and is bidden raise an altar to Athena Hippia and to sacrifice to Poseidon[141]. On the other hand, the intimate part played here by Athena in the process of shamanising seems to deny all that we know of her in later mainland Greece. At first sight these are contradictions. Yet their resolution lies before us. It is to be found in the very fact recorded by Pindar, that Athena gave Bellerophon the bit and bridle that enabled him to control Pegasus. We have observed already that Athena shows signs of once having been a shamanist deity. In the form of shamanism here presented to us there are two elements, contrary moments within the outwardly single manifesta-

---

objects, may easily weigh 40 lbs. Yet he succeeds in dancing in it (ἔπαιζεν), a feat which has astonished modern observers of the Siberian shaman dancing. Lest any persistent 'realist', oblivious of a winged horse and flight through the air, should argue that Bellerophon's armed dance is simply a warrior's dance before battle, it should be pointed out that there is, so far as I know, no evidence that such dances were performed by single warriors, or by horsemen. On the former point see K. Latte, *De Saltationibus Graecorum* (Giessen, 1913), cap. III.

[139] In *Iliad* 6.155 and 190 Bellerophon is called ἀμύμων. It would be worth investigating the use of this adjective with the object of discovering whether it is used especially, or exclusively, of men who were regarded as shamans or at least as possessed of supernatural powers.

[140] Eliade, *op. cit.*, p. 366.

[141] Sophocles, *O. C.* 1070 ff., makes the cults of Athena Hippia and Poseidon characteristic of the Athenians under Theseus.

tion. One is typified by Pegasus, whose sire is Poseidon: the winged horse is the surge of ecstasy, the overpowering force that obliterates the ordinary consciousness. It is a profound psychosomatic disturbance, a winged horse, the wild and powerful thrust of whose hoofs and beating wings imperatively demands the means and the knowledge to control it. This, the bit and the bridle brought by Athena, is the other moment. The bridling of Pegasus must in fact be the act of articulate shamanizing, for Pindar makes the presentation of the bit and bridle end the sleep and sufferings of Bellerophon. The trance-like condition and the acute suffering of candidates for the vocation of shaman precede, among modern shamans, the act of shamanizing, which is reported to bring relief[142]. Some shamans have actually declared that, had they not at this stage been able to shamanize, they would have died[143]. Strange as shamanizing in all its forms may appear, it is nonetheless a kind of articulate expression. It is to this extent a form of rationality, an unfamiliar rationality which shows itself in an ecstasy in which the shaman, following the prescribed forms he has been taught, is never the helpless victim of forces beyond his control. In fact it is rationality in its true aspect, that is, seen against a background of inarticulate power, making two moments, as we have said, in a single manifestation. Eliade[144] emphasizes the remarkable control by shamans of their physical movements in ecstasy, a control particularly noticeable when the ecstatic dance is performed in a crowded *yurt*, and draws attention to their altogether exceptional powers of concentration, large vocabulary and knowledge of poetry. Athena therefore first meets us in Greece wearing her aegis, the fringed coat of the shaman, not as an independent embodiment of rationality, but as a part of the complex of shamanism, in which she provides the possibility of controlling by art and knowledge the primitive inarticulate forces which are called by the name of Poseidon[145]. She teaches the shaman to ride his horse.

[142] Eliade, *op. cit.*, pp. 38 ff.; Findeisen, *op. cit.*, p. 57.

[143] Cf. Czaplicka, *Abor. Sib.*, p. 181.

[144] *Op. cit.*, pp. 40 ff.

[145] This division of the forces at work upon a shaman into superior and inferior influences, of which the latter may be painful or distressing to the shaman, is in fact to be found in modern reports. Miss Czaplicka, *Abor. Sib.*, page 181, quotes the case of a shaman who, when he began to shamanize, saw two spirit protectors, one of whom bade him distrust the other, which had a man's head but a bird's body. Among the Yakuts there may be three kinds of spirits at work upon the shaman, of which, however, one is of minor importance. Of the other two, one, which regularly takes an animal form, as

Bellerophon, like Tantalus and other shamans of Asiatic tradition[146], came into conflict with the supreme deity. In *Iliad* 6. 200 Bellerophon is hated by all the gods. Pindar, *Isthmian* (VI) VII, 64 (44) ff. is more explicit:

ὅ τοι πτερόεις ἔρριψε Πάγασος
δεσπόταν ἐθέλοντ' ἐς οὐρανοῦ σταθμούς
ἐλθεῖν μεθ' ὁμάγυριν Βελλεροφόνταν
Ζηνός.

'But the winged Pegasus threw his master Bellerophon, who desired to reach the folds of heaven, to enter into the assembly of Zeus.'

These two passages are very strong corroborative evidence that in Bellerophon we see the archetypal figure of a famous line of shamans[147]. The desire to be 'with the gods' is a characteristic description of the aim of a shaman, who alone of men can converse with spirits. Equally typical is the shaman's rejection and humiliation[148]. Indeed, the wandering on the Ἀλήιον πεδίον may be a reminiscence of the shaman's narrative of his flight over a wild landscape.

L. Malten believes that the myth dates from the end of the third or from the second millennium B. C.[149]. He comes to no absolutely definite conclusion about Bellerophon's original nature, but is inclined to equate him with a divine lightening-bearing figure associated with a winged horse on some Mesopotamian seals. He actually thinks that the horse was, or may have been, an incarnation of the flash of lightening. Malten, writing in 1925, was still under the influence of the school of thought which tried to interpret religious symbolism and myths in terms of natural forces. It was not then widely perceived that ancient religion had, at any rate in its nascent and vital stages, an inner meaning, based upon experiences accessible only to a few, experiences which found symbolic expression in a macrocosmic imagery which the multitude might be expected to understand. Scholars of the last two or more

---

dog, bear, elk, bull or stallion, may be harmful to the shaman, though at the same time an aspect of his power. The third kind of spirit is constantly helpful; it defends and advises him (pp. 182 f.).

[146] See pp. 142 ff.

[147] See L. Malten, 'Bellerophontes', *Jahrbuch des deutschen archäolog. Instituts*, 40 (1925), p. 126, for the names Bellerophon, Glaukos, Hippolochos, as hereditary in Lycia and Caria.

[148] But sometimes the shaman triumphed: see p. 143 for the first Buryat shaman, who forced, or tricked, God into releasing a girl's soul.

[149] *Ibid.* p. 156.

generations have often only observed the latter aspect of spiritual and religious myths, a very natural limitation of their view, for the myths were widely so understood in antiquity itself. They have therefore tended to interpret one symbol in terms of another, as does Malten in seeing in the winged horse an embodiment of the lightening-flash. Both are in fact symbols, but their interpretation must await another occasion.

It would be wrong to derive 'the gods' solely from shamanist experience, but it is certain that such experience played a very important, if not an essential, part in the development of certain of them. It was an extraordinary experience, charged with numinous presences and deeply affecting the constitution and mentality of those who underwent it. In it the forces which later crystallised into traditional objective shapes such as Athena and Poseidon played directly, without any mediation, upon the shaman's exposed being. The combined training and experience in some cases was accompanied by the development of abnormal powers, powers upon which the whole standing of the shamans was based. While no doubt the lesser shaman used his wits as best he could, the specific capacities with which the greater shamans were endowed were highly prized by the ambitious among them. The acquisition of these powers[150] could, and in some cases evidently did, lead to great pretensions on the part of those who possessed them. The virtuosity of the shaman seemed independent of those more-than-human forces which had made him what he was: between them and him a gulf began to open, a process of mutual alienation which, with the aid of macrocosmic symbols, powerfully helped to generate the Olympian gods and to reduce mortals to a sense of the need for moderation and their dependence upon fate. An arduous experience, touched, it seems, with a light and knowledge not of this world, had been exploited in something like arrogance, so that what had once been vivid and palpable reality began to take on the fixed and distant outlines of a god.

Thus, as we see, I suggest, in the story of Perseus, Athena begins later to separate herself from the Poseidonian forces which called her into being, and becomes an independent power in her own right, directing not the obscure energies of the soul but the obvious warlike tendencies of the city-state. It is only after she has passed into this stage that she appears as the deity whom we all know, the rival, and indeed the enemy, of Poseidon and all he stood for, the goddess of organised warfare, and of the unity and

[150] See Findeisen's phrase quoted on p. 139.

skills of the *polis*. Yet her ancient relationship to the god was not wholly forgotten. In the thirteenth Olympian ode of Pindar we are present both at the birth of a goddess and at the revelation of a struggle within the soul of a man as heavy with destiny as any of which history preserves a record.

Appendix I

Helen

Both Helen and Artemis were, as M. P. Nilsson has shown, connected with a tree-cult. There is indeed at times so close a relationship between the two goddesses that it amounts to something like identity[1]. Plutarch[2] says that Theseus carried off Helen, while still a child, when she was dancing in the temple of Artemis Orthia at Sparta. Menelaus had a spring and a plane-tree near Kaphyae in Arcadia[3]. The name of Menelaus surely implies the former presence of Helen here, and the tree reinforces the inference. Pausanias mentions no memorial of Helen, but says that on a neighbouring hill Artemis was worshipped every year. Furthermore, 'about a stade' from Kaphyae— that is, only 200 yards away—there was a grove and sanctuary of Artemis Hanged[4]. The antiquarian refers to no other shrines or deities in this vicinity. The conclusion that Artemis Hanged may have had a close affinity to the hanged Helen Dendritis (who had a temple on Rhodes[5]) is reasonable. In the light of this apparent close relationship we may understand the fact that while Clytaemnestra's daughter is Iphigeneia, Clytaemnestra herself is the 'sister' of Helen. Iphigeneia is so closely associated with Artemis that the name is to be recognized as a name of Artemis herself. Pausanias indeed tells of a temple at Argos which was said to have been dedicated to Eileithyia by Helen after she herself had given birth to Iphigeneia[6]. In the O d y s s e y [7] Helen coming out of her chamber is compared to golden-arrowed Artemis. At Sparta a temple of Helen's companions, the Dioscuri, and the Charites, stood close to one of Eileithyia, Apollo Karneios, and Artemis Hegemache[8]. It is clear beyond, I think, reasonable dispute that Helen and Artemis were, at times, barely, if at all, distinguished. There is some suggestion that Helen was the mother of Artemis, though this is implicitly denied, and even almost inverted, by Plutarch's story.

Before we go further, one aspect of Helen should be touched upon in order

---

[1] This relationship is not suggested by Professor Nilsson.
[2] *Vita Thes.* 30, 31. Hyginus, *Fab.* 79, says she was carried off from a sacrifice to Artemis.
[3] Paus. 8.23.3.   [4] Ἀπαγχομένη. *Ibid.* 8.23.5.   [5] Paus. 3.19.10.
[6] Paus. 2.22.7.   [7] 4.121 f.   [8] Paus. 3.14.6.

that it may be seen in its proper setting. In the Odyssey[9], Helen, when she was in Egypt, is said to have received from Polydamna, the wife of Thon, a particular drug, which she cast into the wine. It banished, in him who drank it, sorrow and anger; no tear would trickle down his cheek all day long, not even if his mother and father had died, nor even if someone had slain his brother or his dear son. What, to begin with, was this drug?

A bell-shaped female idol from Gasi in Crete[10] wears above the forehead, on a fillet, three seed-heads which are, it seems, beyond doubt those of *Papaver somniferum*. The capsules are deeply incised, as for the extraction of the juice. This shows that the use of opium was known in the eastern Mediterranean in Minoan times, although we can give no name to the goddess. The cultivation of the opium-poppy and its association with religious centres is attested in early archaic Greece. Hesiod[11] calls Sicyon Mēkōnē, 'Poppy Town'. Pausanias[12] says there was a temple of Asklepios there with statues of Sleep and Dream; Kyllene was also named Mekone[13], but is presumably to be associated with Hermes, whose wand could put to sleep. Poppies are an attribute of Demeter in later art. The use of opium is thus not likely to have been restricted to the cult of Helen and is rather to be seen as an index of the importance generally attached to dreams.

Helen therefore shares with other deities a connection with another world than that of everyday reality, a world in which supernatural powers can communicate with human beings in dreams, or in which, through the medium of the drug, men can attain to an analogy of bliss[14]. In the case of Helen we

---

[9] 4.219 ff.

[10] Illustr. S. Marinatos, *Kreta und das mykenische Hellas* (Munich, 1959), p. 128–131. I do not quote the well-known gold ring from Mycenae, found by Schliemann on the site of a shaft-grave, in which a goddess seated beneath a tree holds three stems bearing supposed poppy seed-heads in her hand. Botanical observation makes me virtually certain that they are not poppy-heads but the seed-capsules of the water-lily *Nymphaea lotus,* or of some other water-lily or lotus.

[11] *Theog.* 536.

[12] 2.10.2.

[13] Pauly-Wissowa, *R. E.,* s. v. Μηκώνη.

[14] To believe that a drug-induced condition lay at the root of the cult of Helen would be a fundamental error. This essay does not seek to enter into the inner nature of the cult, though it may be said, briefly and vaguely, that it centred upon, or at least sought, experience of the transcendental. I hope to treat of the matter in the course of a larger work. The use of opium may be regarded as an accretion to the cult, or a degenerate extension of it to a wider public.

hear only of the use of opium (as we may assume the drug to have been) for inducing this latter condition.

Helen can grant immortal life to certain men. In a famous passage in the fourth book of the Odyssey[15] Menelaus tells Telemachus of the prophecy made to him by Proteus, the old Egyptian sea-god:

'For thee, divinely-nurtured Menelaus, it is not fated that thou shouldst die and meet thy fate in horse-breeding Argos, but that the immortals should send thee to the Elysian plain at the ends of the earth, where fair-haired Rhadamanthus dwells. There is life easiest for men; there is no snow or much hard weather nor any rain, but Ocean ever sends, to cool men, the breath of the shrill-whistling west wind. And this shall be because thou hast Helen and in their eyes[16] art the son-in-law of Zeus.'

The Elysian plain, to which the elect may pass without dying, is, as has long been made clear by Nilsson, a Minoan conception; it has nothing in common with Hades, the underworld of bloodless shades, to which, according to Greek religious ideas, all must go when they die.

Helen, as we have said, was worshipped in a tree-cult. An Egyptian painting[17] from a pillar in the tomb of Thutmosis (Thotmes) III gives a most remarkable illustration of the relation of a young prince to the goddess of the tree-cult. It shows the young king being suckled by the divine tree; from the lower branches appears a female breast, supported by a hand and arm which also issue from the tree. Here it is evidently not material nourishment that is imbibed. Thutmosis III belonged to the eighteenth dynasty, reigning from about 1501 to 1448 B.C. To prove the influence of either country in making the tree-cult popular and significant in the other world would be difficult, but it is worth remembering the connection of Helen and Menelaus with Egypt in view especially of the fact that there is no representation of the cult of a tree-goddess in Egyptian art before the eighteenth dynasty[18]. The great

---

[15] 4.561–9.

[16] i.e. in the eyes of the immortals.

[17] Arpag Mekhitarian, *Aegyptische Malerei* (Geneva, 1954), p. 38.

[18] Plutarch, *De Malign. Herod.*, 12, says that many honours were paid to Helen and to Menelaus in Egypt, but he is of course speaking of a later age. Herodotus, 2.112, speaks of the temple of the 'stranger Aphrodite' at Memphis. He judges her to be Helen, although some modern commentators have taken her to be Astarte (see F. Chapouthier, *Les Dioscures au Service d'une Déesse*, pp. 145 f.). The conclusion was probably not (in spite of Chapouthier's observations on συμβάλλομαι) an independent judgement by Herodotus, for the temple was said to be in the precinct of Proteus and Proteus' words in the passage from the fourth book of the Odyssey quoted above seem to suggest that

bulk of Egyptian objects found in Greece belong either to the eighteenth or to the twenty-sixth dynasties; that is, the two periods of lively intercourse between Egypt and Greece are from the 15th to the 13th centuries B. C. and again in the orientalising period from the middle of the 7th century B. C. The former period falls within the Mycenaean age. There is also the possibility of Egyptian influence on Mycenaean religion, for Crete might have acted as an intermediary in this case, if indeed a real influence of the one land on the other is represented here at all. It may well be, however, that the cult of the divine tree reached both countries from a third source[19].

Another painting from the same tomb shows a tree standing by a pool. From the tree an arm emerges, holding a jug, from which a liquid is poured into a cup held by the dead man. The liquid, being poured for a dead man, must symbolise, not abundance of ordinary physical nourishment but the means of sustaining life beyond death. There is evidently, both in the Egyptian goddess of the tree (here Isis) and in Helen, the power to give immortality.

Let us return to the myths about Helen. Helen is said to have been born as the result of the union of Leda with Zeus in the guise of a swan. Why did Zeus take the form of a swan on this occasion? The bird of Zeus is the eagle. The swan, however, although it later became the bird of Aphrodite (whose bird properly is the goose[20]), was transferred to her from Apollo[21]. If we may go by the symbol rather than the name, the father of Helen was not Zeus but Apollo. The substitution of Zeus' name for that of Apollo is in fact not at all unlikely: Apollodorus[22] in his account of the fate of Kallisto (who was

---

the attribution had already been made in archaic times. Why otherwise should the god know Helen so well and esteem her power so highly? Strabo XVII, p. 807, (cited by Chapouthier, *op. cit.*, p. 269, n. 5) refers to what is apparently the same temple of Aphrodite, who, he believes, was considered to be a Greek goddess. But some, he says, declared it to be the temple of Selene.

[19] The suckling of a young pharaoh is not a function of the tree-goddess only; the goddess Hathor is represented as performing this action in the shape of a cow. Nor was there any goddess who was exclusively a tree-goddess; this was simply one form in which a goddess might appear. Thus the goddess suckling Thutmosis III is Isis.

[20] R. Hampe, 'Das Parisurteil auf dem Elfenbeinkamm aus Sparta' in *Festschrift zum 60. Geburtstag von Bernhard Schweitzer (Stuttgart, 1954), p. 82:* 'Der Vogel ist . . . die Gans, wie sie als heiliges Tier der Aphrodite in der griechischen Bildkunst seit dem 7. Jh. häufig abgebildet wurde.'

[21] Erika Simon, *Die Geburt der Aphrodite* (Berlin, 1959), p. 34.

[22] 3.8.2.

an Arcadian form of Artemis), says that some authorities give Zeus, others
Apollo, as her ravisher[23]. The functions of Zeus and Apollo are at times so
alike that the two gods seem almost to merge into one another. In Aeschylus'
Eumenides[24] Apollo declares himself to be, in prophecy, the scrupulous spo-
kesman of Zeus. The lightening is normally flung by Zeus, but it was Apollo
who, when the Argonauts were sailing by night, shot a shaft of lightening
down into the sea[25]. Of the male gods, Apollo seems, after Zeus, to be most
at home on Olympus: the others indeed have plainly taken up residence there
under compulsion. These things are familiar, though we are accustomed to
think of the two gods as wholly distinct, as in classical times they were. There
were, however, occasions when they could be confused. It is therefore not
impossible for us to accept as the true tradition that Helen's father was
Apollo: indeed, the swan seems to show this unmistakably, for the swan was,
until, apparently, the fourth century, sacred to Apollo[26]. He was also, it
appears, her consort, or alternatively, she was at times identified with Leda,
for, in a curiously confused version of the story, Apollodorus[27] says that
Zeus, in the form of the swan, had intercourse with Helen, who laid an egg
which shepherds found and gave to Leda. She was thus her own mother, or,
more simply, the consort of the swan, of Apollo. It is nevertheless difficult
to eliminate Zeus wholly from the myth, and we are reminded of Laumonier's
statement that 'Les Zeus anatoliens ne se distinguent pas toujours nettement
d'Apollon'. The observation may be relevant here.

Helen, however, we have seen, was virtually identified with Artemis, and
Apollo and Artemis are traditionally brother and sister. Yet she was not like
Artemis only, for the same passage of Apollodorus quite clearly tells us that
she was another goddess: as Helen fled from the desirous swan, she turned
herself into a goose. The goose, we have already remarked, is the bird of
Aphrodite. There can be little doubt that we have here Apollo and Aphro-

---

[23] The passage in Apollodorus names Artemis, in addition to Zeus and Apollo, as the
deity given by some writers. This is clearly a late intrusion, the more obvious as such
because the text implies that a child was born of the union. The mention of Artemis
must be due to the later view of Artemis, and consequently of Kallisto, as a virgin,
who would never have allowed a male to approach her so closely. Kallisto's own
goddess, who is indeed she herself, is substituted.

[24] 616 ff.

[25] Apollod. 1.9.26.

[26] E. Simon, *Ibid*. According to Apollodorus, *Epit*. 3.23, Tenes was said by some to be the
son of Kyknos, Swan, and Prokleia, but others said he was the son of Apollo.

[27] 3.10.7.

dite. Helen then has a treble identity, as Helen, as Artemis or perhaps her mother, and as Aphrodite. This treble identity is in fact represented in another legend. Helen, according to Pausanias[28] bore Iphigeneia, and it is implied that Theseus was the father. Here she appears in her aspect as Artemis or the mother of Artemis. In another passage[29], however, Pausanias tells us that Theseus founded a temple of Aphrodite Nymphia when he took Helen as his wife. In Odyssey 4.14 Helen's only child, Hermione, has the appearance (εἶδος) of Aphrodite.

The conclusion at first sight may be startling. Aphrodite and Artemis are traditionally irreconcilable enemies. How are we to understand this situation?

In the fifth book of the Iliad, we find that there are quite clearly two Aphrodites, distinguished by the gods they severally associate with. The one is the consort of Ares, the other of Apollo. The consort of Apollo is warlike: in 5.311 ff. she enters the battle to save Aeneas. When she is wounded, Apollo rescues him. Ares is not in the fight during this episode and this is explicitly stated[30]. It looks as though, when Aphrodite is associated with Apollo, Ares is excluded. It is in this book that Ares and Aphrodite are made *kasignetoi*, brother and sister through their mother Dione. While the Aphrodite who is the consort of Apollo is the protectress of Aeneas (as also of Hector[31]), it seems to be another Aphrodite that protects Paris. At any rate she is no warrior's goddess. It is certainly the Aphrodite who is associated with Paris who converses with Helen in the third book of the Iliad[32]. In this passage Helen bids Aphrodite go and sit beside Paris, desert the ways of the gods, and not return to Olympus: for herself, she will have nothing to do with him. In other words, Helen ranges herself with the Olympians against Aphrodite (and also, as will be seen from the context, with the gods of Greece against those of Asia Minor). Helen thus repeats the attitude of her father, Tyndareos, to whose refusal to sacrifice to Aphrodite was ascribed the marital faithlessness of his daughters, Timandra, Helen, and Clytaemnestra[33]. This 'faithlessness' was, of course, misunderstood in the later age of Aphrodite

[28] 2.22.7.
[29] 2.32.7.
[30] 5.335 f. See Farnell, *Cults of the Greek States,* II, p. 635, and V, 400 f., footnote *d.*
[31] *Il.* 23.185 ff.
[32] 382–420. On this passage see also below, on Niobe.
[33] Schol. Eurip. *Orest.* 249, citing Stesichorus and Hesiod.

Pandemos: as the ground given for it suggests, it was really a matter of hostility to the cult celebrated by their husbands.

Yet Helen herself was a form of Aphrodite, the Aphrodite who is associated, not with Ares or with Paris, but with Apollo, and in the passage in
the Iliad Aphrodite says that she now hated Helen as she had once extravagantly loved her. Once they were intimate, but now they were enemies.
The passage shows linguistic signs of late composition, and the suggestion of
a distinction between Greeks and barbarians in 400-404 points in the same
direction. It was clearly composed at a time when the Olympian gods had
distinguished themselves from the others, but not too late for the former
close connection of Helen and Aphrodite to be remembered[34]. As we have
seen[35], even Herodotus had no difficulty in identifying a certain Aphrodite
with Helen.

Helen was Artemis and she was Aphrodite (or very nearly related to both
of them). As Artemis and Aphrodite she is associated with Apollo, but her
associations go further then this: she seems to have been intimately connected
with the cult of Helios also.

It will be remembered that Pausanias[36] records a legend of Helen's flight
to Rhodes, where she had a temple. The temple must have been of some
importance for its existence to have been known of in the Peloponnese. Rhodes, of course, was the greatest centre of the worship of the Sun in the Aegean
world and Greece proper. Of Helen's presence there we have (as far as I
know) no other record, but if, as we have seen, she was also to be identified
with Aphrodite, then we have ample evidence of her association with the Sun
in Rhodes. Pindar[37] calls Rhodes the daughter of Aphrodite and the bride
of Helios. The scholiast adds that some called Rhodes the daughter of
Aphrodite and Helios[38]. On the mainland of Greece, Corinth was once a

---

[34] F. Chapouthier, *Les Dioscures au Service d'une Déesse*, p. 224, refers to a cosmetic
bowl in the Cairo Museum which bears an inscription which he gives as 'à Hélène,
sœur d'Aphrodite'. At the time of writing, the bowl was apparently unpublished,
although he mentions his correspondent's declared intention to write about it. Chapouthier gives no further details. The bowl is, I assume, late Hellenistic or imperial
work and it may be argued that such evidence is worthless. On the other hand, the
inscription may reflect tradition.

[35] See footnote 18.

[36] 3.19.10.

[37] *Ol.* 7.14 (25).

[38] He also says that Herophilus called Rhodes the daughter of Aphrodite and Poseidon.

considerable centre of the cult of the Sun. Pausanias[39] says that on the way up to the summit of the Akrokorinthos was a temple of Aphrodite, with statues of Aphrodite Armed, Helios and Eros with a bow. This armed Aphrodite is not an unknown figure. She it is, as we have seen, who is associated with Apollo, and together with him she protects Aeneas and Hector. She is present in the battle with Aeneas and is wounded by Diomedes[40]. This goddess is certainly very like Aphrodite Urania, and if on Ida, 'mother of animals', she draws wolves, lions, bears and panthers to follow her, fawning upon her as she goes[41], it is because access to her is only for the religious hero, who can overcome the difficulties and dangers on the way to the height where she dwells. Thus she became the protectress of heroes in battle, but this is for the initiate only an analogy of her true nature. She was never a patroness either of amorous dalliance or of fertility, although, as the heavenly Aphrodite, she may in some sense have been the cause of the world's existence.

We may also quote the evidence of Virgil. When, in *Aeneid* I, 314 ff., Venus meets her son Aeneas, she appears as a virgin in countenance and wearing the dress and arms of a Spartan virgin or of Thracian Harpalyce. She bears a bow and is a huntress. Aeneas asks her (329) if she is the sister of Phoebus.

If Helen is both the celestial Aphrodite and also Artemis, she should be associated with the moon as well as the sun. The Dioscuri are often associated in later Hellenistic art with a goddess who bears the recumbent crescent as an attribute[42]. The temple at Memphis which Herodotus believed to be Helen's was, according to Strabo, said by some to be that of Selene[43]. It is true that references to Artemis' connection with the moon (and the sun) are not to be found in existing epic poetry, but Euripides' Θύγατερ Ἀελίου Σελαναία[44] shows that the connection was known in classical times. Her connection with the night-time sky appears in the Aeschylean fragment:

ᾶς οὔτε πέμφιξ ἡλίου προσδέρκεται,
οὔτ' ἀστερωπὸν ὄμμα Λητῴας κόρης. (Nauck 170).

The phrase from the *Phoenissae* quoted above connects Artemis with Helios

---

[39] 2.4.7.

[40] *Il.* 5.331 ff.

[41] Hom. Hymn. 5.68 ff. It is worth observing that the Zeus whom Agamemnon invoked together with Helios (*Il.* 3.276 f.) also had his seat on Ida.

[42] F. Chapouthier, *Les Dioscures au Service d'une Déesse*, Catalogue nos. 26–37 (pp. 48 ff.).

[43] See footnote 18.

[44] *Phoen.* 179.

also. The connection of Artemis with the sky (quite apart from her relationship to Apollo) is clear. She also sent the winds, and, like Aphrodite, could favour those who made voyages upon the sea. An inscription[45] from Sparta brings the Armed Aphrodite together with Artemis: it informs us that there was an hereditary priestess of Artemis Orthia, the Moirai Lacheseis, Aphrodite Enoplios, Asklepios Schoinatas, Artemis Patriotis, the Dioscuri and the festival of the Dioscureia. It is true that the inscription dates from imperial Roman times, but the priestess was hereditary, and the assemblage of deities is evidently old (except perhaps for Artemis Patriotis). It is to be remarked that once more we have the Dioscuri associated with Artemis (and with Aphrodite Enoplios) without any mention of Helen.

Sun and crescent moon appear together in Mycenaean and Minoan religious scenes. The bronze votive tablet from the Psychro cave which Evans illustrates and discusses[46] shows a rayed disc, evidently the sun, in the top left-hand corner and a sickle moon on its back in the top right-hand corner. In the centre stands a tree, indicated as sacred by the attitude of a worshipper. The mould from Palaikastro[47] appears to show the sun as a toothed wheel and, again, the sickle moon on its back. The 'toothed' wheel may be a fiery wheel (the teeth being stylised flames), by which the disc of the sun was represented in ritual. Alternatively, it may represent the chariot of the sun. From Tiryns is said to come a gold ring[48] showing a seated woman receiving libations from four approaching demons. In the upper panel appear, with four ears of corn, the inverted sickle of the moon and, seemingly, the sun. The sickle moon (upright) and apparently the sun[49] appear in the upper panel of the famous ring found by Schliemann in the grave circle at Mycenae; here they are again associated with a sacred tree. Sometimes one is uncertain whether a star or the sun is intended[50]. Taking this evidence as a whole, however, one can scarcely doubt that the sun and moon in some way were elements in Minoan and Mycenaean religion, and that there was some connection of the heavenly luminaries with a sacred tree. Such a connection we find in Helen too.

---

[45] Boeckh, *CIG.* I. 1444 = *I. G.* V (Laconia), 602.

[46] *Palace of Minos*, I.632 ff. (Fig. 470).

[47] Nilsson, *Gesch. d. griech. Relig.* (2nd. Ed.), I, Pl. 23,1.

[48] Nilsson, *op. cit.*, Pl. 16,4. Some doubt has been cast on the genuineness of this ring.

[49] There seems to be an approximation of the sun's disc to the top of the seed-case of a poppy, or still more closely, to that of *Nymphaea lotus*.

[50] See Nilsson, *op. cit.*, Pl. 13,2.

We may go further afield for supporting evidence. I am indebted to Professor W. Porzig, who holds the Chair of Comparative Indo-European Philology at the University of Mainz, for drawing my attention to the fact that in the *Rigveda* there are a number of allusions to a divine figure, Sūryā, who bears a striking resemblance in certain ways to Helen. She, Sūryā, is the daughter of the sun (Sūryǎ, masculine). Twin brothers called the Aśvinau have her in common as their wife. She travels with them in their broad-tracked chariot[51]. The beauty of Sūryā, whom the Aśvinau (in this passage called the Nasatyas) accompany, is spoken of in 1.116.17. Their beauty is also referred to elsewhere. The twin brothers are addressed in 1.118.5: 'Euren Wagen, Ihr Herren, bestieg die jugendliche Frau, die Tochter des Sūryǎ, da sie daran Gefallen hat. Eure prächtigen fliegenden Rosse, die rötlichen Vögel, sollen im rechten Augenblick herumfahren'. The chariot has three wheels[52] and places for three to ride in it. It can travel in three directions[53]. The three directions, since the chariot is plainly the chariot of the sun, must be the sun's movements from east to west and towards and away from the zenith between the winter and summer solstices.

In 10.85. 8-9 the Aśvinau are suitors of Sūryā, and Soma is her lover. Soma, who has a whole book to himself in the *Rigveda,* is also a drink pressed from the fruit of a plant. The drink induces a stimulated condition, raises the courage, increases procreative power and clarifies the thought. It is drunk by the gods, and also by the chief priest. In 1.184.3. the Nasatyas come to Sūryā's wedding. In 1.117.14 the Aśvinau rescue one drowning; they may be taken as having a *rôle* as helpers in distress at sea.

To see in these figures forms of Helen and the Dioscuri is not at all unreasonable.

The cumulative result of the evidence is the strong probability that Helen was closely connected with the cult of Helios, as also with a doctrine denoted by an attribute resembling the sickle moon.

Helen was above all things beautiful. When in the Odyssey[54] she emerges from her chamber, she is like golden-arrowed Artemis. She is like Artemis because she was either Artemis or the mother of Artemis, but there is surely more than a hint of unearthly beauty here also. She was beautiful, and she could make beautiful. An ugly child that was brought to her temple became

---

[51] K. F. Geldner's German translation, 4.44.1.

[52] 10.85.14 and 16.

[53] 1.118.2 Geldner's translation here is apparently not accurate.

[54] 4.121 f.

the most beautiful woman in Sparta and the mother of King Demaratos[55]. Her beauty must in some way have been comparable to the light of the sun and the moon.

We cannot properly understand the history of Helen in early Greece without making some reference to Niobe. In order to do so, we must remember that cult and dynasty or clan were, in early Greece, very closely connected. Hippodameia, whom Pelops married, is, according to Hesychius[56], a name of Aphrodite. Pelops was beloved of Poseidon, but Oinomaos, the father of Hippodameia, was the son of Ares. The cult of Aphrodite-Hippodameia will have descended matrilineally (as indeed the myth of Oinomaos and Pelops makes clear[57]) and we therefore seem to have the goddess associated first with Ares and then with Poseidon. With this parallel in mind, we may consider Niobe.

The appearance of Niobe in Apollodorus 3.5.6 as a Pelopid or Tantalid and at the same time as wife of Amphion, son of Zeus, is not at first sight easy to understand. In Sophocles[58] she is likewise a daughter of Tantalus, a Phrygian stranger. With 'Niobe' we must certainly hold fast to the principle that identity of name normally implies identity of clan, and that identity of clan carries with it identity of cult. How then are we to reconcile with Pelopid descent the facts, not only that Niobe marries in Amphion a son of Zeus, a deity foreign to the Pelopidae, but that Pausanias[59] records a tomb of Niobe and Argos, 'who thought he was Zeus', while in Apollodorus[60] Niobe, the daughter of Phoroneus and Teledike, is 'the first woman with whom Zeus had intercourse'?

The last passage gives us the clue: Phoroneus, the father of this Niobe, is said by Apollodorus to have reigned over the whole of *what was later called the Peloponnese*. Her brother was Apis, who named the land after himself; she was the mother of Argos. In other words, Niobe belongs to a clan which was in Greece before the Pelopids arrived there and gave their own name to Apia and Argos. This clan (or people) observed a cult of Zeus and Dione (Dione was the mother of Niobe according to Hyginus[61]). In this cult Niobe was the representative of the goddess, was the goddess herself: θεός ... καὶ θεογέννης[62]. A temple of the Dioscuri stood

---

[55] Herodotus, 6.61.   [56] *s. v.* Hippodameia.   [57] See Chapter I, § II.

[58] *Antig.* 824 f.   [59] 2.22.6.   [60] 2.1.1.

[61] *Fab.* 9.

[62] Soph. *Antig.* 834. It is true that Sophocles is here referring to the Tantalid cult, but the fragment of Sappho quoted below and the fact that Niobe was daughter of Dione as

near the tomb of Argos and Niobe, recorded, as we have mentioned, by Pausanias, and a fragment of Sappho[63] tells us that at one time Niobe and Leto were close friends: Λάτω καὶ Νιόβα μάλα μὲν φίλαι ἦσαν ἔταιραι. Later, as we know from the famous myth, they were enemies. The similarity with the situation in the third book of the Iliad[64] in which Aphrodite tells Helen that she now hates her as she once extravagantly loved her, is so close that it can hardly be doubted that the same religious events are referred to. 'Niobe', once apparently representative of a dynasty and divinity akin to Helen-Artemis, (for she is, as we have noticed, associated with Zeus, Leto and, it would seem, the Dioscuri), deserted the traditional religion for that of the Pelopid Aphrodite. The Pelopids came from Phrygia, and in the Homeric passage Helen associates Aphrodite with the cities of Phrygia or Maeonia, and forbids her to tread Olympus.

The Pelopid association with Niobe is therefore relatively late: she was an old Peloponnesian or, rather, 'Apian' goddess and will originally have had no connection with Mount Sipylus or Phrygia. The supposed connection would seem to have arisen only through her later association with the Pelopidae. This view seems to be confirmed by Apollodorus[65], who makes Niobe leave Thebes (her association with Thebes is not clearly explained) after the destruction of her children (*i.e.* after she had made herself into a rival of Leto) and go to her father Tantalus on Sipylus. The tradition that Niobe, 'daughter of Tantalus', married Amphion, son of Zeus, and bore Tantalid children is thus chronologically incorrect. 'Niobe', is, of course, a name which covers a succession of matrilineally-connected representatives of the cult of Dione, spouse of Zeus. In this context a 'Niobe' married an Amphion[66], son of Zeus. Then came the Pelopid immigration into Greece: the new masters, cultivating Poseidon and their own Aphrodite, married the women of the old Dionian line and converted the divinely-descended dynasty of Niobe from its old allegiance to Leto or Dione to a representation of the chthonic Pelopid Aphrodite and to her fertility-cult. Thence arose the story of Niobe's boast. She had become a daughter of Tantalus. To regard the vengeance of Leto and her children upon Niobe and her children as a moral tale bearing

Amphion was son of Zeus make it clear that the words are equally applicable to her pre-Pelopid nature.

[63] Bergk 31; Lobel 27.

[64] 382–420.

[65] 3.5.6.

[66] Amphion is doubtless not a personal name, but a title descriptive of a ritual office.

13*

a warning of the folly of boasting is to read an ancient myth with the eyes of the fifth century. Niobe's offence was not that she rivalled Leto in fertility: it was that she became a fertility-goddess at all.

The dynasty, having become 'Pelopid', remained matrilineal in spite of its desertion of the old allegiance, no doubt because the Pelopid men had been accustomed in their home in Asia Minor to a similarly matrilineal religious dynasty. Indeed, as we have suggested, they probably remade Niobe, as they remade Hippodameia, in the sacred image of their traditional line of queens. Hence sprang the hatred borne towards the Pelopidae by the syncretic Artemis, who represents Dione and Leto and Helen and Niobe.

How completely we may identify Dione, Leto, Helen, Niobe, Artemis and the celestial Aphrodite in very early Greek religion is a question which I shall not pursue further. What is certainly common to them all is that they represented a celestial cult, and what set Artemis and Helen against Aphrodite, and Leto against Niobe, was the defection of 'Aphrodite' and 'Niobe' from the celestial cult. Aphrodite and Niobe associated themselves with chthonic religion, in the case of Niobe apparently as the result of the seizure of certain Greek centres by the Poseidon-worshipping Pelopids, who were ever pursued by the hatred of Artemis. The true nature of the events concealed in the seduction of Helen by Paris is less clear. The relationship of Helen, Menelaus and Agamemnon needs a separate investigation. The author of the conversation between Helen and Aphrodite in the third book of the Iliad[67] evidently wished to bring Helen, Agamemnon and Menelaus, as true Greeks, into the circle of the Olympians and their worshippers. Outside it were barbarians. In the event however Niobe perished, Helen dwindled, Aphrodite was never truly at home on Olympus, and the old high goddesses, Dione and Leto, began to fade in the light of a common day.

[67] 382–420.

Appendix II

Names Beginning with Alk-

Pindar, *Pyth.* IV, 172 f., says

δοιοὶ δ' ὑψιχαῖται
ἀνέρες, Ἐννοσίδα γένος, αἰδεσθέντες ἀλκάν.

We have already noticed (Chapter I, footnote 187) the apparent connection between the two Ajaxes in the Iliad and the cult of Ares; they are twice called servants of Ares and are noticeably associated with *alke*. The word *alke* seems to be even more closely associated with Poseidon. Of the 23 names beginning with *Alk-* in Apollodorus' *Bibliotheca*, five are of undeniable Pelopids (Alkathos, 'son of Pelops' (3.12.7); Alkestis, daughter of Pelias and Anaxibia or Phylomache; Alkides (i. e. Herakles), son of the Pelopid Alkmena; Alkyone, daughter of the Pelopid Nikippe); one, Alkippe, daughter of Ares, mated with the son of Poseidon, Halirrhothios; Alkimenes, 'some say', was the name of the brother of Bellerophon, whose steed was Pegasos, the offspring of Poseidon and Medusa (2.3.1). Alkinos and Alkon, the sons of Hippokoon, seem to be worshippers of Poseidon: they fought for Neleus, the son of Poseidon (Apollod. 2.7.3.), and the Heraclidae, against whom they fought, are said by Pausanias (2.18.6), to have been Perseids by origin (i. e., presumably, if their descent were reckoned patrilineally). As Hippokoon is also said to have expelled Tyndareos, it is clear that they opposed all the main Peloponesian cults and clans except the Tantalid. We may therefore presume their attachment to Poseidon and to the Pelopids. A second Alkippe was the mother of Daedalus, who constructed the labyrinth for the bull of Poseidon, and the wooden cow to enable Pasiphaë to mate with the bull (3.15.8.). Alkyone, daughter of Atlas and Pleione, was the mother of Aithousa by Poseidon. Alkyoneus, a Titan, seems fairly clearly to have been a volcano, which suggests a connection with the Earth-shaker. One Alkyone said that her husband was Zeus and he said that she was Hera: this is the only case in the list where there is definitely no connection with Poseidon. Thus, of the 23, we may be fairly sure that eleven were closely connected with Poseidon. One was also a daughter of Ares. Alkyoneus, the Titan, may have been connected with Poseidon. One, an Alkyone, cannot be linked with Poseidon at all. Of the remaining nine we do not know enough to make any assertion.

INDEX

PLATES

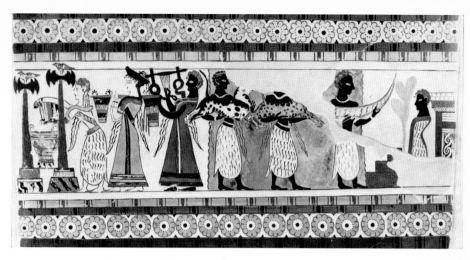

Plate I. A side panel of the Hagia Triada sarcophagus

Plate II. Aegisthus about to slay Agamemnon, with Clytaemnestra

Plate III. Hermes carrying the 'three-leafed' caduceus

Plate IV.   Hermes' caduceus with cross-bar

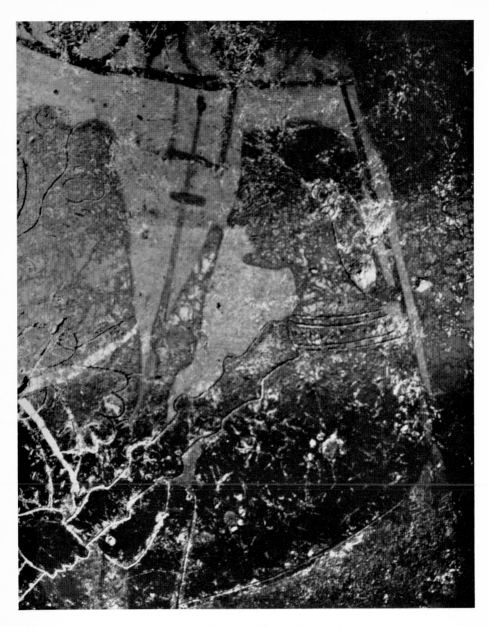

Plate V. Poseidon and trident with cross-bar

Plate VI. Poseidon and trident with cross-bars

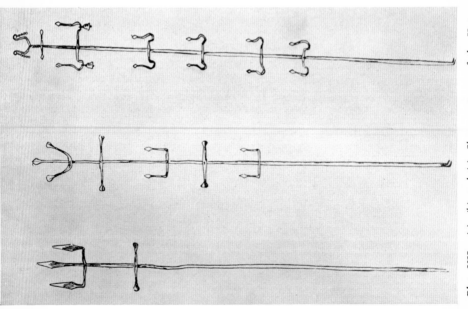

Plate VIII. Shaman staff of the Kets fitted to the masthead of a boat

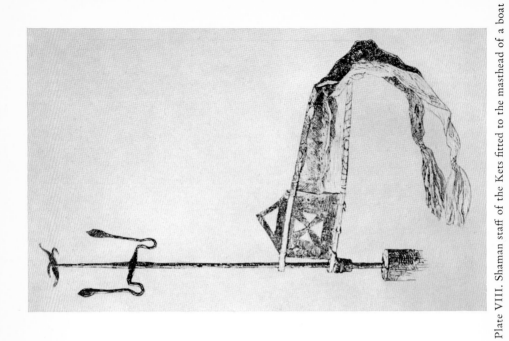

Plate VII. (a), (b) and (c). Shaman staves of the Kets

Plate IX.   Mongolian Cham dancer with trident-headed sceptre

Plate X. Tibetan medium, with trident, entering into trance

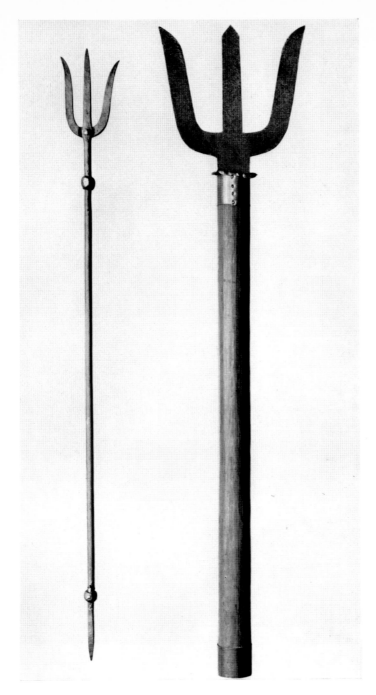

(a) Trident from pariah altar, S. India.   (b) Shaman's staff from Korea

Plate XI.

Plate XII Siva holding trident, with Parvati (India)

Plate XIII.   Siva as Bhairava, holding trident (India)

Plate XIV.   Siva as Bhatara Guru, with trident (Java)

Plate XV.   Masked dancer at festival of Kali (India)

Plate XVI. Solon shaman with bronze mirrors on dress (N. W. Manchuria)

Plate XVII. Robe with mirrors, head-dress and drum of shamaness (N. W. Manchuria)